THE NUBIAN
PHARAOHS OF EGYPT

THE NUBIAN PHARAOHS OF EGYPT

THEIR LIVES AND AFTERLIVES

AIDAN DODSON

The American University in Cairo Press

Cairo   New York

First published in 2023 by
The American University in Cairo Press
113 Sharia Kasr el Aini, Cairo, Egypt
420 Lexington Avenue, Suite 1644, New York, NY 10170
www.aucpress.com

ISBN 978 1 649 03163 1

Library of Congress Cataloging-in-Publication Data

Names: Dodson, Aidan, 1962- author.
Title: The Nubian pharaohs of Egypt : their lives and afterlives / Aidan
    Dodson.
Identifiers: LCCN 2023009033 | ISBN 9781649031631 (hardback) | ISBN
    9781649031648 (adobe pdf)
Subjects: LCSH: Egypt--History--Third Intermediate Period, ca. 1071-ca. 650
    B.C. | Egypt--Kings and rulers. | Nubia--Kings and rulers.
Classification: LCC DT90 .D63 2023 | DDC 932--dc23/eng/20230228

1 2 3 4 5   27 26 25 24 23

Designed by Sally Boylan
Printed in China

To Jules . . .
for four decades of friendship

Assyrian term "Melukhkha." "Kush" is used to refer to the indigenous polity that ruled some or all of this region, although in the ancient Egyptian language it was a geographical term essentially synonymous with Nubia.

In writing the names of the Nubian kings who ruled in Egypt, for simplicity and transparency I have used the forms that reflect a direct transcription of the actual hieroglyphs, rather than using forms that interpret them in light of later Meroitic usage (so "Shabataka" rather than "Shabitku"). Similarly, I will be using the form Pi(ankh)y for the name of the great Kushite conqueror, to reflect the ongoing debate as to whether the *'nḫ*-sign should actually be read (see page 27). For later rulers of Napata and Meroë I have, however, followed general practice in using "Nubian" forms.

Thanks are due to Essam Nagy, the late David Moyer (and, as ever, Martin Davies) for providing images and Patricia Usick for information. In addition, my continuing thanks goes to my army of proofreaders, led by my wife, Dyan Hilton, together with Ali Ball, Victoria Baylis-Jones, Reg Clark, Vanessa Foott, Anne Hilton, Sid and Mary Kitchell, and Cindie Lovelace. All remaining errors and infelicities remain, however, my sole responsibility.

CONTENTS

PREFACE

The Twenty-fifth Egyptian Dynasty is interesting for a range of reasons. It saw a restoration of Egypt's fortunes after an extended period punctuated by economic and political troubles, which had culminated during the late ninth and eighth centuries BC in fragmentations of the Egyptian state and civil conflict within and between some of these emergent local kingdoms. The fallout from this included a rebirth of monumental art and architecture. This incorporated an archaism in representation and discourse that would also be a feature of the immediately succeeding dynasty. But the aspect that has received the most attention has been the fact that the dynasty comprised kings who were simultaneously the rulers of Egypt's immediate southern neighbor, Nubia—anciently called Kush.

That region's destiny had been intimately linked with that of Egypt since the earliest times, but for most of prior history Nubia had been so chiefly as a target for Egyptian plundering, colonialism, and imperialism. This had culminated in its absorption into the pharaonic kingdom as a formal viceroyalty during the sixteenth through eleventh centuries—the Egyptian New Kingdom. However, now it was kings of this formerly despised people who brought an end to the squabbling among Egypt's assorted regional rulers, and imposed order for a century, before being driven out by foreign invasion. Then, back in their southern heartland, the Kushite kings would maintain their entangled Nubian–Egyptian culture through the fourth century AD.

For modern researchers, the Nubians' identity as an unequivocally "African" people—in contrast to the Egyptians, whom some have equivocally characterized as "in Africa, but not of Africa" (an oversimplification of Egypt's role as a bridge between Asia and Africa, but with a core of truth)—has been a matter of particular interest. This racial identity of the Kushite kings has led, especially since the late nineteenth century, to assessments that have been implicitly, and sometimes explicitly, racist, in both their origin and mode of expression. While some of the more gross statements (e.g., those quoted on pages 158 and 165, with the aim of illustrating the mores of the times) are—thankfully!—no longer to be found in the literature, their malign influence nevertheless lingers. Thus we find ongoing negative assessments of the Kushite kings' foreign policy and military prowess which find no support in any objective assessments of the available data (see page 156), attesting to the long-term poisoning of the historical discourse by the racist attitudes of some of the founding fathers of Nile valley history writing.

Accordingly, the reception of the Kushite kings is an important theme in the latter part of the present book, as is the author's aim to strictly "follow the evidence" as far as possible—not only in the reconstruction of ancient events, but also assessing them. This evidence is particularly interesting in that key parts of the story have to be reconstructed from a combination of Egyptian, Assyrian, and biblical sources—with a leavening of Classical ones as well—in a way that is generally not the case for Egypt's earlier periods. During these previous eras, biblical and cuneiform sources on occasion contribute to matters of chronology via synchronisms, or to the reconstruction of specific episodes (e.g., the affair of the Hittite prince after the death of Tutankhamun; Rameses II's Battle of Qadesh), but are not crucial to the main narrative. Now, however, the collapse of Kushite rule in Egypt has to be reconstructed almost entirely through the lens of Assyrian texts, which have also provided key data toward a revision of the structure of the Twenty-fifth Dynasty. They have additionally, with some help from the Old Testament, defined the dynasty's foreign engagements. While not as fundamental, the Classical sources provide, for the first time, data that, although generally corrupt, reveals some knowledge of Egyptian history that can, with care, be useful.

The Kushite kings of Egypt are thus to be viewed through rich seams of information, concerning both their lives and their afterlives: the ways in which they have been treated by posterity ancient and modern. Accordingly, they form a particularly interesting topic for this latest volume in my series of pharaonic biographies. Its narrative perforce reaches back into the periods preceding the Kushites' imposition of their authority over Egypt, including a reassessment of the scanty evidence for the establishment of the monarchy that would achieve this feat, and also the disintegrations of Egypt that would pave the way for the Nubian takeover. While I also provide a summary overview of the history and funerary practices of the Nubian kings who ruled after the evacuation from Egypt, the book is, nevertheless, fundamentally focused on those who actually ruled in Egypt, and their presentation in the context of their role as rulers of the short-lived dual kingdom of Egypt-Kush.

As to the matter of terminology, I have generally used the term "Nubia" to refer to the region stretching from Aswan to a little north of Khartoum, and to translate the

ABBREVIATIONS AND CONVENTIONS

Ashmolean	Ashmolean Museum, Oxford, UK
Athens	National Archaeological Museum, Athens, Greece
BegN/S	Meroë-Begarawiya North/South tomb
Berlin	Ägyptisches Museum, Berlin, Germany
BM	British Museum, London, UK
Cairo	Egyptian Museum/Grand Egyptian Museum, Cairo, Egypt
Florence	Museo archeologico, Florence
Hamm	Gustav-Lübcke-Museum, Hamm, Germany
ISACM	Institute for the Study of Ancient Cultures Museum (formerly Oriental Institute Museum), Chicago, USA
Ku	El-Kurru tomb
Louvre	Musée du Louvre, Paris, France
MFA	Museum of Fine Arts, Boston, USA
MMA	Metropolitan Museum of Art, New York, USA
NMS	National Museums Scotland, Edinburgh, UK
Nu	Nuri tomb
SNM	Sudan National Museum, Khartoum, Sudan
TT	Theban Tomb
Turin	Museo Egizio, Turin, Italy
*	biography of individual available in Bierbrier 2019

In tabulations of royal names, the following abbreviations apply:
H = Horus-name; Nb = Nebti-name; GF = Golden falcon; P = Prenomen; N = Nomen

Under Egyptological convention, kingly and high-priestly homonyms are distinguished by upper-case roman numerals (e.g., Osorkon III), while lesser individuals are distinguished by upper-case letters (e.g., Osorkon F) or lower-case Roman numerals (e.g., Pamiu i).

In translations, transcriptions, and transliterations, restorations/lacunae/interpolations are enclosed by square brackets and glosses by parentheses; ⌜…⌝ indicates that the reading of the enclosed material is uncertain.

INTRODUCTION

Nubia is the section of the Nile valley that extends some eight hundred kilometers southward from Aswan to the general area of modern Khartoum. A feature of the region is a series of "cataracts"—points at which the flow of the Nile through the sandstone bedrock is interrupted by incursions of igneous rock, making navigation often almost impossible. As such, they form an important element of the historical punctuation of the region, with the Second Cataract marking the division between Lower and Upper Nubia, and also the political boundary dividing the modern states of Egypt and Sudan.

For much of its history, ancient Egypt's attitude toward Nubia was a negative one. Countless pharaohs raged against "vile Kush," regarding it officially as little more than a source of slaves and exotic raw materials, and the principal conduit of trade items from more remote parts of Africa. On more than one occasion, Egypt occupied large portions of the area, absorbing it into the Egyptian kingdom between the sixteenth and eleventh centuries BC. However, Nubian rulers turned the tables on at least two occasions and threatened the rulers of Egypt; the final one resulted in their becoming the kings of both Egypt and Nubia for the best part of a century.

This feat was aided by a cultural entanglement of the two regions that went back beyond the first political unification of Egypt at the beginning of the third millennium BC. That event was closely followed by what seems to be the first recorded major episode of Egyptian aggression against their southern neighbors. This saw a confrontation between an early ruler of the Egyptian First Dynasty (probably Djer) and the Nubian A-Group culture, which had existed from 3500 BC, but all but vanished from Lower Nubia around 2900 BC. Lower Nubia was then seemingly depopulated for over half a millennium, being reduced essentially to an Egyptian-controlled buffer zone and a source of, and conduit for, raw materials. In particular, Egypt coveted the gold and exotic stones present in the Nubian deserts. For example, a quarry beyond Toshka was the source of a diorite-gneiss that was used for royal statuary during the Old Kingdom—including the famous statue of Khaefre from Giza.

In the meantime, the focus of Nubian civilization became Kerma in Upper Nubia, its eponymous culture continuing for a millennium and a half. Lower Nubia was reoccupied from around 2400 BC by the C-Group culture,[1] and contemporary Egyptian texts mention the regional polities of Setju, Irjet, and Wawat,[2] the latter eventually becoming the name for the whole of Lower Nubia. However, around 2000 BC the Egyptians began the formal occupation of the area, establishing a fortified hard border at the Second Cataract (fig. 1).

The latter process seems to have begun under the Twelfth Dynasty's Senwosret I, but it was Senwosret III who was responsible for the final complex of forts in the area. These comprised a mixture of truly military structures and others that were essentially storage facilities, since a key part of the Egyptian strategy was to monopolize trade across the Second Cataract:

> Southern boundary, made in Year 8 under the person of the Dual King Khakaure, given life forever and eternity, to prevent the crossing of it by any Nubian traveling north, by land or with a ship, or any Nubian herds apart from a Nubian who shall come to trade at *iqn* (Mirgissa), or anything good that may be done by them, or with a message, in any case without letting a ship of the Nubians pass that sails north past *ḥḥ* (Abu Sir), eternally.[3]

The attitude of the Egyptian king to the Nubians is made explicit by Senwosret III in another text (fig. 2):

> The Nubian listens to the word of mouth. Answering him is making him retreat. If one shows aggression toward him, he turns his back. (But if one) retreats, he will act aggressively. For they are not respectable people. They are wretches with broken spirits. My person has seen them: it is no lie.[4]

This episode of Egyptian colonial rule in Lower Nubia continued into the Thirteenth Dynasty. However, the number of occupied Second Cataract forts diminished until soon after the time of Neferhotep I, from whose reign comes the last royal seal impression found at Mirgissa, as well as a faience plaque at Buhen.[5] Then, or soon afterward, Egyptian forces appear to have withdrawn, most probably owing to escalating problems north of Aswan. In particular, there was the increasing domination of the north of Egypt by Palestinian elements, which would culminate in the establishment of the Hyksos Fifteenth Dynasty.

FIGURE 1 The Second Cataract at Semna in 1962.

The whole of Nubia was now apparently under the control of the polity based at Kerma, which now reached its height of prosperity. The city itself, which seems to have had a population of some ten thousand at this time, was centered on a massive brick cult structure, now known as the Western Deffufa (fig. 3).[6] An extensive cemetery to the east included a series of huge tumuli, clearly the burial places of the kings of Kerma.[7] These each contained not only the royal interment, but also large numbers of sacrificed retainers, and in some cases items of Egyptian origin, including large items of sculpture. This material seems to have been the loot from one or more raids into Egypt: that some such

FIGURE 2 The stela
of Senwosret III from
Uronarti (SNM 451).

incursions penetrated as far north as Asyut is suggested by the presence of statues of that
city's Twelfth Dynasty nomarch Hapidjefa and his wife in a royal tomb at Kerma. A reference to one such invasion is to be found in a Second Intermediate Period tomb-chapel
at El-Kab.[8]

FIGURE 3 The Western Deffufa at Kerma.

The Kingdom of Kush was at this point an antagonist of the rump Egyptian royal line (Sixteenth/Seventeenth Dynasties). This had been concentrated in the Theban region following the Hyksos takeover of much of the north of Egypt. The situation of the Egyptian king is indicated by the lament of Kamose, on the eve of his campaign against the Hyksos: "To what end do I know my (own) strength? One chief is in Avaris, another in Kush, and I sit cheek by jowl with an Asiatic and a Nubian: each man has his piece in this Egypt and so the land is partitioned with me."[9] Once the campaign had been launched, the Egyptians captured a messenger traveling from the north to Kerma via the western oases, with a letter from the Hyksos king Apepi. This missive proposed that the Kushite king invade from the south while Kamose was attacking the Hyksos in the north, and that the whole of Egypt should then be partitioned between them.[10]

A Theban reaction seems to have secured control of Lower Nubia as far as Toshka, some two hundred kilometers south of Aswan, before the end of the reign of Kamose, which was maintained into the reign of the next Egyptian king, Ahmose I,[11] who was also responsible for the expulsion of the Hyksos. The Egyptian return was marked by the inauguration of the post of Viceroy of Kush (*s3-nsw n kš*), the first holder of the office possibly being Ahmose-Sitayet.[12] Control over Nubia was then extended farther upstream, Thutmose I fixing the southern boundary at Kurgus, on the Abu Hamed reach of the Nile above the Fourth Cataract.[13] The vast majority of Nubia thus came under Egyptian control, and remained so until the end of the New Kingdom.

During this period the colonial administrative-military organization was elaborated, with the viceroyalty divided into Wawat, embracing the area between the First and Third Cataracts, and Kush, stretching up to the limit of Egyptian control. Overall governance was exercised by the Viceroy, with a deputy responsible for each of the subdivisions.

The Viceroy himself was based at Aniba, 150 kilometers from Aswan, but the ceremonial center of his territory was over four hundred kilometers farther south, where the city of Napata (most likely modern Sanam) and the ritual center of Gebel Barkal[14] were established, probably under Thutmose III, as the Nubian counterpoint to Thebes in Egypt. Thus, the holy mountain of Gebel Barkal (figs. 4, 24) was regarded as the dwelling place of a specifically Nubian version of the god Amun, increasingly distinguished from his northern manifestation by having the head of a ram, rather than that of a man wearing double plumes (fig. 53).

A series of temples were built at the foot of the mountain over the coming centuries. The major temple of Amun (B500—figs. 23, 24) was, interestingly, originally built by Akhenaten, presumably as an Aten sanctuary.[15] It was subsequently extended by various rulers down to Meroitic times. Elsewhere in Nubia, extensive temple-building was undertaken throughout the New Kingdom, including "temple-towns," some of which seem to have been intended to project Egyptian prestige into sparsely populated areas (fig. 5). At Kerma, the ancient center was abandoned in favor of its suburb of Dukki Gel, a kilometer to the northeast.

Although under a formal colonial regime, local Nubian rulers continued to exercise some authority, for example Heqanefer, Prince of Miam, who was buried at Toshka-East.[16] Interestingly, in his tomb, Heqanefer is depicted as though a conventional Egyptian, but in his contemporary depiction in the tomb-chapel of Amenhotep-Huy, Viceroy under Tutankhamun (TT40), Heqanefer is shown as a caricatured Nubian (fig. 6). Egyptian military activity continued in Nubia throughout the New Kingdom, but it is often unclear whether actions were against actual rebellions within the borders of the viceroyalty, or farther south in the "near abroad" of Irem, where the local inhabitants may have opposed Egyptian interests.

FIGURE 4 Gebel Barkal.

FIGURE 5 Top: the temple of Amenhotep III at Soleb; bottom: Abu Simbel as reconstructed after the flooding of its original site by the lake of the Aswan High Dam.

The viceregal structures survived throughout the New Kingdom, and were an important source of wider power for the incumbents. On at least one occasion, they may have been the basis for a seizure of the kingship, if the usurping Nineteenth Dynasty king Amenmeses has been correctly identified as the former Viceroy Messuwy.[17] During the collapse of the New Kingdom, Nubia was the venue for a conflict of uncertain basis, in which the principal protagonist was a certain Piankh, who combined the viceroyalty with the high priesthood of Amun at Karnak. These hostilities have generally been regarded as a war against a renegade former Viceroy, Panehsy, who had lost office something over a decade earlier, but this is by no means certain. Indeed, after Piankh's sudden disappearance, Panehsy may have returned to office for a period before the viceroyalty passed to another High Priest of Amun, Herihor, whose pontificate seems to have been interrupted by Piankh's incumbency.

FIGURE 6 The presentation of Nubian tribute, with detail of Heqanefer, Prince of Miam, in the tomb-chapel of the Viceroy of Kush, Amenhotep-Huy (TT40, reign of Tutankhamun).

Herihor was apparently the last substantive holder of the title of Viceroy of Kush, although a few decades later, during the pontificate of Menkheperre, a Third Prophet of Amun, Aakheperre, held the title,[18] as still later did Nesikhonsu, a wife of the High Priest Panedjem II.[19] These two cases may simply have denoted that these individuals benefited from residual revenues from Nubia, as there is no evidence for any Egyptian activity in Nubia following the events under Piankh. The viceregal title now vanished, except for a single known revival in the early eighth century BC, when the Vizier Pamiu i held the dignity (see page 20). Interestingly, this was not long before Thebes was absorbed by the Kushite kingdom. One wonders whether he was responsible for liaison between the contemporary Theban regime and the Kushite king.

So, by the second third of the eleventh century BC, Nubia appears to have once again lost its Egyptian overlords, never for them to return. Three and a half centuries later, it would be Nubians who would be the overlords of Egypt.

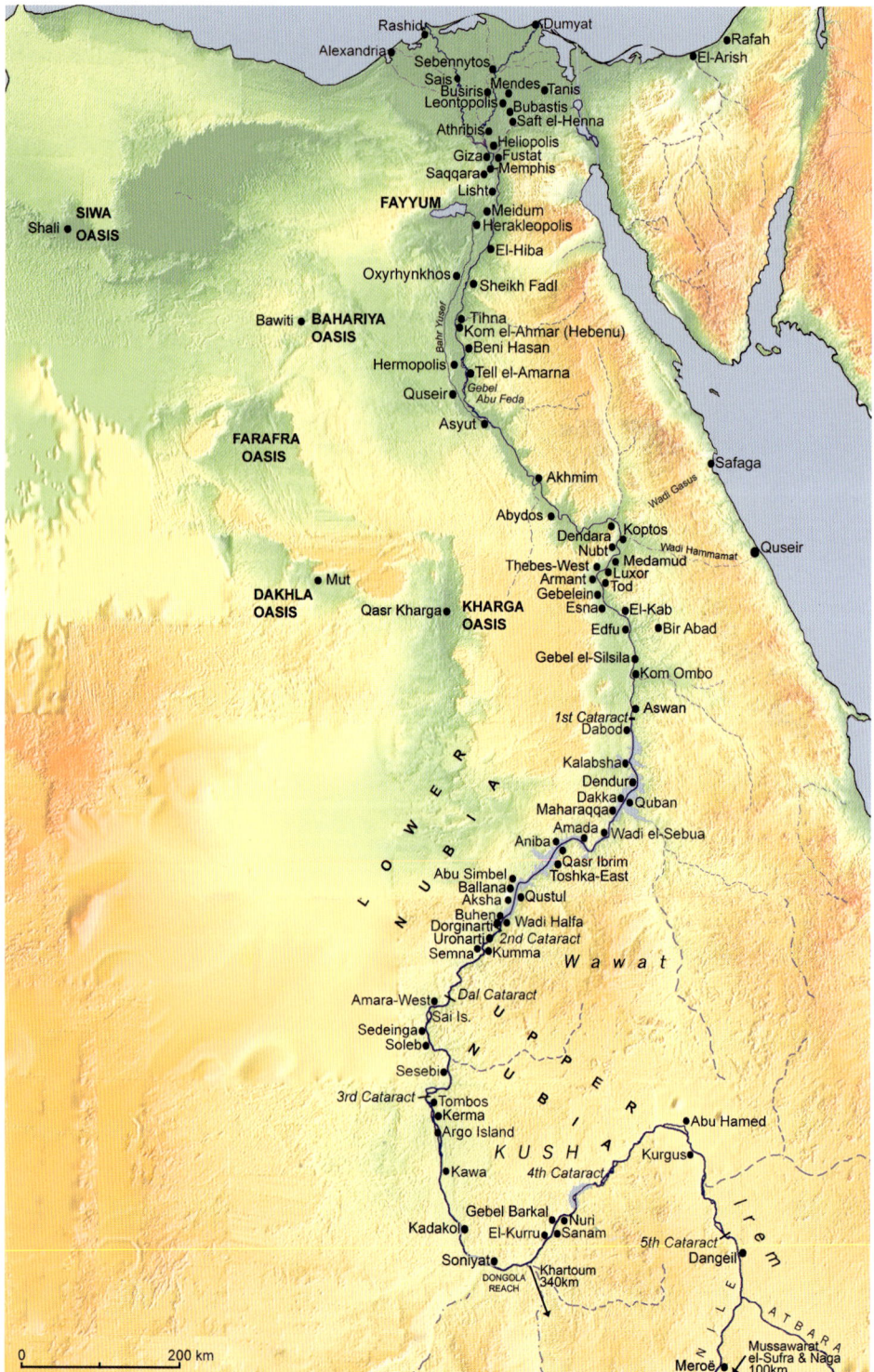

FIGURE 7 Map of Egypt and Nubia.

1 KUSH AFTER THE EGYPTIANS AND EGYPT BEFORE THE KUSHITES

Post-imperial Nubia

First-millennium BC Nubia was a postcolonial society. While many time-hallowed aspects of Nubian culture still flourished, the impact of five hundred years of Egyptian rule meant that the region's customs and practices had become intimately entangled with those of Egypt. In particular, the Nubian elite were now literate, and had before them the Egyptian models of the state, divine kingship, and public religion. Thus, when the first representatives of a new Kushite kingship emerge from the archaeological record, they are very much in an Egyptian mode, from the points of view of names, titulary, representation, and the use of the Egyptian language and hieroglyphic script.

Two kings with prenomina reminiscent of those of late New Kingdom/early Third Intermediate Period Egyptian monarchs are known from Nubia. One, Usermaatre-setepenre Iry-meryamun ⌷⌷⌷⌷, seems to have built Temple B at Kawa (figs. 67, 128), where two of his stelae were found, recording work there (fig. 8a–c).[1] The second, Menmaatresetepenamun ⌈Qa⌉tiaa⌈t⌉ ⌷⌷⌷⌷,[2] is known from material from Gebel Barkal (fig. 8d)[3] and Nuri,[4] the core of the later independent Kushite state. These kings have generally been placed in the late fourth/early third century BC (see page 167), but on stylistic and archaeological grounds it seems difficult to accept such an attribution.[5]

On the basis of their prenomina, it seems far preferable to place Iry and ⌈Qa⌉tiaa⌈t⌉ somewhere during the late eleventh through early ninth centuries, in the wake of the Egyptian withdrawal. Also to be placed among this group is a King's Great Wife Katimala,[6] the author of a tableau[7] added to the façade of the New Kingdom temple at the Second Cataract fort at Semna-West (fig. 9). Its inscription is dated to a Year 14

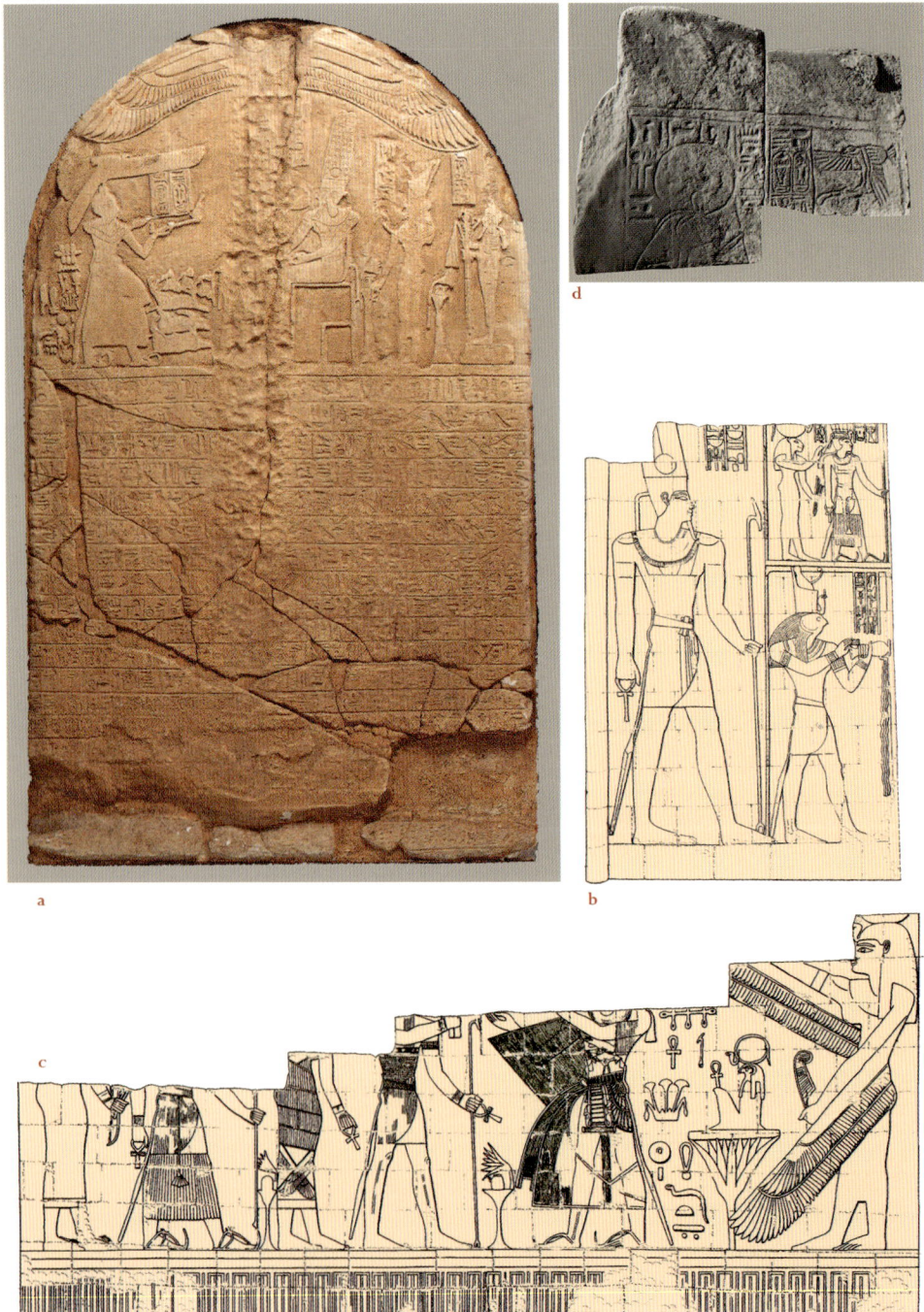

FIGURE 8 a. Stela of Iry from Kawa (Ny Carlsberg ÆIN 1709). b. The north face of the east pylon of the Temple at Kawa. c. West wall of the sanctuary of Temple B—Sanc W Wall Kawa II pl vi vii. d. Fragment of scene of ⌈Qa⌉tiaa⌈t⌉ (SNM 5227).

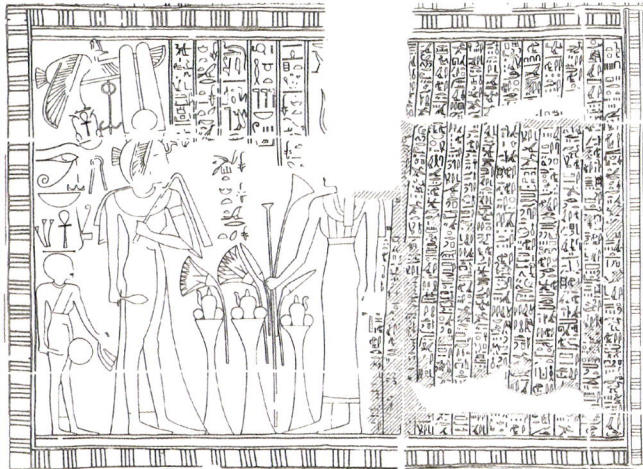

FIGURE 9 a. The New Kingdom temple of Semna, shown in 1962 while still standing in the Middle Kingdom fortress at the site; b. detail of the figure of Katimala, as seen in recent years in the Sudan National Museum; c. drawing of the whole Katimala tableau.

and records the events resulting from a rebellion against an unnamed king. The style of the figures and language of the text suggest that it was carved in parallel with the Egyptian Twenty-first/early Twenty-second Dynasty (essentially the tenth century).[8] Whether the two kings already noted above and Katimala (and her unnamed husband) formed part of a single line, controlling the whole area between (at least) the Second and Fourth Cataracts, or represented separate polities existing in parallel, is wholly obscure. Other evidence for royal activity during the ninth/eighth centuries is provided by radiocarbon dates from fortification work at the hilltop stronghold of Qasr Ibrim in Lower Nubia (fig. 10).[9]

Just downstream from the New Kingdom centers of Napata and Gebel Barkal is the cemetery of El-Kurru, which contains a series of tombs extending back from the mid-seventh century (fig. 91).[10] Typologically, there is a clear sequence from simple tumuli (KuTum1–6, Ku19—fig. 11), through early pyramids (Ku9–14)[11] to later pyramids (Ku8, 15–18, Ku51–55).[12] However, what is far less clear is how the pre-pyramid monuments should be spread through time. A "conventional" view long assumed pairs of husband/wife tombs belonging to a single royal line. On this basis, a simple

FIGURE 10 Qasr Ibrim in 1962; inset: in 2013, almost entirely submerged by the waters of Lake Nasser.

generation count would take the sequence back to the mid-ninth century.[13] However, other views have assumed that all tombs belonged to a single line of males, thus doubling the number of generations and allowing the series to be taken back to the early eleventh century.[14] That the latter option may be the more likely is indicated by some of the material found in the tombs. This includes items of New Kingdom type, some forms suggesting manufacture and/or import a considerable time before they were buried.[15] Another option is that the cemetery is chronologically discontinuous, with at least some of the tumulus tombs actually contemporary with the mid–New Kingdom.[16] The early pyramids would then begin considerably later, perhaps around 900, if one were to assume around twenty-five years per generation.

Only in the middle of the eighth century can anything definitive be said about the history of Nubia (see chapter 2). At this time, the Egyptian-derived concept of monarchy seen in the texts of Iry, ⌐Qa⌐tiaa⌐t⌐, and Katimala was still extant, and material from then and later demonstrates the way in which this and other Egyptian and Nubian elements became commingled to produce the distinctively Kushite monarchy that would endure down to the fourth century AD.

FIGURE 11 Tumulus tomb KuTum6 at El-Kurru.

Post-imperial Egypt

The so-called Bronze Age Collapse of the twelfth century BC affected the entire eastern Mediterranean world, with long-standing cultures disappearing altogether, or surviving only in a much reduced form.[17] Egypt escaped the physical invasions suffered by many other polities, but the country had already been weakened by civil conflict during the first decades of the century, exacerbated by the contemporaneous dislocation of international trade and relations. The last decades of the Twentieth Dynasty saw economic and social upheavals, manifest in the large-scale looting of tombs in the Theban necropolis and a split in the unity of the country. This continued into the Twenty-first Dynasty. Furthermore, although the kingship was eventually reunified, the southern part of Egypt remained essentially independent under a hereditary sequence of individuals who combined the role of High Priest of Amun with that of Army Leader.

Before the end of the dynasty, the kingship had fallen to a man of Libyan ancestry, Osorkon the Elder. Four decades later a new Twenty-second Dynasty began, composed entirely of kings whose Libyan background was proclaimed by their names of Shoshenq, Osorkon, and Takelot. In addition, many local and regional roles were taken by individuals with both Libyan names and titles, in particular Chief of the Ma(shwesh)—one of a number of Libyan tribes.

Initially, the dynasty reimposed central control, with its founder, Shoshenq I, ending the hereditary succession of the High Priests of Amun in favor of the direct appointment of a royal son. However, as time progressed, fissiparous tendencies reasserted themselves, and in the middle of the ninth century the result was the establishment of a separate southern kingship once again, based on Thebes. This ran in parallel with the old "national" line, based at Tanis in the Delta, but was itself subject to civil conflict between two sets of claimants to both the southern kingship and the high priesthood of Amun.

Victory eventually fell to the High Priest Osorkon B, son of a former Theban king, Takelot II. The initial result was a brief reunification of the kingship in the person of the Tanite Shoshenq III (who also seems to have been subject to a challenge in the north from an ally of Osorkon's opponents). He was recognized for the rest of his life as the king of the whole of Egypt, but after Shoshenq's death, Osorkon finally followed his long-dead father as king in Thebes (fig. 12 left). The now–Osorkon III then ruled the south for some thirty years. During this time, his son Takelot (later King Takelot III) served as High Priest, while the king's daughter, Shepenwepet I, occupied the parallel post of God's Wife of Amun.

This latter office had originated as a subsidiary role of the queen back in the Eighteenth Dynasty. However, under Rameses VI it had been definitively separated from queenship, to become an office normally held by a senior daughter of a king. The status

FIGURE 12 Depictions of Osorkon III (left) and Takelot III (right) in the chapel of Osiris-Heqadjet at Karnak (figs. 31–32).

of the God's Wife varied over time, and seems to have declined between the Twenty-first Dynasty and the reign of Osorkon II. After this it revived, with Shepenwepet being the first of what would come to be a sequence of particularly prominent women.

The last decade of Osorkon III's reign saw his son Takelot III (fig. 12 right) ruling alongside him as fully fledged king. Such coregencies are rare after the Middle Kingdom,[18] and may in this case have been prompted by the extreme age of Osorkon III, given that his career as High Priest and then as king spanned some seventy years. Takelot's place as High Priest of Amun was taken by a certain Osorkon F, of unknown origins, while Shepenwepet I continued as God's Wife.

Lower and Middle Egypt
The Tanites remained for the time being the principal power in the north, in the persons of Shoshenq III and his successors Shoshenq IV, Pamiu, Shoshenq V, and Osorkon

IV. From the middle of the eighth century, we find radical changes being introduced as regards royal titulary and artistic style, which are first found on the monuments of Shoshenq V, Osorkon IV, and Takelot III.[19] These innovations involved an attempt to recapture the spirit of the remote past, by following the patterns of royal naming used during the Old and Middle Kingdoms, and drawing on models from the same periods for new artistic productions. Thus, royal names, which had over the previous centuries grown into sprawling compounds of names and epithets, were greatly simplified. To support the new artistic approach, ancient monuments—including the Step Pyramid at Saqqara—were opened in what can only be described as archaeological excavations, and reliefs gridded for precise replication.[20] Ancient modes of expression also began to be used in contemporary texts, including the "republication" of ancient works and the creation of new ones purporting to be such copies. This whole complex of archaism continued into the seventh century, although by then direct imitation of ancient artistic styles had been replaced by an approach which combined ancient models of form with modern innovations, particularly as regards portraiture.

Around the middle of the eighth century the divisions of the country widened yet further (fig. 18), with kingdoms arising at Herakleopolis (Ihnasiya el-Medina) and Hermopolis (Ashmunein) in Middle Egypt, alongside lesser independent or quasi-independent entities. Similar fresh divisions also arose in the Delta, new polities including a Chiefdom of the West, based at Sais, which came to be the dominant power in the northwest of Egypt, with wider political aspirations as well.

2 KUSH COMES TO EGYPT

Kashta

It is as Egypt was undergoing its progressive disintegrations that it becomes possible to pick up the threads of events in Nubia—which now directly impinged on those in Egypt. From Elephantine, on the historic border between the two territories, comes a fragmentary stela of a King Kashta (fig. 13).[1] His names are found written as follows:

P.		$(n-)m^{3c}t-r^c$	One who belongs to the *maat* of Re
N.	/	$k^3 \check{s}t^3$	Kashta

The prenomen is the core form of a name employed by many kings since the time of its first bearer, Rameses II, including the shadowy Iry, as well as Osorkon III of Thebes, and Shoshenq III, Pamiu, and Osorkon IV of Tanis.

From the temple complex of Karnak (fig. 15) comes an even more striking illustration of the way in which the Nubians had burst onto the Egyptian scene. This is a fragmentary entry, dated to Kashta's Year 1, in the temple's Priestly Annals, which stretch back to the Twenty-first Dynasty.[2] The existence of such an entry implies that Kashta was the ruler of Thebes at the time in question, and that the line of Takelot II and Osorkon III had now been displaced from their former capital.

Exactly when this had occurred is not wholly clear. Significantly, Takelot III was not followed on his throne by any of his known sons. His brother Rudamun is known to have become a king, although evidence of the latter's presence at Thebes is limited to painted cartouches in the chapel of Osiris-Heqadjet at Karnak, a structure built

FIGURE 13 Elephantine island at Aswan and the stela of Kashta from the site (Cairo JE41013).

by Osorkon III and Takelot III (figs. 12, 31). This may suggest that it was at the death of Takelot III—or very soon afterward—that much of the southern part of Egypt passed under Kushite control.

There is no evidence of any hostility toward the memory of Osorkon III and Takelot III by the Kushites—their names and images remained intact on their monuments—and Shepenwepet I continued in office as God's Wife, albeit with a Kushite princess installed as her heiress (see next page). Also, a son-in-law of Rudamun is to be found later as a Kushite ally (pages 29–33). All this suggests a negotiated handover of power. This may also have been the background to the adoption of the ancient title of King's Son of Kush, moribund since the beginning of the Twenty-first Dynasty, by a son-in-law of Takelot III, the Vizier and Third Prophet of Amun Pamiu i.[3]

It is possible that it was Kashta who achieved this feat single-handedly soon after his accession in Nubia. However, a King Alara is presented in later retrospectives as perhaps the originator of the northern extension of the power of the renewed Kingdom of Kush.[4] Although no contemporary remains naming Alara are known, his daughter, Tabiry,[5] was married to Kashta's successor, Pi(ankh)y, thus making Alara the likely predecessor of Kashta, given that there is no sign whatsoever of Alara in Egypt.[6]

Very little is known of Kashta, and apart from the aforementioned Elephantine stela and the Karnak Priestly Annal, only an aegis and a necklace,[7] the pedigree of his daughter Amenirdis I,[8] and a stray fragment found at El-Kurru[9] bear his name. The latter would suggest that Kashta was buried there, and on the basis of its size and position, tomb Ku8 (fig. 93) has been attributed to him.

Whether or not Alara had some involvement in the initial stages of the takeover of southern Egypt, Kashta's primacy in the absorption of Thebes is suggested by the fact that it was his daughter, Amenirdis I, who was adopted by Shepenwepet I as her heir to the position of God's Wife. In doing so, Kashta would be following the historical precedent of kings presenting their senior daughter to fulfill the role.[10] Although the direct evidence for formal adoption as the mechanism for succession to the office of God's Wife only comes from the Twenty-fifth and Twenty-sixth Dynasties, it is likely to have been in place much earlier, perhaps going back to the point at which the office was definitively separated from queenship.

There is evidence, however, to suggest that the princess's actual arrival at Karnak only came under Pi(ankh)y, perhaps as a consequence of her young age, or her father's premature death (given the paucity of material relating to his reign). This comes from a group of blocks from the temple of Mut at Karnak recording the arrival of an heir to the God's Wife of Amun (fig. 16).[11] As these blocks now stand, they incorporate texts of Sematawytefnakhte, Shipmaster of Herakleopolis, who served under Psamtik I, founder of the Twenty-sixth Dynasty. These texts seem to refer to the arrival of Psamtik's daughter, Neitiqerti I, at Thebes in the king's Year 9 (cf. pages 97–98). However, it has been suggested that the Sematawytefnakhte texts are secondary and that the blocks originally referred to the installation of Amenirdis I as heir under Pi(ankh)y—potentially in his Year 5.[12] Certainly, Amenirdis's first clear attestation names her (and Shepenwepet I) alongside Nimlot, king of Hermopolis,[13] who was a contemporary of Pi(ankh)y (see below, pages 32–33). On the other hand, it may be more likely that the lady arriving is Shepenwepet II, daughter of Pi(ankh)y, coming to be adopted in turn by Amenirdis I as her heir. Shepenwepet II would, however, only come into office many years later, after the successive deaths of her adoptive grandmother Shepenwepet I and her adoptive mother, Amenirdis.[14]

Kashta's relationship to Pi(ankh)y is unclear. Kashta married a lady named Pebatjma, with whom he had at least two daughters, the aforementioned Amenirdis I and Peksater, who married Pi(ankh)y.[15] It remains a moot point[16] whether Pabatjma is identical to a King's Daughter, King's Sister, and Mother of the God's Adoratrix Paabtameri who was the mother of a generalissimo Pegatterru-Irpaakhqenqenenef.[17] However, Pegatterru is not called a King's Son, which would be expected if he were the son of Kashta. Another possibility is that he may have been the offspring of a second marriage by a widowed queen.[18] Yet another option could be that, as seems to have been the case at other points in the past, the title of King's Son was applicable only during the lifetime of the king in question.[19] That Paabtameri had been married to a king is suggested by the fact that she was the mother of a God's Adoratrix—all of whom at this period were king's daughters.

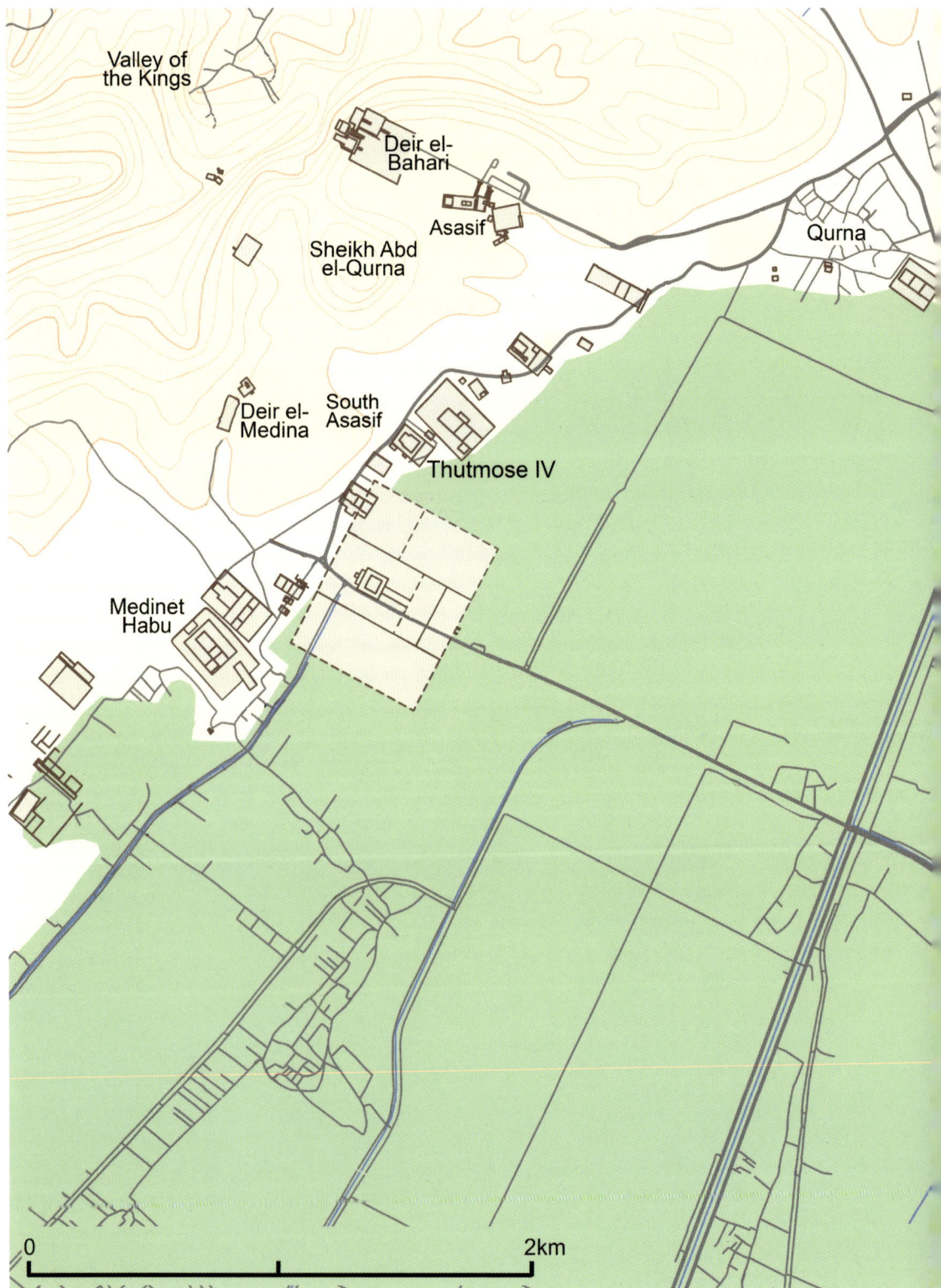

Valley of
the Kings

Deir el-
Bahari

Asasif

Qurna

Sheikh Abd
el-Qurna

Deir el-
Medina

South
Asasif

Thutmose IV

Medinet
Habu

0   2km

FIGURE 14 Map of Thebes.

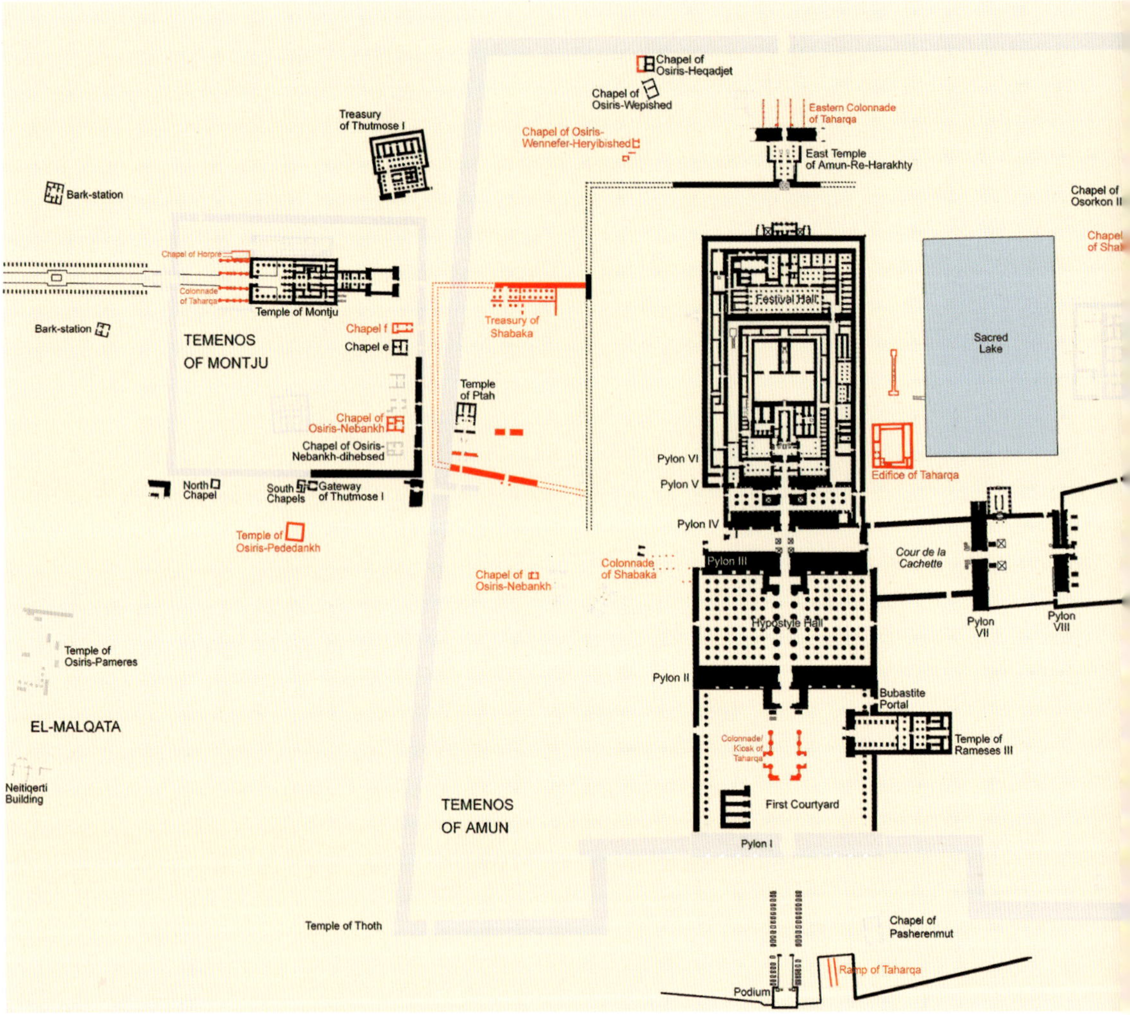

FIGURE 15 Plan of Karnak, showing Twenty-fifth Dynasty additions in red.

She could thus have been a spouse of Pi(ankh)y (father of Shepenwepet II),[20] of Kashta (father of Amenirdis I), or even Taharqa (father of Amenirdis II), if her stelae could be dated sufficiently late.[21] A certain Neferukakashta may, on the basis of her name, have been another daughter of Kashta.

A later king, Shabaka, has been suggested as a son of Kashta, since Amenirdis I is referred to on one monument as a "King's Sister of Neferkare" (Shabaka).[22] However, the term "sister" (*snt*) had wider usage in ancient Egypt,[23] and here may simply indicate Amenirdis's status vis-à-vis her kinsman-king.[24] A clear example of such a usage is to

N

Temple of
Nakhthorheb

Chapel B

Sanctuary of
Amun-Kamutef

Temple A

Temple of Mut

Temple of
Osiris-Ptah-Nebankh

Porch of
Taharqa

Contra-temple

Sacred Lake

Gateway of Taharqa

Pylon
X

TEMENOS
OF MUT

South Temple
of Rameses III

Karnak-Luxor Sphinx Avenue

e of Khonsu

Colonnade
of Taharqa

Chapel of
Neferhotep

Temple
of Opet

100 meters

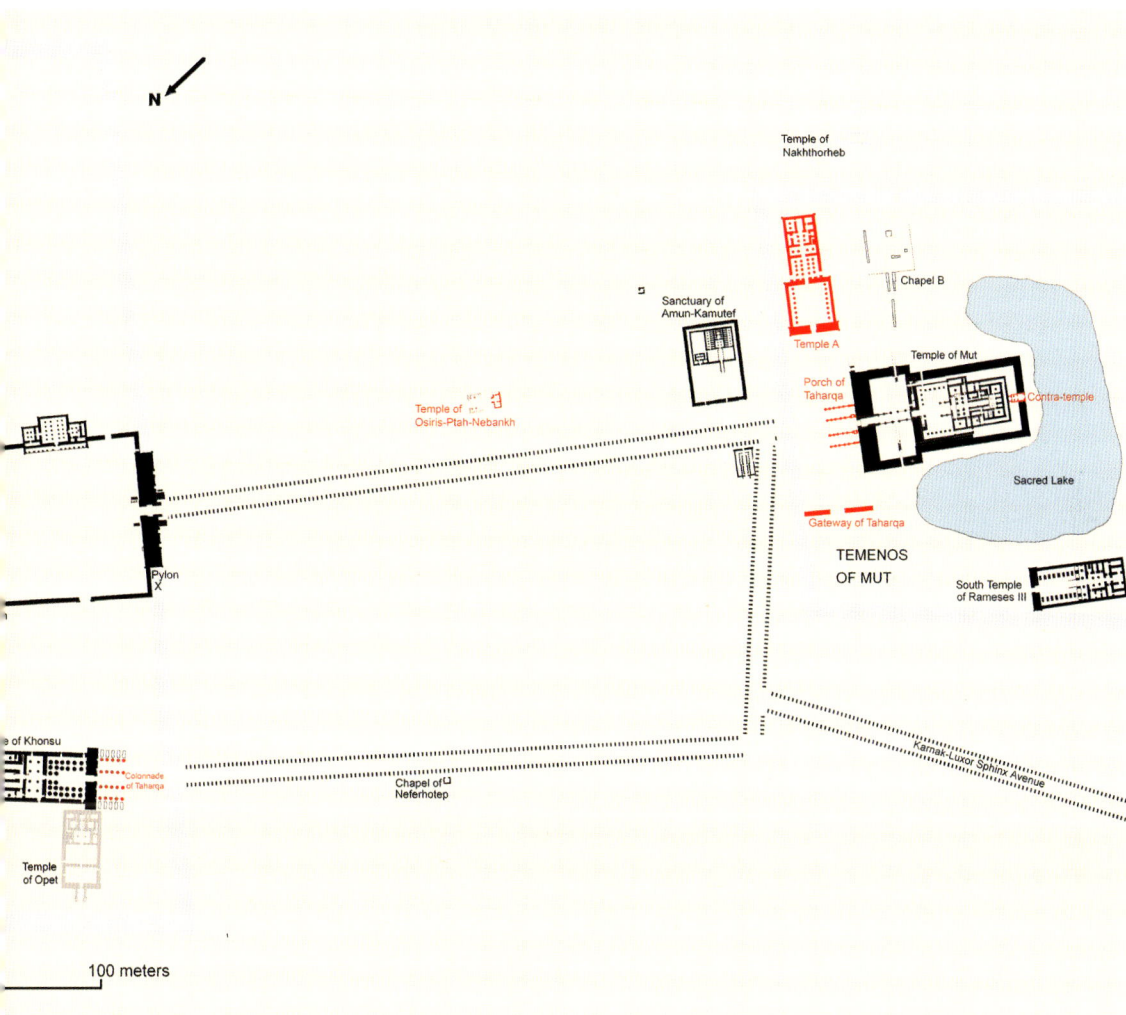

be seen in the case of Hatshepsut and Thutmose III, where the latter is referred to as Hatshepsut's "brother," yet was most certainly actually her nephew.[25] A parallelism of status between Amenirdis and Shabaka is certainly a key feature of the context in question, the decoration of the chapel of Osiris-Nebankh at Karnak-North (fig. 124).[26]

It has been proposed[27] that the so-called "Excommunication Stela" from Gebel Barkal (fig. 17 top)[28] relates the aftermath of Kashta's death. The stela dates to Year 2 of a king whose name and figure have been erased, with the latter crudely restored. He has conventionally been assumed to be Aspelta (Kashta's ninth successor), whose monuments

FIGURE 16 Blocks probably originally depicting the arrival of the prospective God's Wife of Amun, Shepenwepet II, and later adapted to show the arrival of Neitiqerti I; from temple of Mut at Karnak (Cairo JE31886).

were the subject of attack (cf. pages 104–105, fig. 83). However, it has been pointed out that the composition of the lunette, consisting of the king offering to the Amun-triad without any supporting members of the royal family, is inconsistent with stelae of the time of Taharqa and later. In addition, the erasure-followed-by-crude-restoration of a Napatan king's figure is otherwise found only on the Sandstone and Victory Stelae of Pi(ankh)y (see figs. 17 bottom, 19), suggesting that the Excommunication Stela should also be dated to his reign.

The stela relates that

His Person proceeded to the temple of his father, Amun of Napata who dwells in Gebel Barkal, to expel that family whom the god hates . . . because of that deed—it is an abomination to even utter it—which they did in the temple of Amun. They did a deed which the god had not ordered. They made a plot in their hearts, namely killing a man whose crime did not exist . . . . He slaughtered them, and made (them) into a burnt offering . . .

It has been argued that the "abomination" might have been the murder of the previous king.[29] This might be supported by the severity of the punishment and the fact that the author of the stela is given the epithet "eldest son who protects his father, who answers on the occasion of replacing (him) on his throne." The first part is an epithet of Horus, as avenger of his murdered father, Osiris, while the second part is extremely unusual. If so, the crime would seem not to have been recognized immediately (poisoning?), given that retribution was not meted out until Year 2 of the next king.

Pi(ankh)y

That Pi(ankh)y was indeed a child of Kashta is not susceptible to proof, but seems likely. As noted in the preface, the reading of the king's nomen, which is written ⬚, presents problems. The issue concerns whether the ʿnḫ-sign, which is found in all hieroglyphic writings of the name, but is omitted in hieratic ones, should be read, or be regarded as some kind of determinative.[30] The cartouche is sometimes expanded by epithets, either just "beloved of Amun," or further by a proclamation of the king as "son of Bastet."[31] This latter kind of expansion had been common in Egypt since the time of Osorkon II. However, most attestations of the king's nomen are in its simple form, without epithets.

Two prenomina are definitely known for Pi(ankh)y: Usermaatre[32] and Seneferre (used toward the end of the reign).[33] The former name went back to the time of Rameses II, and had been used by Kashta, but the latter was a fresh formulation, although names of the s-nfr-X-rʿ type are known from the Second Intermediate

FIGURE 17 Top: the "Excommunication Stela," possibly of Pi(ankh)y (Cairo JE48865); bottom: the "Sandstone stela" of Pi(ankh)y (SNM 1851); both from Gebel Barkal.

Period. Pi(ankh)y may have used the prenomen Menkheperre at the beginning of the reign, depending on whether the partly erased nomen on a stela[34] should be restored as [Pi(ankh)]y or [In]y (an obscure local king of the same general period). In favor of Pi(ankh)y being this "Menkheperre" is the fact that on the so-called Sandstone Stela from Gebel Barkal (see further below)[35] he employs Horus, Nebti, and Golden Falcon names that are taken directly from those of Thutmose III (with the substitution of "Napata" for "Thebes" in the Horus name).

Like most kings between the early New Kingdom and his time, Pi(ankh)y also employed alternate Horus and Nebti names, including alongside the "Thutmose III" Horus name on an obelisk from Kadakol.[36] One example of more remote historicism is seen in the occasional use of the Horus name *sm3-t3wy*, originally used by Montjuhotep II, reunifier of Egypt at the beginning of the Middle Kingdom. Pi(ankh)y's full titularies thus appear to run as follows:

H.	*k3-nḫt ḫꜥ-m-npt*	Strong bull appearing in Napata
	sm3-t3wi	Uniter of the Two Lands
	sḥtp-t3wy.f	He who pacifies his Two Lands
	k3-t3wi.f	Bull of his Two Lands
	k3-nḫt ḫꜥ-m-w3st	Strong Bull appearing in Thebes
Nb.	*w3ḥ-nsyt-mi-rꜥ-m-pt*	Enduring of kingship like Re in the sky
	ms-ḥmwt	Creator of crafts
	ḥq3-kmt	Ruler of Thebes
G.	*dsr-ḫꜥw sḥm-pḥti*	Whose appearances are divine, whose might is powerful
	sꜥš3-qnw	Multiplier of brave soldiers
P.	*mn-ḫpr-rꜥ*	Established of form like Re
	wsr-m3ꜥt-rꜥ	Strong of *maat* like Re
	snfr-rꜥ	Whom Re makes vital
N.	*p{ꜥnḫ}y-mr-imn*	P(ankh)y beloved of Amun
	p{ꜥnḫ}y-mr-imn-s3-b3stt	P(ankh)y beloved of Amun, son of Bastet
	p{ꜥnḫ}y	P(ankh)y
	py	Py

The aforementioned "Sandstone Stela" (fig. 17 bottom) was found in the outer court-yard of the Great Temple of Amun (B500—figs. 23, 24), a structure originally founded back in the New Kingdom (page 6). To this, Pi(ankh)y added a southern annex (B520) and two successive pylons and courtyards (B501 and B502). The earlier of these (B502) was ultimately transformed into a hypostyle hall.

The stela is undated but would seem to belong to the beginning of the reign, as it relates the following speech by Amun:

> "I said of you in your mother's womb that you would be ruler of Egypt; I knew you in the semen, while you were in the egg, that you were to be lord. I made you receive the great crown . . . ."

The king responds, saying:

> "Amun of Napata has caused me to be ruler of every foreign country. He to whom I say 'You are Chief,' he is to be Chief; he to whom I say 'You are not king,' he is not king. Amun-in-Thebes has caused me to be ruler of Egypt. He to whom I say "Appear (as king)," he shall make his appearance. He to whom I say "Do not appear (as king)," he shall not make his appearance . . . ."

Taken together, this would appear to fit well with the picture seen later in Pi(ankh)y's reign (see just below), with the king as sole ruler of the southern part of Egypt, and as overlord of the rest of the country, which was ruled by a patchwork of kings, chiefs, and mayors.

A fragmentary stela from Gebel Barkal, dated to II *3ḫt* in Year 4,[37] records some kind of activity which involved northward travel, and mentions an "[ar]my of the northland." It may record a visit by the king to Egypt, or it may indicate some fighting in Egypt, but the context remains wholly obscure.

It is not until Pi(ankh)y's Year 21 that we have a further record of events, related on a further Barkal stela dated to that year, and presumably covering events of the immediately preceding year or two (fig. 19).[38] Pi(ankh)y's authority had by now expanded northward to at least the mouth of the Fayyum, where Herakleopolis was under the rule of King Peftjauawybast (fig. 20), a son-in-law of Rudamun, and a loyal vassal of the Kushite ruler. However, Pi(ankh)y, in Upper Nubia, now received a report:

> One came to inform His Person that the Prince of the West . . . Tefnakhte . . . had seized the entire West from the coastal marshes to Lisht, sailing south with

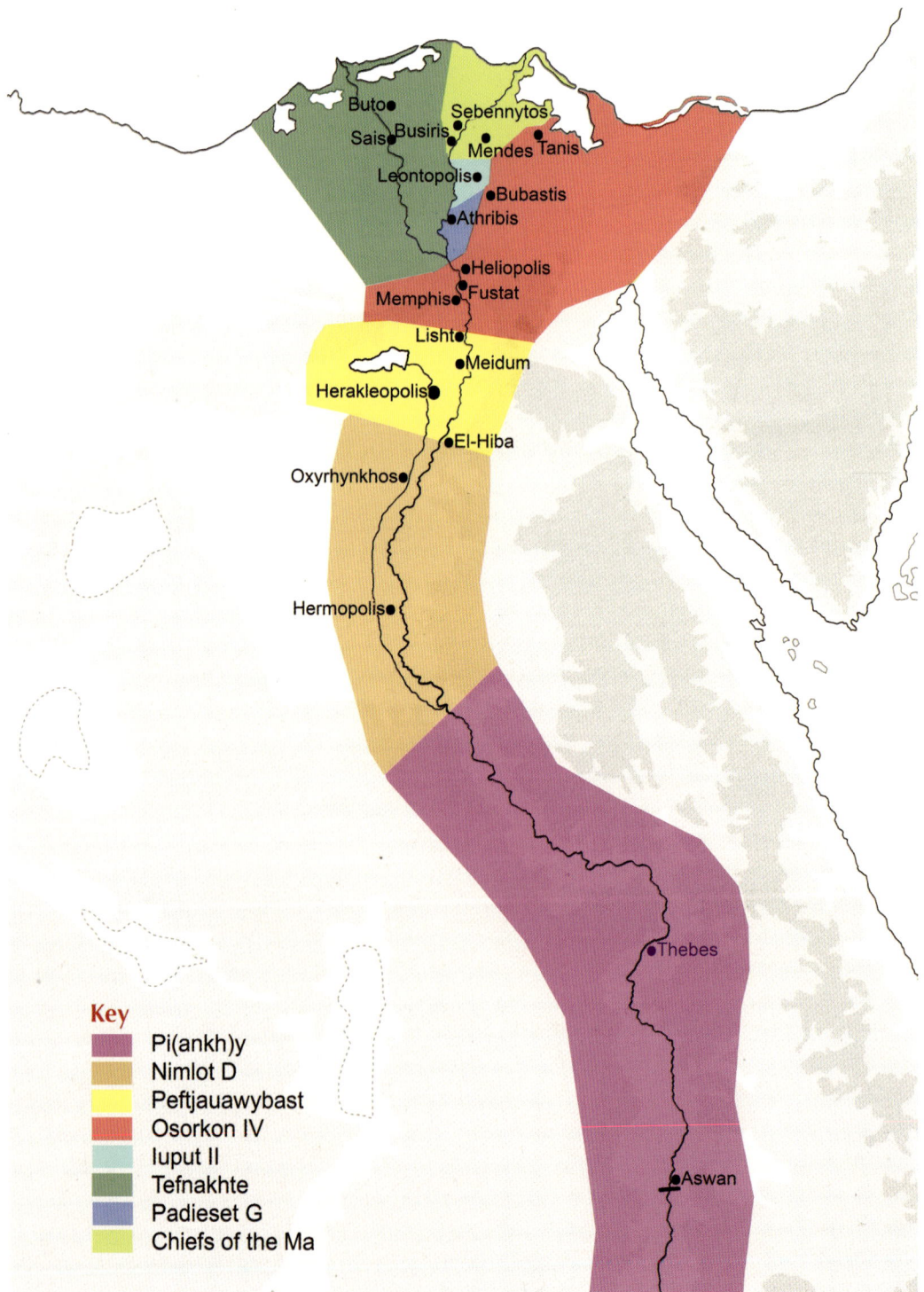

FIGURE 18 Political map of Egypt at the time of Pi(ankh)y's northern campaign.

a great army, the two lands being united in following him, the mayors and rulers of compounds being dogs at his heels. No fortress of the nomes of the south had closed (their gates) . . . every town in the west had opened its gates in fear of him.

He had turned back against the nomes of the east and they had opened to him . . . . He was ⌜closing in⌝ on Herakleopolis, he had surrounded it without allowing anyone to leave or enter, fighting every day.

FIGURE 19 The Victory Stela of Pi(ankh)y; from Gebel Barkal (Cairo JE48862).

FIGURE 20 Peftjauawybast, King of Herakleopolis (MFA 1977.16).

In contrast to Peftjauawybast's loyalty, two hundred kilometers to the south—and thus closer to Pi(ankh)y—Nimlot, king of Hermopolis, had "gone off to be [Tefnakhte's] footman, [having] betrayed His Person."

In response, Pi(ankh)y ordered his Egypt-based commanders, Pawarema and Lamerskny, to immediately lead their forces to Hermopolis and put it under siege. A further army was then put together, to be led northward from Nubia. The king gave detailed strategic and tactical instructions to this force, enjoining it to pay its respects to Amun while passing through Thebes. Having done so, the combined Kushite armies engaged with enemy forces which were proceeding by ship upriver from the north. Successful in combat against them, the Kushite generals sent prisoners south to Pi(ankh)y, who had remained in Nubia. They then pushed on to Hermopolis, where Nimlot had been joined by Kings Osorkon IV (Tanis and Bubastis) and Iuput II (of Leontopolis), and Chiefs of the Ma Shoshenq E (of Busiris), Djedameniufankh (of Mendes), and Nesnayisu (of Hesebka).

During the battle that followed, the Kushite army

made a great bloodbath among them, greater than anything. Their fleet was captured on the river. The remnant crossed over, mooring on the west bank . . . . At first light, His Person's army crossed over against them: army mingled with army, then they slaughtered many men among them and innumerable horses. Trembling arose among the rest, and they fled toward the northland from the great blow . . . . King Nimlot fled southward when told that Hermopolis was ⌐confronted⌐ by the hostility of His Person's army . . . and entered Hermopolis while His Person's army was on the riverbank . . . .

The Kushites then laid siege to Hermopolis and its surrounding territory, sending a full report on the action to date back to Pi(ankh)y. He was enraged that total victory had not been achieved, and resolved to proceed to Middle Egypt to take personal command of his forces. However, he was not prepared to do so until he had celebrated the New Year- and Opet-Festivals at Thebes, leaving his commanders to continue to direct operations in the interim.

Three fortified towns (modern locations unknown) had been taken, a son of Tefnakhte being among the dead, before Pi(ankh)y finally began his journey to Egypt. Having celebrated the Theban festivals, he entered the theater of operations and, having personally berated the army for their failure to bring matters to an end, the king had earthworks created overlooking Hermopolis, to allow fire to be directed down into the city itself. At length, it

> placed itself on its belly, beseeching [Pi(ankh)y], envoys coming out and de-scending, bearing everything that is good to see, gold, all kinds of fine stones, clothing in a chest, the crown that had been on [Nimlot's] head . . . for many days . . . . Then was caused to come [Nimlot's] wife, the King's Wife and King's Daughter Nestjent, to beg to the king's wives, the royal harem, the king's daugh-ters [of Pi(ankh)y]. She lay on her belly in the house of the king's wives before the king's wives: "Come to me, king's wives, king's daughters, king's sisters; may you placate Horus, lord of the palace [Pi(ankh)y]!"

Finally, Nimlot himself came to Pi(ankh)y to offer his own submission, accompanied by a mass of tribute, of "silver, gold, lapis lazuli, turquoise, bronze, and many fine stones." Furthermore Nimlot gifted a horse, led to Pi(ankh)y by Nimlot himself.

Pi(ankh)y then entered Hermopolis and made sacrifices at the city's temple of Thoth (fig. 21), before proceeding to Nimlot's palace. There, he studiously ignored the royal women's attempts to offer homage, and then went to the stable, where he was shocked to find that the horses had gone hungry during the siege, berating Nimlot that this was "much more evil in my heart that my horses have been made to hunger, than any evil you have done in the meanness of your heart." This great regard for horses would be found among later Kushite rulers as well, down to the very end of paganism.

The fall of Hermopolis had been accompanied by the lifting of the siege of Herakleopolis. The city's King Peftjauawybast now brought gifts to Pi(ankh)y, lamenting how he "did not find a friend in [his] day of distress, who would stand on the day of battle," yet now re-joicing that Pi(ankh)y had "driven darkness from" him, and pledging Herakleopolis to him.

From Herakleopolis, Pi(ankh)y proceeded deeper into the Fayyum. He also besieged and took the submission of a number of towns back in the Nile valley, including Meidum and Lisht, prior to appearing in front of the city of Memphis, calling on the inhabitants:

Don't shut yourselves in; don't fight . . . he that would enter, let him enter; he that would come out, let him come out. Those who would depart shall not be hindered. I shall give an offering to Ptah and the gods of Memphis . . . . I shall sail north in peace, [having left] Memphis safe and sound . . . .

Why, look at the nomes of the south: not a single person has been slain there, except for rebels who cursed god . . . .

However, the gates of Memphis were closed against the king, and a force sent out against Pi(ankh)y's army, including a number of conscripted civilians. Tefnakhte arrived at Memphis at night, managed to enter, and exhorted its inhabitants to hold out, as the city was well stocked with foodstuffs, had strong—and newly reinforced—fortifications, and abutted the Nile on its eastern side. He then mounted a horse and rode north, to bring back reinforcements.

Having inspected the city's defenses, Pi(ankh)y called a meeting of his senior advisors to debate means of overcoming the apparently impregnable fortifications. The approach adopted was to mass every available ship and boat against the river defenses of Memphis and use their masts to scale them, allowing the city to be stormed at night and "seized like a cloudburst, with many slain or brought as living captives to the place where His Person was."

FIGURE 21 The temple area at Hermopolis.

The next morning, the king sent men to ensure the safety of the holy places of Memphis, made libations, returned the priests to their temples, and made his way to that of Ptah to make offerings. Moving then to the royal palace, he received there King Iuput II of Leontopolis, the Chief of the Ma Akanosh of Sebennytos, Prince Padieset G of Athribis, and various other northern leaders, all bearing gifts. At dawn the next day, Pi(ankh)y crossed the river to offer to Atum at Fustat, and then pushed on to Heliopolis to be purified and make sunrise offerings in its great temple. After this, he visited the sanctuary of the *bnbn*-fetish and bark-sanctuaries of Re and Atum, resealing the doors with his own seal. It was at Heliopolis that Pi(ankh)y received King Osorkon IV, who had "come to see the vitality of His Person."

The next destination for Pi(ankh)y was Athribis, whither he sailed before pitching his tent on the eastern side of the town. Here, there paraded before him "those kings and mayors of the northland, all the chiefs who wear the (Libyan) feather, every vizier, every chief, every royal acquaintance from the west, from the east, and from inland islands, to behold the vitality of His Person." As the local ruler, Padieset led them in pledging his palace and his possessions to Pi(ankh)y, including the choice of the horses in his stables.

> Then these kings and mayors said to His Person: "Dismiss us to our cities so we (can) open our treasuries: choose according to what your heart desires. (We) will bring to you the best of our stalls, the foremost of our horses." Then His Person did so.

A raid on Athribis by troops loyal to Tefnakhte seems then to have taken place, which was bloodily repulsed by the troops of Padieset, assisted by Kushite forces.

In the wake of this event, Tefnakhte sent a messenger to Pi(ankh)y presenting his submission.

> Be appeased! I cannot look upon your face in the days of shame: I cannot stand before your flame. I dread your awesomeness. Indeed, you are Nubti, foremost of the southland, Montju, the bull of the strong arm. As for any city toward which you turn your face, you will not find this humble servant <there> before I have reached the islands of the sea in fear of your might . . . . Cleanse (your) servant of his fault. Let my property be received into the treasury, of gold and every precious stone, even the foremost of the horses . . . . Let a messenger come to me quickly that he may drive fear from my heart. Then I shall go to the temple in his presence and cleanse myself by a holy oath."

Pi(ankh)y sent General Pawarema and the Chief Lector Priest Padiamennesuttawy as his delegates to Sais, who received Tefnakhte's tribute and oversaw his oath: "I will not go against a royal decree; I will not thrust aside what His Person says; I will not do harm to a mayor without your knowledge; I will do as the king says; I will not go against what he has decreed."

In the wake of Tefnakhte's act, the remaining areas that had not yet submitted to Pi(ankh)y did so. This was followed by an early-morning event at which the four local Egyptian kings formally pledged their loyalty—not just the three who had sided with Tefnakhte, but also the loyal Peftjauawybast (fig. 19, lunette). But only Nimlot was received into Pi(ankh)y's residence: the other three had to remain outside "because they were uncircumcised and fish-eaters . . . , an abomination to the king's house."

With this, Pi(ankh)y loaded his ships with the tribute he had received and sailed for the south, "his heart swelling, the riverbanks on both sides . . . singing and shouting, saying: 'O mighty ruler, O mighty ruler, Pi(ankh)y, O mighty ruler! You have come from establishing rule over the northland. You have made bulls into women. Happy is the heart of the woman who bore you and the man who begot you!'"

The king did not institute personal rule beyond his previous Nubian/south Egyptian domain. Rather, he left the existing dynasts and other local potentates, all now bound to him by oath, in place to govern Middle and Lower Egypt. In particular, Osorkon IV (fig. 22), ruling from Tanis, adjacent to Egypt's eastern land border, seems to have been left responsible for foreign relations. On this basis, he is likely to have been "So, king of Egypt" to whom the Israelite king Hoshea sent (unsuccessfully) for aid against Shalmaneser V of Assyria in 726/5.[39] Osorkon was probably also the ruler who sent his army commander "Re'u" to aid a Palestinian rebellion against the new Assyrian king, Sargon II, in 720—only to be defeated in battle at Rafeh.[40] However, the Assyrian depiction of the battle[41] seems to include a Nubian.[42] This may suggest that the force commanded by "Re'u" was actually a joint Egyptian–Kushite one, reflecting the fact that Osorkon IV's realm was now a dependency of Kush.

A few years later, in 716, Osorkon IV was probably the "Shilkanni, king of Egypt" who sent a gift of horses to Sargon II of Assyria, whose forces had at that time penetrated as far as El-Arish in the northeastern Sinai.[43] It is unknown when Osorkon's reign terminated, but he would appear to have been succeeded in his local kingship by a series of monarchs, including Shepseskare-irenre Gemenefkhonsubak and Sehetepib(en)re Padubast (III), both known from items found at Tanis.[44] The latter king is also known

FIGURE 22 Block from Tanis, showing Osorkon IV in Third Dynasty style.

from a statue at Memphis (fig. 72)[45] and was probably the king of that name who was ruling from Tanis at the end of the 670s (see below, pages 86–87).

Prior to his northern campaign, Pi(ankh)y had perhaps already begun the great hypostyle hall (B502) at the Gebel Barkal Amun temple (fig. 23). This was apparently erected on foundations originally prepared under Rameses II, but subsequently abandoned. Its walls in any case now provided a canvas for tableaux relating to the king's recent campaign, but only a few fragments of these reliefs now survive (fig. 24 top).[46] An outer peristyle court (B501) was also added to the temple, within which was erected the king's great stela. To mark the approach to the greatly enlarged temple, a series of six ram statues were taken from the temple of Amenhotep III at Soleb and placed in front of a new outer pylon (fig. 24 bottom).

Following the inauguration of the hypostyle hall, Pi(ankh)y seems to have adopted the prenomen Seneferre, superseding the previously used Usermaatre (which appears in the hall),[47] to judge from a votive piece of linen dated to Year 20 or later (fig. 25).[48] This piece is the key evidence for determining the minimum length of Pi(ankh)y's

FIGURE 23 The temple of Amun (B500) at Gebel Barkal, and columns in hypostyle hall B502, with the nomen of Pi(ankh)y on the surviving abacus.

FIGURE 24 Top: north wall of hall B502 of the temple of Amun, showing Pi(ankh)y and Queen Peksater greeting the bark of Amun. Bottom: Pylon I and rams before the temple of Amun, with a view to peak B350, which was conceived as, and was enhanced to further resemble, a rearing cobra. Visible below are columns before Taharqa's temple B300 (figs. 53, 69, 70).

FIGURE 25 Linen inscribed with the highest known year date of Pi(ankh)y (BM EA6640).

reign, with the most likely reading of its damaged date apparently "Year 30," rather than the "Year 40" that has also been suggested.[49] Pi(ankh)y would thus seem to have survived his great expedition by at least a decade, and perhaps more (see page 43). From Year 23 comes a stela from Dakhla,[50] which has a protagonist, the Chief of the Shamin, Nesthuty, who had previously been attested in office back in Year 13 of Takelot III.

In addition to Tabiry, discussed above (page 20), Pi(ankh)y seems to have had at least three other wives: Khensa,[51] Peksater,[52] and Abar. The latter was the mother of the later king Taharqa, born around two decades before Pi(ankh)y's death (see page 47, below). It is unknown, however, which wives bore Pi(ankh)y's remaining known children: two sons, Khaliut[53] and Har,[54] and at least six daughters. The latter were headed by the future God's Wife, Shepenwepet II, identified as Pi(ankh)y's daughter on various of her monuments,[55] along with Arty, a spouse of Shabataka (see page 45, below), Qalhata, a wife of Shabaka (see page 56, below), and Naparaye and Takahatamun, sister-wives of Taharqa (see page 71, below). Tabakenamun, who was a King's Daughter, Wife, and Sister, may have been Pi(ankh)y's offspring, but this is unclear since the identity of her husband is uncertain—perhaps Shabaka or Taharqa.[56]

As already noted, Pi(ankh)y seems to have allowed the status quo to continue in Middle and Lower Egypt. However, this was seemingly once again disturbed by Tefnakhte, probably not long after Pi(ankh)y's return to Nubia. The evidence for this is the existence of material belonging to a Tefnakhte who bore full royal titles and the prenomen Shepsesre and reigned for at least eight years (fig. 28).[57] While it has been suggested that this Tefnakhte was not Pi(ankh)y's erstwhile opponent, but instead a later "Tefnakhte II," possibly the "Stephinatês" listed by the third-century BC historian Manetho as one of the precursors of the Twenty-sixth Dynasty,[58] the older view seems on balance to be the better one. The implication would accordingly be that, as soon as Pi(ankh)y was safely back in Nubia, Tefnakhte resumed his expansionist career, albeit now with full royal titles.[59]

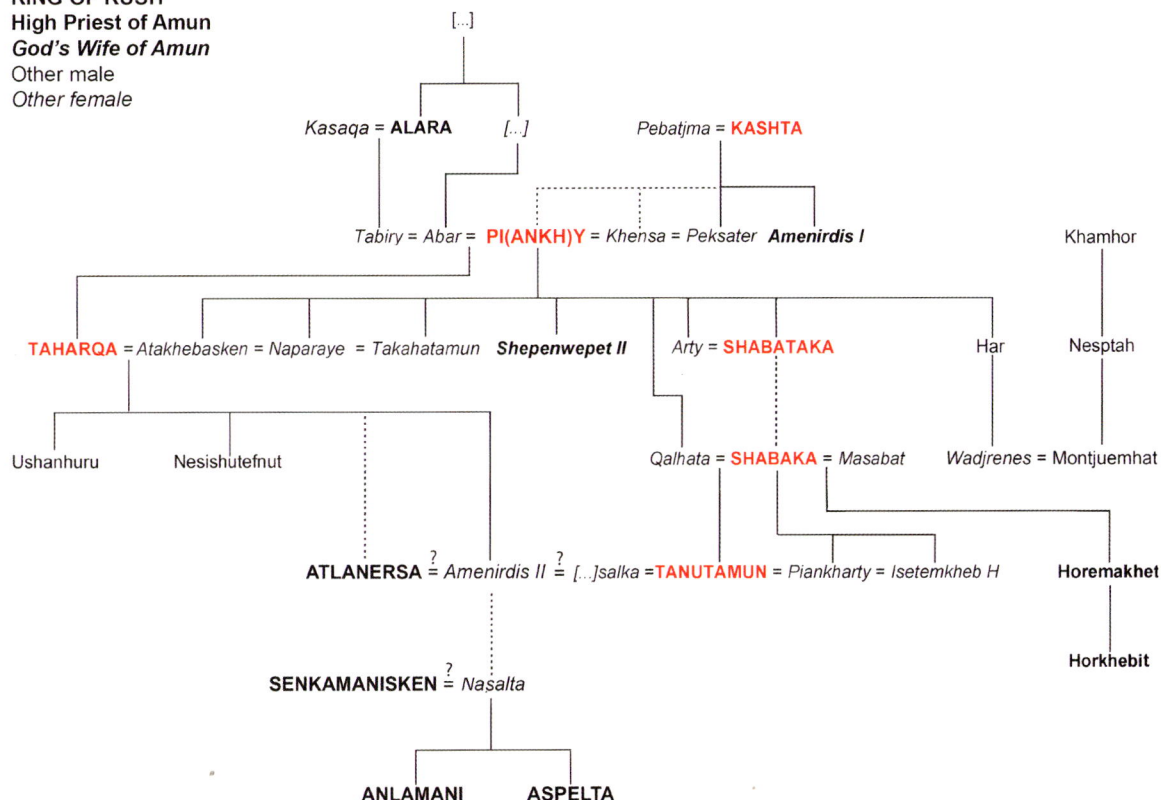

Key

KING OF EGYPT-KUSH
KING OF KUSH
High Priest of Amun
God's Wife of Amun
Other male
Other female

FIGURE 26 Provisional family tree of the Twenty-fifth Dynasty.

That Tefnakhte's area of kingly control included Memphis is suggested by the fact that his successor, Wahkare Bakenrenef, was responsible for the burial there of an Apis bull in his Year 6. It is generally assumed that Bakenrenef was a son of Tefnakhte. This is supported by a later tradition that made Bakenrenef the offspring of "Tnephtichthus," and praises him for his wisdom and as a lawgiver.[60] It is by no means clear how he attained this posthumous fame,[61] or what lay behind a further late tradition that during his reign a lamb spoke, prophesying the future.[62] Apart from various items related to the Apis burial,[63] a donation stela, perhaps from the eastern Delta,[64] and a fragment from Tanis[65] are also known. Among smaller pieces are two faience vases and a scarab that were found in tombs in Italy, which may link into the king's Classical reputation.[66]

KUSHITES	THEBES		TANIS	SAIS	HERAKLE-OPOLIS	LEONT-OPOLIS	HERMO-POLIS	ASSYRIA
	High Priest of Amun at Karnak	God's Wife of Amun at Karnak						

BC	KUSHITES	THEBES HP	THEBES GW	TANIS	SAIS	HERAKLEOPOLIS	LEONTOPOLIS	HERMOPOLIS	ASSYRIA	BC
760		Takelot III / Osorkon F	Shepenwepet I	Shoshenq V 20					Ashur-dan III	760
759				21						759
758				22						758
757				23						757
756				24						756
755	Kashta			25						755
754				26					Ashur-nirari V	754
753				27						753
752				28						752
751				29						751
750				30						750
749	Pi(ankh)y 1			31						749
748	2			32						748
747	3			33						747
746	4			34						746
745	5			35	Tefnakhte (as Chief/ Prince)				Tilgath-pileser III	745
744	6			36						744
743	7			37						743
742	8			38						742
741	9									741
740	10			Osorkon IV						740
739	11									739
738	12									738
737	13									737
736	14									736
735	15									735
734	16					Peftjauawybast				734
733	17									733
732	18									732
731	19						Iuput II	Nimlot D		731
730	20									730
729	21									729
728	22				Tefnakhte (as King) 1					728
727	23				2				Shalmaneser V	727
726	24				3					726
725	25				4					725
724	26				5					724
723	27				6				Sargon II	723
722	28				7					722
721	29				8					721
720	30									720
719	31									719
718	32				Bakenrenef 1					718
717	33				2					717
716	34				3					716
715	35				4					715
714	36				5					714
713	Shabataka 1				6					713
712	2									712
711	3									711
710	4									710
709	5									709
708	6		Amenirdis I							708
707	7									707
706	8									706
705	Shabaka 1	Horemakhet							Sennacherib	705
704	2									704
703	3									703
702	4									702
701	5									701
700	6									700
699	7				"Stephinates"					699
698	8									698
697	9									697
696	10									696
695	11									695
694	12									694
693	13									693
692	14									692
691	15									691
690	Taharqa 1			Gemenef-khonsubak						690
689	2									689
688	3									688
687	4									687
686	5									686
685	6									685
684	7		Shepenwepet II		Nekauba					684
683	8									683
682	9									682
681	10								Esarhaddon	681
680	11									680
679	12									679
678	13									678
677	14									677
676	15									676
675	16									675
674	17									674
673	18									673
672	19									672
671	20									671
670	21									670
669	22				Nekau I				Ashurbanipal	669
668	23									668
667	24			Padubast III						667
666	25									666
665	26									665
664	Tanutamun 1				Psamtik I 1					664
663	2				2					663
662	3				3					662
661					4					661
660					5					660
659		Horkhebit			6					659
658					7					658
657					8					657
656					9					656

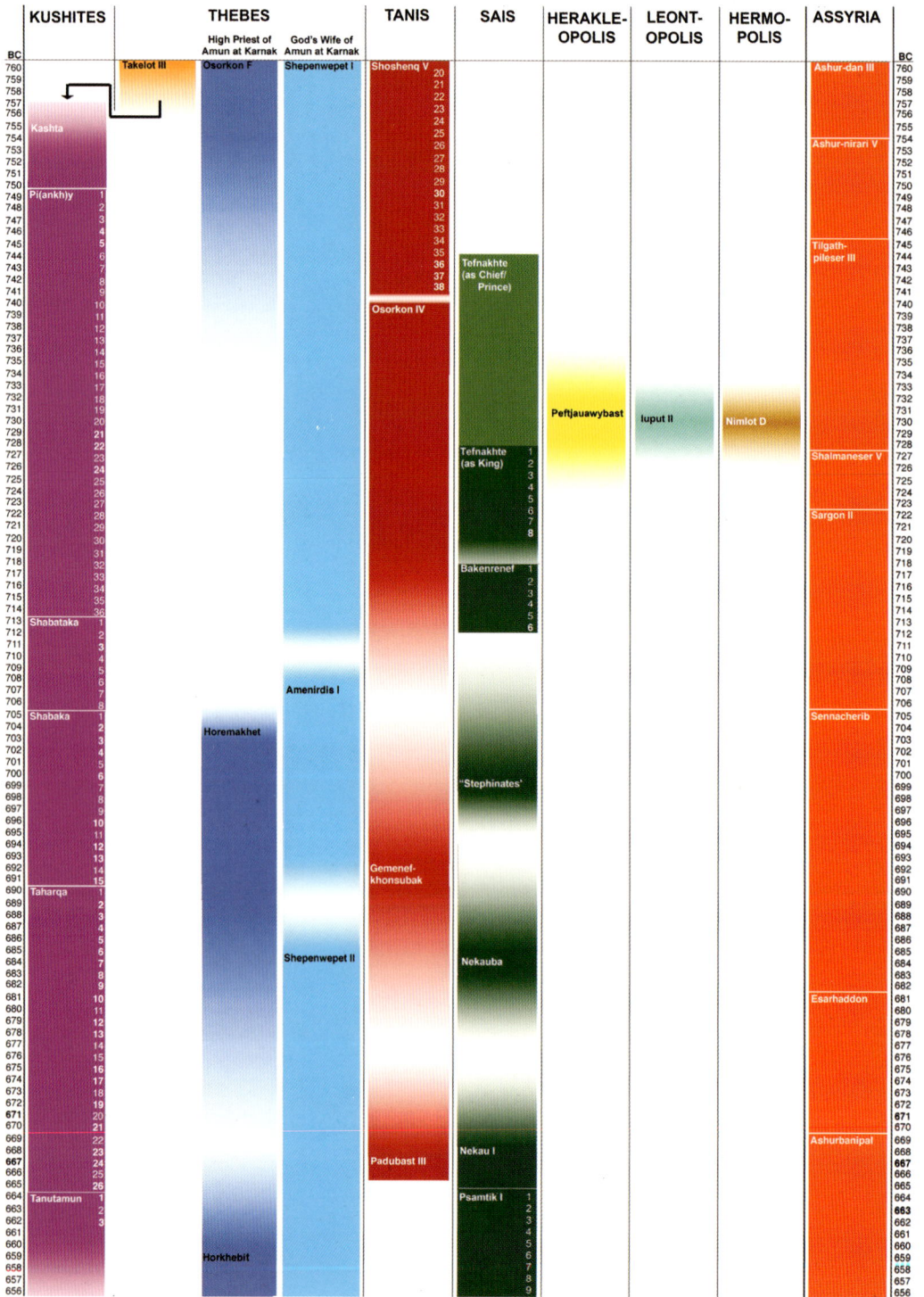

FIGURE 27 Chronology of the late eighth and early seventh centuries BC.

FIGURE 28 Donation stela dated to Year 8 of Tefnakhte (Athens 32).

It would have been during Bakenrenef's reign that the aged Pi(ankh)y died in Nubia. If the Tefnakhte of the stela was indeed his erstwhile opponent, his minimum of eight years, plus most of the six of Bakenrenef, would place Pi(ankh)y's death late in the fourth decade of his reign. He was buried in the ancient cemetery at El-Kurru (see pages 113–26), leaving it to his successor to take the next step in Nubia's engagement with Egypt.

3 THE UNITED KINGDOM OF EGYPT AND KUSH

Shabataka

As will be explored in Chapter 7 (pages 170–73), for many years it was assumed that Pi(ankh)y was succeeded by a King Neferkare[1] Shabaka. However, since 2013 there has been a shift toward the view that Pi(ankh)y was actually followed on the Kushite throne by Djedkaure Shabataka. He seems to have been a son of Pi(ankh)y, to judge from a later text of King Taharqa, who was definitely a son of Pi(ankh)y, where Taharqa refers to himself as a "brother" of Shabataka (see page 47). Shabataka certainly had a wife who was a daughter of Pi(ankh)y, named Arty, who may have been buried in pyramid Ku6 at El-Kurru.[2]

Shabataka's titulary ran as follows:

H.		*k3-nḫt ḫꜤ-m-w3st*	Strong bull appearing in Thebes
		ḏd-ḫꜤ(w)	Enduring of appearances
Nb.		*Ꜥ3-šft-m-t3w-nb(w)*	Great of renown in all lands
		sḫꜤ-m3Ꜥt-mry-t3wi	Who makes *maat* appear, beloved of the Two Lands
		ḏd-ḫꜤ	Enduring of appearances
G.		*Ꜥ3-ḫpš ḥw-pḏt-9*	Great of strength who smites the 9 bows
		hrw-ḥr-nḫtw	Satisfied with victory
P.		*ḏd-k3(w)-rꜤ*	Enduring of the *kas* of Re
N.		*š3b3t3k3-mr-imn*	Shabataka beloved of Amun
		š3b3t3k3	Shabataka

FIGURE 29 Head probably representing Shabataka (Nubian Mus ex-CG1291).

At the beginning of his reign, Shabataka employed names of the expansive kind used since the New Kingdom, but in his later monuments his names followed the "minimalist" approach that had appeared during the preceding decades in titularies adopted by kings in Tanis and Thebes. Thus, the king's nomen was shorn of its epithet, and the Horus name *k3-nht-h'-m-w3st*, employed by many kings since the Eighteenth Dynasty, was replaced by *dd-h'(w)*. This appellation went back to Isesi of the Fifth Dynasty. Isesi had already provided one variant of Shabataka's prenomen, although the *k3*-element was sometimes turned into the plural.

As Pi(ankh)y's successor, Shabataka (fig. 29) would be the King "Sabacôn," who Manetho states captured Bakenrenef and burned him alive. Bakenrenef may have been replaced by a Kushite governor, to judge from Manetho's listing of "Ammeris the Nubian" as the first ruler of the Twenty-sixth Dynasty line at Sais. However, the listing after him of a "Stephinatês"—presumably a writing of the name "Tefnakhte" (cf. page 40, above)—may suggest that the Saite line was then revived, the following "Nechepsôs" apparently being the King Nekauba known from a single contemporary object.[3]

Whether or not Bakenrenef indeed suffered a fiery death at his hands, it does seem that Shabataka was, unlike Pi(ankh)y, a hands-on ruler of Egypt, rather than a remote suzerain. The record of the height of the inundation in Shabataka's Year 3 at Karnak speaks of the king "appearing as king in the enclosure of Amun, where he caused that he appear to the Two Lands like Horus on the throne of Re"[4]—possibly a formal Egyptian coronation following the defeat of Bakenrenef.

A further indication of Shabataka's role as re-conqueror of Egypt may be seen in his use of the epithet *hq3 w3st it t3wy m m3't*, "ruler of Thebes who truly seized the Two Lands."[5] His status as king of both his dominions was henceforth indicated by his placing twin uraei on his forehead, something that would be continued by the later rulers of the dynasty. While the Saite Twenty-fourth Dynasty, the Nubians' key rival for dominion over Egypt, was deposed, other local kings—in particular Osorkon IV and his successors in the northeast—continued to reign, as they would until the end of Kushite rule in Egypt.

It was probably to undertake this "reconquest" of Egypt that Shabataka summoned north an army, including his twenty-year-old[6] brother, the later king Taharqa. As was later recounted:

> Now, when [Taharqa] was in Nubia as a handsome youth, a king's brother, sweet of love, he came sailing northward to Thebes in the midst of recruits for whom His Person, King Shabataka, true-of-voice, had sent to Nubia, in order that he (Taharqa) might be there with him, because he (Shabataka) loved him more than all his brothers.[7]

The victory over Bakenrenef may have been achieved soon after the burial of an Apis bull in Bakenrenef's Year 6, given the discovery of the remains of a text of Shabataka close to the bull's burial room in the Saqqara Serapeum.[8]

Shabataka built at least one chapel at Karnak, erected just south of the southeast corner of the Sacred Lake, with scenes of the king offering to the gods (figs. 30, 62).[9] He also added an outer court to the chapel of Osiris-Heqadjet, originally built by Osorkon III and Takelot III (fig. 31). The new section included images of the God's Wife Shepenwepet I, and also of her successor Amenirdis I (fig. 32), the transition between the two ladies thus occurring during the reign of Shabataka.[10] Scenes were also added to the exterior of the rear wall of the Luxor temple (fig. 33 top).[11] Away from Thebes, Shabataka is attested by blocks from a structure at Edfu (fig. 33 bottom),[12] a donation stela, probably from the Delta (fig. 34 left),[13] together with a headless seated statue[14] and two blocks[15] from Memphis—as well as the aforementioned Serapeum text.

All the king's men

The holder (if any) of the high priesthood of Amun at Shabataka's takeover of Egypt is unknown. No incumbent is known between Osorkon F, probably appointed when Takelot III became king (page 17), and Horemakhet, a son of Shabataka's successor, Shabaka (page 63).

While no Second Prophet is directly datable to Shabataka's reign, the post was probably held by one Patjenfy, since he had a son named Amenemhat who was certainly active under Shabaka. The office of Third Prophet is likely to have been in the hands of Padiamennesuttawy A/B—like Patjenfy a scion of an old Theban family. As far as the office of Fourth Prophet is concerned, the Theban Djedkhonsiufankh D, the son of Nakhtefmut B who had held the office under Takelot III, was followed by a Kushite,

FIGURE 30 Scenes from the Karnak chapel of Shabataka.

FIGURE 31 The chapel of Osiris-Heqadjet at Karnak.

FIGURE 32 Eastern interior wall of the forecourt of the chapel of Osiris-Heqadjet at Karnak, added by Shabataka. The upper register shows Shepenwepet I on the left, and Amenirdis I on the right, offering respectively to Amun and Mut. The lower register depicts Amenirdis I before Amun and Mut. The depiction of Shepenwepet I is posthumous, suggesting that she died while the forecourt was under construction, and was commemorated in this way by her successor.

Karabasken, who combined the role with that of Mayor of Thebes. Karabasken's dating is based on the decoration and structure of his tomb (TT391—fig. 35),[16] which seems to have been the very first in a sequence of monumental private tomb-chapels that continued into the Twenty-sixth Dynasty.[17] The construction of such a sepulcher may be seen as a marker of an upswing in local fortunes under the Kushites, contrasting with the very modest burial places that had been usual since the end of the New Kingdom,[18] as well as the insertion of Nubians into the senior ranks of local clergy and administration.

FIGURE 33 Top: reliefs of Shabataka on the rear wall of the temple of Luxor. Middle and bottom: reliefs of Shabataka from a dismantled structure at Edfu.

Karabasken's tomb was constructed in a hitherto unused area now known as the South Asasif, which would be employed for a handful of other burial places over the next few decades. Probably the next to be constructed was that of a certain Karakhamun (TT223),[19] like Karabasken the possessor of a Nubian name. Interestingly, although he held the very highest "ranking" titles[20] of the period, the lack of any attested substantive offices may suggest that he may have been some kind of intimate advisor of the king.[21] "Ranking" titles are particularly to be found in the titularies of the Stewards of the God's Wives of Amun who, by virtue of their mistresses' standing at the apex of sacerdotal

FIGURE 34 Left: fragment of donation stela of Shabataka (MMA 65.45). Right: stela of Namenekhamun, dating to the reign of Shabataka (NMS A.1956.150).

authority at Thebes, clearly played a key role in the local administration. The first known such official was Harwa (fig. 36), who served Amenirdis I, probably from the moment she succeeded Shepenwepet I. His exalted status is made clear by his very large tomb-chapel (TT37),[22] which was constructed eight hundred meters to the north of the sepulchers of Karabasken and Karakhamun, beyond the intervening Sheikh Abd el-Qurna hill, on the main Asasif. This would later become the burial place of most subsequent stewards of the God's Wife and other senior figures (fig. 37) into the Twenty-sixth Dynasty.

As far as the southern vizierate was concerned, one Ankhhor is dated to the time of Pi(ankh)y by the marriage of his daughter to Akanosh, the ruler of Sebennytos at the time of the Kushite king's northern campaign.[23] Around the same time are to be placed three further Viziers: Nespaqashuty B, nephew of an earlier Vizier Padiamenet (himself the son of the Vizier Pamiu i), who was a son-in-law of Takelot III; Padieset; and Khamhor, the latter pair sons of another earlier Vizier, Horsieset F. Also to be placed in the second half of the eighth century is the Vizier Nebnetjeru,[24] son of a Vizier Hor x, and grandson of the Vizier Nakhtefmut, both known to have served Osorkon III. Nebnetjeru was the owner of a monumental tomb occupying part of the site of the ancient memorial temple

FIGURE 35 Aerial view of the first Twenty-fifth Dynasty high-status cemetery, stretching from the South Asasif to the site of the memorial temple of Thutmose IV, with the temple-tomb of Nebnetjeru. The numbered tombs are those of the Twenty-fifth Dynasty Karabasken (TT391), Karakhamun (TT223), and Ramose (TT132), plus the Twenty-sixth Dynasty sepulcher of Iretiru (TT390) and the anonymous TTC14 of the same period.

of Thutmose IV—directly east of the South Asasif necropolis initiated by Karabasken (fig. 35). Unfortunately, none of their incumbencies can be precisely dated, other than by generation, Khamhor being the grandfather of Montjuemhat, who was Fourth Prophet of Amun and Mayor of Thebes under Taharqa (for whom see page 74).

FIGURE 36 Statues of Harwa, Steward of the God's Wife of Amun (left: Nubian Museum ex-JE37386; right: Louvre A84).

Kush and Assyria

As already related, in 716 BC, Sargon II of Assyria had approached Egypt's northeastern border, where he had received a gift of horses from Osorkon IV, presumably to help dissuade him from advancing any farther. Then, in 712, a certain Iamani seized the rule of Ashdod from an Assyrian nominee, and attempted to put together a coalition of Levantine vassals of the Assyrians against their overlord. He also sent presents to a king of Egypt (probably Osorkon IV, given his previous engagement with Assyria and geographical location) to tempt him into joining them.[25] However, Iamani was soon forced, in the face of a swift Assyrian reaction, to flee "to the land of Egypt, which now belongs to Nubia, and live there like a thief" (fig. 38).[26] This would seem to imply that the Kushite takeover of Egypt had only recently taken place. Sargon's annals further characterize Nubia as "in an inapproachable region" which had "never—from remote days until now—sent messengers to enquire after the health of my forefathers."[27] The appearance of the Kushites on the world stage was thus a novelty for the Assyrians, and presumably the other rulers of the Levant as well.

However, a few years later, certainly no later than 706, "Shapataku, ruler of the land of Nubia, heard of the mig[ht] of the gods Ashur, Nabû, (and) Marduk which [Sargon II] had [demonstrated] over all lands" and sent Iamani in chains to the Assyrian king. Sargon's account of this act of "appeasement" by Shabataka is followed by a mention

FIGURE 37 Top: view of the Twenty-fifth/sixth Dynasty necropolis on the Asasif, viewed from the northwest, with the tombs of Harwa (TT37) and Montjuemhat (TT34—see fig. 60). Bottom: the "light court" of the tomb of Harwa; the pylons in the background belong to TT34 and TT197 (Padineith, a Steward of the God's Wife of Amun in the later Twenty-sixth Dynasty).

of the Assyrians defeating "the vanguard of the army of Egypt," in the context of an Assyrian attack on the king of Gaza.[28] Whether this deployment of an Egyptian army to southern Palestine indicates that Shabataka now had a change of heart regarding his approach to the Assyrians, or that it reflected the accession of a new king of Egypt-Kush, is unclear. Nevertheless, the death of Shabataka around 705 BC is indicated by the fifteen known regnal years of his successor, Shabaka (page 68), and the securely fixed accession of the latter's successor, Taharqa, in the year 690 BC—the earliest wholly unambiguous absolute date in Egyptian history.[29]

FIGURE 38 The Tang-i Var
inscription of Sargon II.

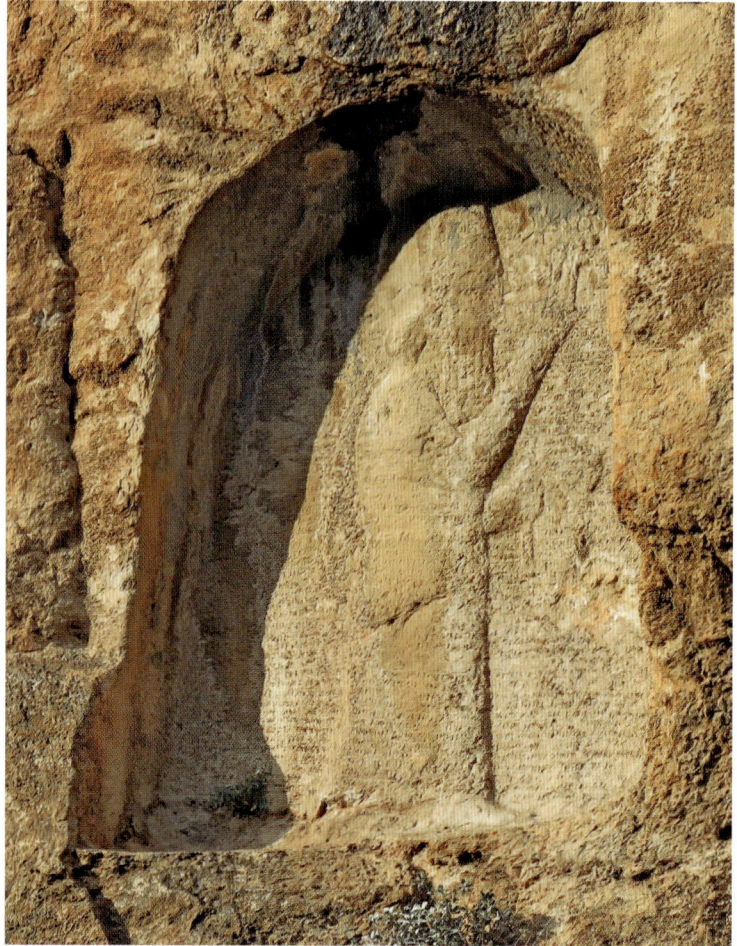

Shabaka

The new king, Shabaka, was long regarded by most as a brother of Pi(ankh)y but, as al-
ready discussed (pages 24–25), the evidence for this relationship is distinctly equivocal.
It seems more likely that he was a son of Shabataka—a relationship explicitly stated in
Manetho, although the latter's statements in such matters are frequently demonstra-
bly wrong and thus cannot be taken wholly at face value. The option is supported by
Shabataka being named on a statue of Horemakhet, High Priest of Amun, and a son of
Shabaka, something difficult to explain unless Shabataka was an ancestor of Horemakhet.

Horemakhet's mother was the King's Wife Masabat.[30] Another wife of Shabaka was
Qalhata,[31] who was the mother of his second successor, Tanutamun. No Egyptian text
explicitly states that Shabaka was Tanutamun's father, but one Assyrian account does

FIGURE 39 Map of the Near East.

(another calling him a son of Taharqa's sister).[32] This is corroborated by the fact that Queen Isetemkheb H, who is explicitly called a daughter of Shabaka, also bore the title of King's Sister,[33] of a monarch who can only have been Tanutamun. Also potentially in favor of the latter being a son of Shabaka is the fact that, although the royal cemetery had been removed from El-Kurru to Nuri by Taharqa (pages 117–21), Tanutamun returned to El-Kurru for his burial, in a tomb directly next to that of Shabaka.

In his titulary, Shabaka embraced the now-standard minimalist approach, with the exception of the occasional addition of "beloved of Amun" to his nomen:

H.		*sbq-t3wi*	He who blesses the Two Lands
Nb.		*sbq-t3wi*	He who blesses the Two Lands
G.		*sbq-t3wi*	He who blesses the Two Lands
P.		*nfr-k3-rˁ*	Vital of the *ka* of Re
N.		*š3b3k3 mr-imn*	Shabaka beloved of Amun
		š3b3k3	Shabaka

FIGURE 40 Donation stela of Year 6 of Shabaka (MMA 55.144.6). The piece is interesting in that the main text is written in hieratic.

His dittographed Horus/Nebty/Golden Falcon name had apparently not been used before, although it is of an ancient formulation. In contrast, his prenomen had first been used by the long-reigned Pepy II at the end of the Old Kingdom, and perhaps because of this association had been used regularly over the following centuries. The most recent users were Rameses IX of the Twentieth Dynasty, Amenemnisu of the Twenty-first, and Pi(ankh)y's ally Peftjauawybast.

In Year 2 of Shabaka, a text was written in ink in the Serapeum at Saqqara, but it is unclear whether it was actually associated with a burial.[34] It is likely, however, that a group of stelae including one of an anonymous "Year 4"[35] should be attributed to an interment under Shabaka. There is also a Nile Level record from Shabaka's Year 2,[36] and a donation stela of the same year from the Delta (possibly Hurbeit), dedicated by the Great Chief of the Ma, Patjenfy, one of the local rulers who had submitted to Pi(ankh)y two decades earlier.[37] Further donation stelae from the north of Egypt are dated to Years 3,[38] 4,[39] and 6 (fig. 40).[40]

Various architectural elements from Memphis attest to Shabaka's building work there, including a chapel in the southwest of the temenos of Ptah,[41] as well as statuary.[42] Of unknown original provenance (see page 148), but probably originally set up at Memphis, is a slab bearing an important theological text, the so-called Shabaka Stone or Memphite Theology (fig. 41).[43] This was either a genuine copy of an ancient text or a pastiche imitating Old Kingdom concepts. In either case, its existence highlights the antiquarian nature of Twenty-fifth Dynasty thought, which is also seen in the continuation of the archaizing art styles already present under the later Libyan pharaohs (page 18, fig. 22).

However, it is at Thebes that the largest assemblage of Shabaka's monuments is to be found, as well as blocks deriving from them (fig. 42).[44] Particular attention was given during his reign to the area directly north of the main Amun temple.[45] Here, Shabaka added two gates (II and IV) to the temple of Ptah (fig. 43), which he incorporated into a new

walled precinct that abutted what was then the northern wall of the enclosure of the Amun temple itself. The axis of this precinct lay just south of that of the Ptah temple, its outer gate fronted by a pair of columns, and with a further gate in alignment with the façade of the inner part of the temple. It culminated in a "treasury" (*pr-ḥd-ʿ3*—fig. 44 top), but other structures within the precinct have yet to be identified. It was presumably to mark the beginning of the route to/from the Ptah temple from the cross-axis of the Amun temple that a colonnade was erected directly west of the latter's Pylon III (fig. 44 bottom).

FIGURE 42 A block of Shabaka reused by Taharqa in his "Edifice" at Karnak.

FIGURE 43 Counterclockwise from the top: view of the temple of Ptah at Karnak; Shabaka's gate II; scene from the north interior wall of gate II; image of Shabaka, with erased cartouche and serekh, from the outer face of the south jamb of gate IV.

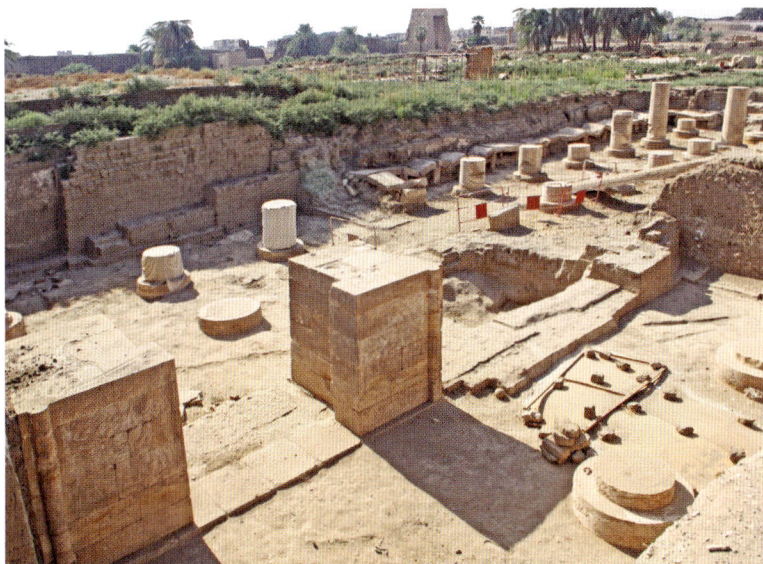

FIGURE 44 Top: the Treasury of Shabaka, southeast of the Ptah temple at Karnak. Bottom: the king's colonnade to the north of Pylon IV of the Amun temple.

Shabaka also added a new approach to the temple at Luxor, comprising a colonnade or kiosk,[46] and a new doorway for the old pylon of Rameses II (fig. 45).[47] He also initiated the construction of a pylon at the small temple at Medinet Habu (figs. 46, 110).[48]

Farther south in Egypt, a naos found at Esna (fig. 47)[49] indicates work by Shabaka there; there are also traces of his activity out at Bahariya Oasis.[50] Back in Nubia, work was carried out in Temple B at Kawa,[51] as well as a rebuilding of the Ramesside Central and Eastern temples at Kerma-Dukki Gel; further work was carried out there under his successors.[52]

FIGURE 45 The eastern jamb of the gateway added by Shabaka to the pylon of Rameses II at Luxor. All royal names have been carefully erased and smoothed for reinscription by Psamtik II.

Officialdom under Shabaka

As already noted (pages 52–53), it is difficult to allocate precise dates to the various viziers known to have served during the Twenty-fifth Dynasty. Nevertheless, it is likely that Khamhor and his sons Pahrer-Horsieset and Nesmin B, and perhaps the unrelated Nespaqashuty C, bridged the reigns of Shabataka and Shabaka. The mayoralty of Thebes seems to have been separated out again after Karabasken's incumbency, as it was given to Nesptah A, another son of the Vizier Khamhor. He would later pass the role to his nephew Raemmakheru, before it reverted to Nesptah's son Montjuemhat under Taharqa.

FIGURE 46 The Twenty-fifth Dynasty pylon of the Thutmosid small temple at Medinet Habu, decorated under Shabaka and Taharqa.

At Karnak, Shabaka's son Horemakhet (fig. 48 left) was appointed to the high priesthood;[53] as already noted (page 47), the identity of his immediate predecessor is uncertain. The office of Second Prophet was probably still held by Patjenfy, and that of Third Prophet now by Djedinhurufankh, but nothing is known of the status of the Fourth Prophetship. Amenirdis I (fig. 48 right) was certainly still in office as God's Wife in Shabaka's Year 12 (fig. 49),[54] but exactly how long she lived after that is unknown, although she was probably dead by the early years of Taharqa (cf. page 73).

FIGURE 47 Naos of Shabaka from Esna (Cairo CG70007). It displays the full range of later mutilations of Kushite kings' monuments, from the erasure of the second uraeus and the royal cartouches, to the partial erasure of a royal image.

Kush in Palestine

Around the time of Shabaka's accession, Sargon II died in battle in northern Iraq, and was succeeded by his son Sennacherib, meaning that within a short period of time both Assyria and Egypt-Kush had new kings. This near-simultaneous change of rulers is likely to have been a catalyst for significant shifts in the relationship between the two powers, although there is no indication that Shabaka proactively sought to intervene in Palestine.[55] His forces would nevertheless be drawn into conflict with Assyria as a result of appeals for help from Palestinian elements seeking to extricate themselves from Assyrian hegemony—or to avoid absorption into it.

In 701, Sennacherib launched a campaign into Palestine, and the authorities of Ekron (Khirbet el-Muqanna)—who had just overthrown their pro-Assyrian ruler—"called for help upon the kings[56] of Egypt and the bowmen, chariotry, and cavalry of the king of Nubia, an army beyond counting."[57] At the subsequent battle of Eltekeh (Tell el-Shalaf, near Ekron?), the Assyrian king claimed to have inflicted a defeat on this force, and "captured alive Egyptian charioteers . . . and charioteers of the king of Kush." However, a

FIGURE 48 Quartzite statuette of the High Priest of Amun, Horemakhet, a son of Shabaka, and a calcite statue of the God's Wife of Amun, Amenirdis I; both from Karnak, with their findspots shown respectively in figs. 126 and 124 (Nubian Museum ex-CG42204; Cairo CG565).

lack of the kind of detail normally given by the Assyrians in such cases may suggest that the victory was not crushing, and that the Egypt-Kushite forces may have withdrawn in good order. Having done so, they possibly combined with reinforcements coming from Egypt, given that subsequent events suggest that strong Egypt-Kushite forces continued to exist.

Sennacherib successfully captured both Eltekeh and Ekron itself, killed those who had rebelled, and reinstalled the former ruler, who had been held prisoner in Jerusalem by Hezekiah, King of Judah. The Assyrians then laid siege to and plundered forty-six Judean towns, and blockaded Jerusalem itself to force Hezekiah to submit. The Old Testament narrative of events[58] includes a mocking speech to the Jerusalemites by an

FIGURE 49 The Wadi Hammamat, a key route from the Nile valley to the Red Sea, and a major source of stone. Among its many graffiti is this one of Amenirdis I, dating to Year 12 of Shabaka, and her last dated attestation. His cartouche has been erased (except for the *b3*-hieroglyph, perhaps felt to be a divine image), as has that of Amenirdis's father, Kashta.

Assyrian official, the Rabshakeh: "What is this confidence of yours? . . . Here now, you put your trust in this broken/bruised reed-staff, in Egypt: that if someone leans upon it, it pierces his palm and punctures it. That is Pharaoh, King of Egypt, to all who put their trust in him." The Rabshakeh then ridicules any inhabitant of the city who might nevertheless put their trust in their god Yahweh.

This image of Egypt as a "broken reed" is often put forward as a commentary by the biblical author on the feebleness of Egypt under the Kushites, and has been quoted extensively in modern deprecations of the Twenty-fifth Dynasty kings (cf. page 156).

However, this ignores the fact that the Old Testament author has put these words into the mouth of the *enemy*, who *also* speaks negatively of the power of the Jewish god, Yahweh, whom the biblical writer would most certainly have had no wish to denigrate! Indeed, it is to Yahweh that the ultimate defeat of the Assyrian plans is credited (see just below). Accordingly, the implication would seem to be that the speech was composed to highlight the forces that *would* bring about victory and punish the Assyrian hubris that had denigrated them. Therefore, for the biblical author, Egypt was probably the exact *opposite* of a "broken reed," and *would* indeed contribute to foiling the Assyrians' designs.[59]

Linked with this, further on in the Old Testament narrative, Sennacherib is said to have "received a report about Tirhakah, king of Kush [sic: see just below], saying that 'he is coming to fight against you,'"[60] and subsequently withdraws the Assyrian troops and returns to Nineveh.[61] A supernatural proximate cause of this departure is given in the biblical text—the killing of 185,000 Assyrians by the "angel of the Lord," thus giving credit to Yahweh. But it has been suggested that the passage including this is a later interpolation, and that the original text directly juxtaposed the warning of the approach of the Kushites with the Assyrian decision to withdraw, thus removing what was originally a direct connection.[62] Accordingly, it seems likely that it was the threatened intervention of an Egypt-Kushite force (perhaps survivors of Eltekeh, augmented by fresh troops, or a separate army) that was a key factor in the Assyrian decision to withdraw, given the inherent vulnerability of a besieging force to external intervention.

Both the Old Testament and the Assyrian annals indicate that Hezekiah subsequently paid tribute to the Assyrians, and lost territory to his Assyrian-supporting neighbors, but that Jerusalem itself remained unconquered and independent. This all suggests that this outcome may have been in the context of a negotiated settlement, quite likely a result of the presence of an Egypt-Kushite army that Sennacherib had no desire to test in battle. Such a conclusion would also fit with the minimal amount of substantive Assyrian activity attested in Palestine over the following few years.[63]

While the aforementioned Assyrian and biblical accounts mesh sufficiently well to strongly suggest that they both refer to the campaign of 701, the Old Testament description of Taharqa as "king of Kush" has given pause, since in 701 he was certainly *not* "king of Kush," and would not be until 690. Some have proposed that, while the campaign recorded in the Assyrian annals was that of 701, the one described in the Old Testament was part of another conflict that took place between Taharqa's accession in 690 and Hezekiah's death in 687/6. However, the more general view is that Taharqa's designation as "king of Kush" in the Old Testament is a simply a later gloss, identifying the Kushite general in 701 as the man who would soon be a well-known king.[64] In favor of the latter supposition is the lack of any clear Assyrian or biblical data for more than one campaign.

FIGURE 50 Jar sealing of Shabaka from Nineveh (BM WA84884).

That Taharqa would have been a likely leader for an Egypt-Kushite intervention in Palestine is suggested by his known military experience, going back to his participation in the reconquest of Egypt a decade earlier under Shabataka (page 47).

Indications of more peaceful interactions between Egypt-Kush and Assyria are provided by seal impressions bearing the image of Shabaka found at Nineveh (fig. 50).[65] There seems little doubt that the sealings derive from storage jars, the mud element matching the internal traces found on contemporary undoubted jar closures. The fact that these examples bear both Egyptian *and* Assyrian seal impressions suggests, however, that the contents of the jars were not simple trade items. Instead, the double impressions may imply some verification or approval of the contents by an Assyrian official present in Egypt at the time of packing.

The end of the reign of Shabaka

Shabaka's highest surviving date is Year 15 (fig. 51),[66] which fits well with his accession occurring soon after the extradition of Iamani in 706, and the known assumption of the throne by Taharqa in 690.[67] An interesting tradition is preserved in a gloss by the fifth-century AD author (St.) Jerome to his Latin translation of Eusebius's fourth-century AD *Chronikon*, the Egyptian part of which is based on the work of Manetho (cf. pages 140–41). Jerome's gloss states that Shabaka died by violence:[68] "after Sebicos was killed, Tarachus ruled over the Egyptians." One version of the gloss even accuses Taharqa of the deed: "Tharacus . . . led an army from Nubia, killed Sebion and ruled the Egyptians himself." Whether it was truly the case that Shabaka was murdered (and if so, whether Taharqa was truly guilty) is impossible to know, but such circumstances might explain why it was Taharqa who became king, rather than Shabaka's son Tanutamun. It could also explain a rather strange statement in one of Tanutamun's texts relating to his accession (page 90). It is interesting that while Taharqa mentions Shabataka by name in one of his autobiographical texts (page 47), and speaks warmly of him in another without mentioning his name, Taharqa's only reference to Shabaka is to obliquely state that he (Taharqa) "received the crown in Memphis after the falcon (i.e., Shabaka) went up to the sky."[69]

In any case, the question of the mechanism of the royal succession of the Kushite kingship has long been a matter of debate,[70] and it remains wholly unclear whether the Kushites had adopted what seems to have been the Egyptian system—succession by the senior surviving son, who may have undergone some formal ceremony of nomination[71]—or something different. The prominence of the female line in the ancestry of King Aspelta on his Enthronement Stela (fig. 83; cf. page 104) may hint at a matrilineal component. But the sheer number of potential mechanisms for royal succession, and variations on them, seen at various times and places during human history, makes it difficult to devise a working hypothesis in which one can have any confidence.

Taharqa

The ancestry of Taharqa (figs. 52, 53)[72] is not a matter for significant debate. He is described as the brother of the God's Wife of Amun Shepenwepet II in the later Neitiqerti Adoption Stela (pages 97–98), and as Shepenwepet was undoubtedly the daughter of Pi(ankh)y, Taharqa must thus also have been his offspring. As already noted (page 40), his mother was Abar (fig. 54), a daughter of a sister of Alara. This line of descent from Alara seems to have been important to Taharqa.[73]

FIGURE 51 Block statue of Iti, with its inscription dated to Year 15 of Shabaka (BM EA24429).

FIGURE 52 Head of Taharqa; from Thebes (Nubian Museum ex-CG560).

FIGURE 53 North wall of the outer hall of Gebel Barkal temple B300 (figs. 69, 70), showing Taharqa and Tekahatamun before Amun and Mut, who are shown within the mountain, the uraeus being represented by the peak B350 (fig. 24, bottom). The top image is a colored rendering made by Richard Lepsius in 1844, the lower shows the state of the wall in 2013.

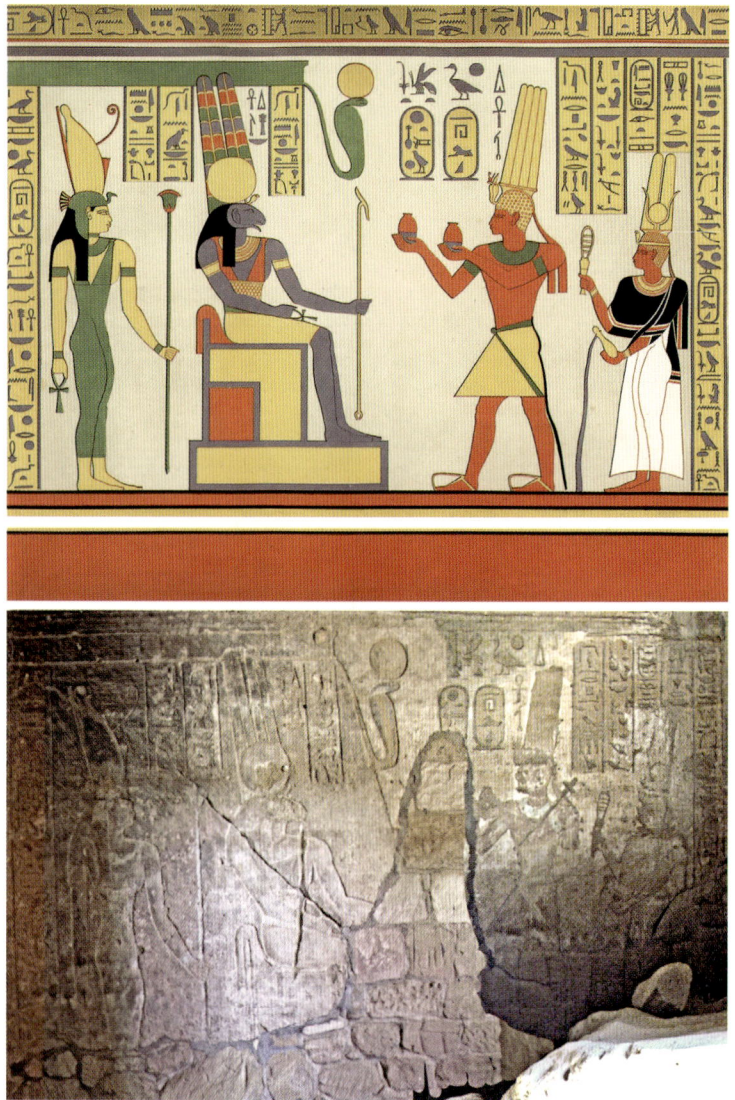

For his titulary, Taharqa adopted the name forms that were typical of the period:

H.		$q\jmath$-$\underline{h}^cw$	Lofty of appearances
Nb.		$q\jmath$-$\underline{h}^cw$	Lofty of appearances
G.		$\underline{h}w$-$t\jmath wi$	Protector of the Two Lands
P.		$\underline{h}w$-$nfrtm$-r^c	Nefertum is protector of Re
N.		$t\jmath hrq$	Taharqa

The Golden Falcon name had been used back in the Thirteenth Dynasty as the Horus name of Sobekhotep III, but all the other names were new, the prenomen being unusual in citing two deities, with only one other element, contrasting with the normal X-Y-Re format.

Taharqa may have had at least four wives: Takahatamun is shown with Taharqa in temple B300 at Gebel Barkal (fig. 53),[74] where she is called his sister and First King's Great Wife; Atakhebasken, of unknown antecedents but bearing the title of King's Great Wife, was buried next to Taharqa (page 126) and was therefore probably his wife.[75] Also likely to have been a spouse of the king is the King's Sister and King's Wife Naparaye,[76] as may have been the king's sister, Tabakenamun (see page 40). While various individuals have been suggested as having been offspring of Taharqa, only Nesishutefnut and Amenirdis II (see just below) were unequivocally his, together with "Ushanhuru," the eldest son who was later to be captured by the Assyrians (page 84, below).[77]

At some point during the first half-decade of the reign, Taharqa's mother Abar came to visit him from Nubia (fig. 54).[78] This was the first time that he had seen her in over two decades, since he had left at the age of twenty to bring an army to Shabataka. Taharqa's account of her visit presented her in the guise of Isis vis-à-vis Horus, "joyful [at] seeing the beauty of His Person after he had been a youth in the nest of Khemmis."[79]

Probably also to be placed during Taharqa's early years as king is a race run by the king's troops. This took place on a desert road that ran southwest from Memphis, starting

FIGURE 54 Lunette of Kawa stela V, showing Taharqa and his mother, Abar (Ny Carlsberg ÆIN 1712).

just south of the pyramid of Isesi at Saqqara, and linking up with the desert route to the Fayyum which comes from the north.[80] Accompanied by Taharqa himself either on horseback or in a chariot, the soldiers left Memphis "in the ninth hour of the night, (and) reached Lake Qarun in the first hour of the day, and returned to the Residence in the third hour of the day," after which the king awarded prizes to the winners of the race.

Throughout Egyptian history, the annual Nile inundation has been a crucial factor in the prosperity of the country; indeed, excessive or inadequate flood levels were certainly factors in the collapse of central authority at the end of the Old Kingdom, and probably at other times as well.[81] A particularly high flood occurred in Taharqa's Year 6, but in this case it had a positive outcome.[82] According to a contemporary stela,

> His Person had been praying for an inundation from his father Amun-Re-nebnesuttawy in order to prevent poverty happening in his time . . . . When the time for the beginning of the inundation came, it continued greatly every day and it passed many days rising at the rate of one cubit a day. It penetrated the hills of the southland, it overtopped the mounds of the northland, and the land was (like) the primaeval waters . . . without land being distinguishable from river. It rose to a height of 21 cubits, 1 palm and 2.5 fingers at the harbor of Thebes. His Person had the annals of the ancestors brought to him, to see the inundations that had happened in their time, and the like was not found there . . . . [The inundation] made the entire countryside lush, it killed the vermin and snakes that were in it, it prevented the devouring of locusts . . . .[83]

That the rains that fed the inundation extended beyond their normal limits of the Ethiopian headwaters of the Blue Nile and Atbara is indicated by the text's further remark that it even rained in Nubia—a most unusual event.

The exceptional height of the Year 6 inundation is verified by the Nile-level records on the Karnak waterfront (fig. 55 bottom),[84] which show that it was the highest preserved there, beating the previous record, of Year 3 of Osorkon III. The flood of Taharqa's Year 7 equaled that of Year 6, but those of the next two years dropped to more regular levels. As well as adding Nile-level marks among older records, the reign of Taharqa also saw modifications to the structure of the Karnak waterfront itself. These included changes to the access ramp that formed part of the river wall, dividing it into three by adding a central ramp that extended farther into the Nile (fig. 55 top).[85] Such changes were necessitated by the ongoing retreat of the river westward, the Nile bank having already shifted by over two hundred meters since the original foundation of the Karnak complex during the Middle Kingdom, some 1,300 years earlier.[86]

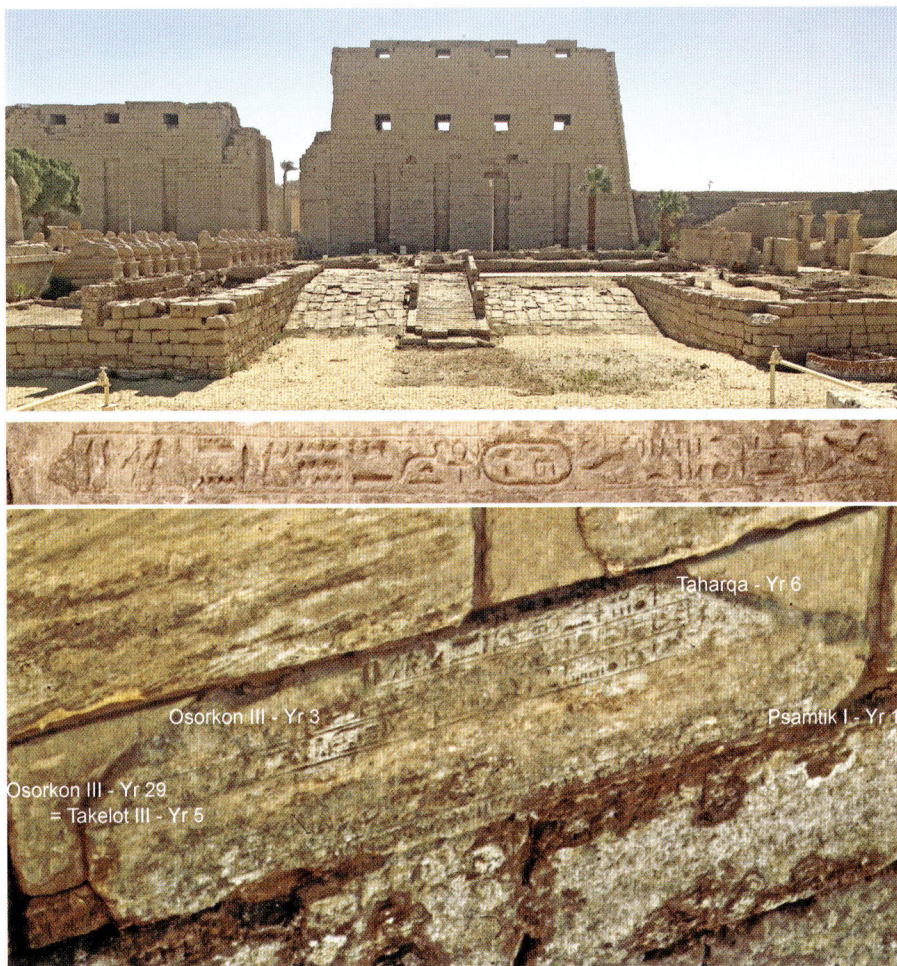

FIGURE 55 Top: the Twenty-fifth Dynasty waterfront at Karnak, with the ramp of Taharqa in the center; the podium is visible on the far left, with its obelisk of Sethy II. Bottom: Nile-level records on the south face of the podium, with a close-up of Taharqa's Year 6 record.

Administrations

Administratively, the matrix of local kings, chieftains, and mayors continued to wield regional authority in northern Egypt. In the Thebaid, power was in the hands of the High Priest, the God's Wife, and the Mayor, together with their subordinates. The pontificate continued to be held by Horemakhet, but Taharqa's sister Shepenwepet II (fig. 56) had certainly succeeded Amenirdis I as God's Wife by the early part of his reign; the new heir to the role was Amenirdis II, a daughter of Taharqa (fig. 57). The steward of Shepenwepet II was Akhamenru (fig. 58),[87] who would stay with her into the reign of Tanutamun, and quite possibly beyond. Like his predecessor Harwa, he had a large tomb-chapel, TT404, on the Asasif, sharing the forecourt of Harwa's sepulcher (fig. 37).

FIGURE 56 Head of sphinx of Shepenwepet II; from Karnak (Berlin ÄM7972).

The royal family's grip on the Amun priesthood was reinforced by the appointment of Taharqa's son, Nesishutefnut, as Second Prophet of Amun.[88] The position of Third Prophet seems initially to have continued in the hands of Djedinhurufankh, before he was succeeded by Padiamennesuttawy C, who would remain in office until between Years 9 and 14 of Psamtik I. His family would hold the post into the sixth century.

The office of Fourth Prophet of Amun was given to Montjuemhat, the son of the former Mayor Nesptah A.[89] He also held his father's post, thus perpetuating the union of these key civic and sacerdotal roles seen back in the days of Karabasken and the beginning of the Kushite supremacy. The new man (fig. 59) not only married two Egyptian women, but also allied himself with the Kushite royal family, espousing Wadjrenes, a daughter of Taharqa's brother, Har.[90] Of the other major posts, the southern vizierate was held successively by Nespaqashuty C (buried in tomb D13 at Abydos)[91] and his son

FIGURE 57 Fragment of relief showing Diesethebsed, sister of Montjuemhat, standing behind Amenirdis II; from Medinet Habu (ISACM 14681).

Nespamedu (Abydos D57).[92] Unlike the viziers, Montjuemhat constructed his own huge tomb (TT34—fig. 60) on the Asasif plain, close to the Harwa-Akhamenru tomb complex (fig. 37), and where a further series of major sepulchers would be built through the Twenty-sixth Dynasty.

The builder-king

While Shabaka had undertaken significant building activities around Egypt, Taharqa worked even more extensively, commissioning structures the whole length of his dual realm. In Egypt, the temple at Athribis was rebuilt[93] and some work undertaken at Tanis,[94] Memphis,[95] Hermopolis,[96] and Akhmim.[97] At Memphis, Year 14 saw the burial of an Apis bull,[98] the successor to the one apparently interred in Year 4 of Shabaka; the next bull was a short-lived specimen, and would die in Taharqa's Year 24 (see page 88). However, the largest number of Taharqa's known Egyptian constructions are at Thebes.

FIGURE 58 Block statue of the Steward of the God's Wife of Amun, Akhamenru (Louvre A25).

FIGURE 59 Statues of Montjuemhat in a number of different styles. The image at top left is heavily influenced by Old/Middle Kingdom art, whereas that at bottom left displays a new naturalistic style, and that on the right is of a traditional steleopherous form; all from Karnak (Cairo CG42236; CG647; BM EA1643).

FIGURE 60 The pylon and
light court of the tomb of
Montjuemhat (TT34).

Most prominent were the colonnaded elements that he added in front of four key cardinal approaches to the northern/central elements of the Karnak complex (fig. 15).[99] Before Pylon II was built a great kiosk, with columns 19.75 meters high (fig. 61 top), and at the opposite (eastern) extremity, a colonnade fronting the temple of Re-Horakhty (fig. 61 bottom).[100] Further colonnades were placed in front of the temple of Khonsu in the south and in front of that of Montju in the north. In the core of the Amun precinct, the king was also the author of the enigmatic "Edifice of Taharqa," at the northwest corner of the Sacred Lake (fig. 62).[101] Just to the west of the chapel of Osiris-Heqadjet was erected a sanctuary dedicated to Osiris-Wennefer-Heryibished in the names of Shepenwepet II and (the probably recently deceased) Amenirdis I.[102] Shepenwepet took sole responsibility for a chapel of Osiris-Nebankh to the north of Pylon III (fig. 63 top).[103]

FIGURE 61 Top: the kiosk of Taharqa in the courtyard in front of Pylon II of the temple of Amun at Karnak; the court dates from the reign of Shoshenq I. Bottom: Taharqa's colonnade in front of the temple of Re-Horakhty at the opposite end of the main axis of the Karnak complex.

FIGURE 62 The main Karnak complex from the south, showing the location of Taharqa's "Edifice," and his eastern colonnade, shown in the previous figure. The chapel of Shabataka (fig. 30) lay just beyond the bottom right of the image.

FIGURE 63 The chapel of Osiris-Nebankh at Karnak, erected by Shepenwepet II, whose image may be seen embracing Isis on the right-hand side of the door, balancing one of Taharqa (embracing Osiris) on the other. The lintel is also balanced between the God's Wife and the king, underlying their equivalence in status at Karnak.

In addition to adding the colonnade to the north of the Montju temple, in between the latter sanctuary and the temple of Ptah, inscriptions were placed on the façades of chapels e and f,[104] and farther to the northwest was built the small temple of Osiris-Pededankh.[105] At the opposite end of the Karnak complex, the addition to the Mut temple of a colonnaded porch (fig. 64 top) was accompanied by considerable work carried out under the direction of the Fourth Prophet and Mayor, Montjuemhat.[106] In the same area, the New Kingdom Temple A was completely rebuilt—possibly continuing work begun under Shabaka—the new decoration including a "divine birth" sequence for Taharqa (fig. 64 bottom). The approach to this temple from the west was marked by a gateway in the king's name (fig. 65).[107] Yet farther south, at Luxor, a small chapel to Hathor was erected just to the east of the beginning of the processional route to Karnak, later adorned with sphinxes.[108] Across the river, the new pylon at the small temple at Medinet Habu, begun by Shabaka (fig. 46), was completed, and a gateway erected to the north; various other inscribed items of Taharqa's reign have come from the same area.[109]

On the border of the Twenty-fifth Dynasty homeland of Nubia, Taharqa may have been the first king to build on what would become the sacred island of Isis at Philae (fig. 66).[110] Deeper into Lower Nubia, a number of rock inscriptions are known,[111] while the clifftop fortress at Qasr Ibrim (fig. 10) was renewed and a temple erected there;[112] at the Middle Kingdom Second Cataract fortress at Semna was built a huge brick temple (now lost).[113] Some kind of construction also seems to have been undertaken at or near Sedeinga.[114]

FIGURE 64 Top: Taharqa's
porch in front of the temple
of Mut at Karnak, and a
depiction of the king making
an offering on the north wall
of the nearby Temple A.

The main Nubian concentrations of Taharqa's monuments are, however, between the Third and Fourth Cataracts. He worked at Dukki Gel, and at Tabo, on Argo Island, a large temple was built.[115] Farther south, at Kawa (ancient Gempaaten), Taharqa seems to have taken a particular interest in restoring and expanding the site. A stela from a new temple that he erected there recalls a visit the king made in his youth, while bringing the army to Shabataka (page 47, above).

He passed by way of this district of Amun-(of)-Gempaaten, so that he might kiss the earth at the double-doors of the temple, together with the army of His Person that had sailed north with him. He found that the temple had been built in brick and that the sand-hill around it had reached its roof, being covered by earth.[116]

The temple referred to was probably that built by Tutankhamun (A) in an area prone to sanding up—and/or Iry's adjacent Temple B (fig. 67 top). The text continues:

His Person's heart became sorrowful about it, until His Person arose as king . . . (and) he remembered this temple, which he had seen as a young man, in the first year of his having arisen as king. So His Person said to his companions: "See, my heart is set on (re)building the temple of my father Amun-Re-of-Gempaaten, because it is built of brick and covered with earth, not a good thing in minds."

As a result of benefactions made in Years 3 through 10,[117] not only was the old Tutankhamun temple[118] restored and extended, but a wholly new structure (Temple T)[119] was erected a short distance to the east (figs. 67 bottom, 68). It was inaugurated in Year 10.

FIGURE 65 Taharqa's gate at the Mut complex, leading toward Temple A.

FIGURE 66 The Ptolemaic temples of Philae, with an altar and a block naming Taharqa, found there and suggestive of his having some role in the inauguration of worship there.

In the capital territory just above the Dongola Reach, Taharqa built a near-replica of Kawa Temple T, dedicated to Amun-Re, at Sanam,[120] and made significant additions to the sanctuaries at Gebel Barkal. These included placing a new bark stand in the Amun temple (B500),[121] and the construction of two sanctuaries of Mut (B200 and B300, figs. 52, 69, 70).[122] Above them, Taharqa undertook work on refining the appearance of the peak that had for centuries been seen as a giant uraeus (fig. 24 bottom).[123]

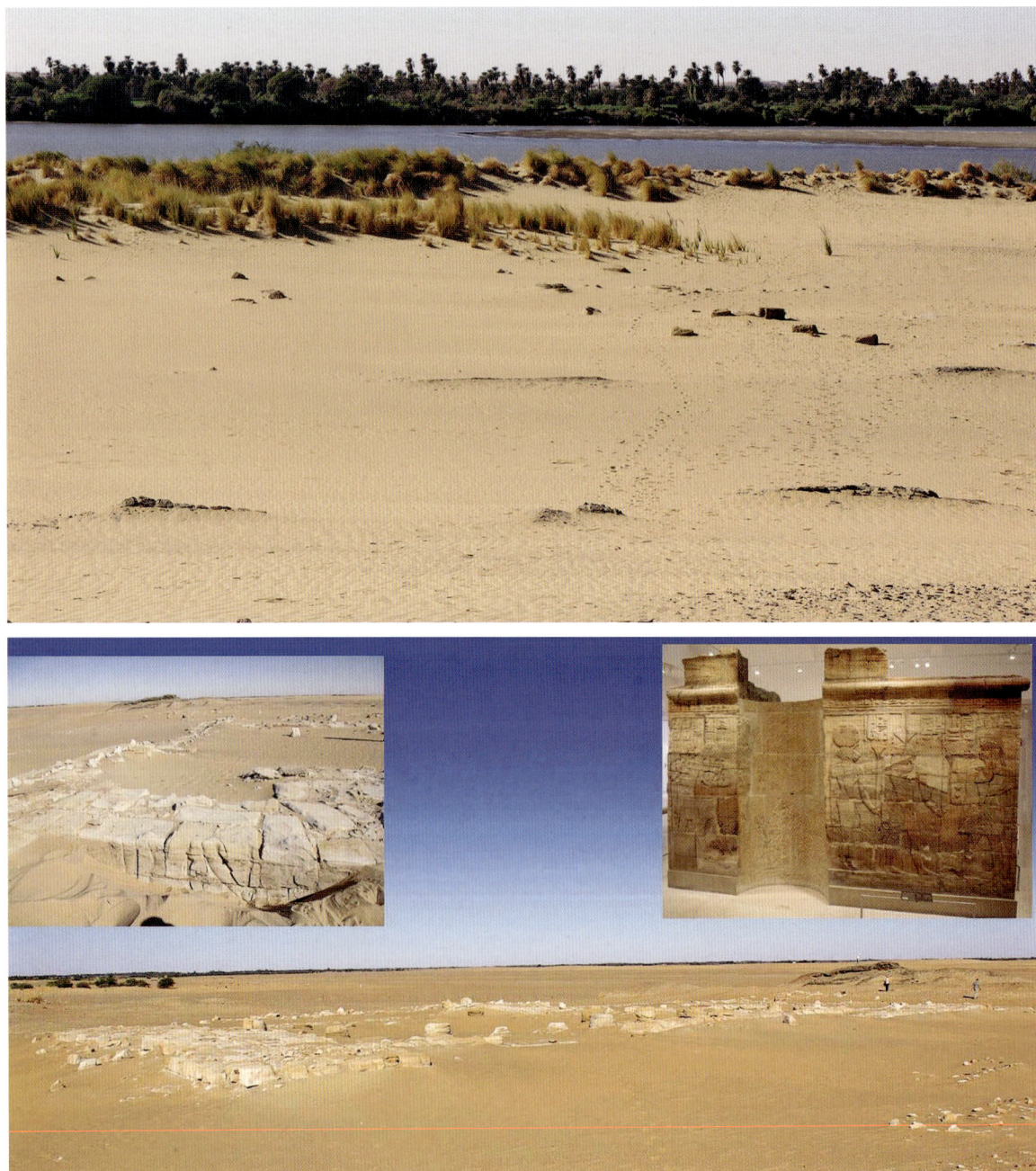

FIGURE 67 Kawa. The upper image shows the site of Temples A and B (fig. 128), and the lower Taharqa's Temple T. The insets in the latter show part of the decoration of its pylon and the chapel that was erected in its hypostyle hall (Ashmolean 1936.661).

Nemesis

The first decade and a half of the reign of Taharqa seems not to have seen any renewal of conflict with Assyria. The latter had in any case been distracted by events closer to home, culminating in the murder of Sennacherib in 681 and an ensuing civil war, which was won by Esarhaddon. Egypt-Kushite relationships with parts of the Assyrian empire may, however, be indicated by such things as a faience plaque of Taharqa from Palmyra in central Syria.[124] Nevertheless, by the mid-670s Assyrian suzerainty over much of Syria-Palestine had been restored, and early in 674 "the army of Assyria was defeated in a battle in Egypt."[125] Clearly an attempt had been made to bring the Nile valley under Assyrian control—or at least to neutralize the power of Egypt-Kush.

Three years later, however, things went much less well for Egypt. Taharqa had allied with potentates in the Levant, who included the first victim of a new Assyrian campaign, the tenth launched by Esarhaddon, which was begun in the spring of 671. The Assyrian king's account (fig. 71) runs as follows:

FIGURE 68 Sphinx and ram of Taharqa, from Kawa Temple T (BM EA1770; EA1779).

I threw up a (siege-)earthwork against Balu, King of Tyre, who had put his trust upon his friend Tarqû, king of Kush, and had thrown off the yoke of Ashur, my lord, answering with insolence. I withheld from [the Tyrians] the food and water that sustained life. I removed my camp . . . and marched directly towards Melukhkha . . . as far as the town of Rafah . . . . I advanced to the town of Ishkhupri[126] . . . and from the town of Ishkhupri to Memphis, his royal residence, a distance of fifteen days, I fought daily,[127] without interruption, very bloody battles against Tarqû, king of Egypt and Nubia, the one accursed by all the great gods. Five times I hit him with the point of arrows (causing) wounds (from which he should) not recover, and I laid siege to Memphis, his royal residence, and conquered it in half a day by means of mines, breaches and assault ladders; I destroyed (it),

FIGURE 69 Rock-cut temples B200 and B300, constructed at Gebel Barkal by Taharqa.

tore down (its walls) and burnt it down. His queen, the women of his palace, Ushanhuru, his crown prince, his other children, his possessions, horses, large and small cattle beyond counting, I carried away as booty to Assyria. All Nubians I deported from Egypt, leaving not even one to do homage. Everywhere in Egypt, I appointed new kings, governors, officers, harbor overseers, officials and administrative personnel. I initiated regular sacrificial dues for Ashur and the great gods, my lords, for all times. I imposed upon them tribute due to me as overlord, annually without ceasing.[128]

FIGURE 70 The outer hall of Gebel Barkal temple, B300, with one of its colossal figures of Bes (cf. fig. 122 bottom right).

At least some of the "new kings, governors, officers, harbor overseers, officials and administrative personnel" were the current scions of long-standing lines of local kings, chiefs, and nobility.[129] The kings comprised Nekau (I) of Sais[130] (to judge from Manetho the successor/replacement of Nekauba)[131] and Padubast III (fig. 72)[132] at Tanis. The rest included Shoshenq F of Busiris, Nimlot E at Hermopolis, Nespamedu A at Thinis—and Montjuemhat at Thebes.

This initial Assyrian hegemony was, nevertheless, short-lived. By 669, Taharqa had returned to Memphis, prompting Esarhaddon to march west once more—only to

FIGURE 71 Left: Stela of Esarhaddon from Zencirli (Berlin VA2708), one of a series set up to commemorate his Egyptian campaign of 671 BC; the small kneeling figure, wearing a uraeus and with Nubian features, has been identified as both Taharqa and his heir, "Ushanhuru," who was captured by the Assyrians at Memphis. Below: the Rassam Cylinder from Nineveh (BM WA91026), a key source for Ashurbanipal's 667 campaign.

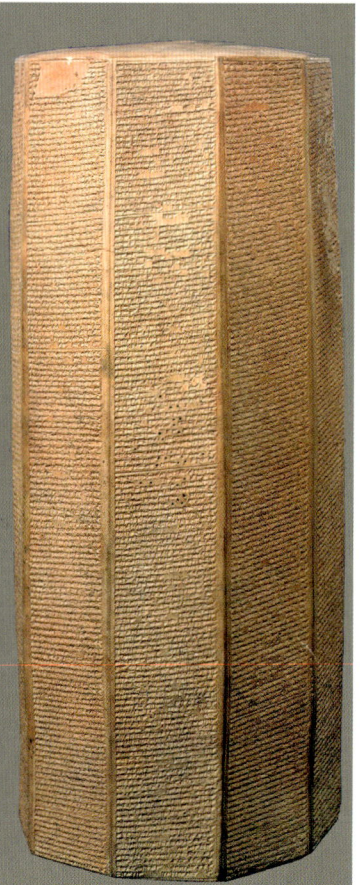

FIGURE 72 Statue of
Padubast III at Memphis.

fall ill and die that November, while still in Palestine. Although this provided Taharqa with a brief respite, the new Assyrian king, Ashurbanipal, initiated a fresh invasion in 667/666.[133] As the king put it in the document shown in figure 73, bottom,

> Tarqû (had) forgot(ten) the might of Ashur, Ishtar and the great gods, my lords, and put his trust upon his own power. He turned against the kings (and) regents whom my own father had appointed in Egypt. He entered and took residence in Memphis, the city which my own father had conquered and incorporated into Assyrian territory. A fast messenger came to Nineveh to report to me. I became very angry on account of these happenings, my soul was aflame. I lifted my hands, prayed to Ashur and to the Assyrian Ishtar. I called up my mighty armed forces which Ashur and Ishtar have entrusted to me and took the shortest road to Egypt and Nubia . . . .

Quickly I advanced as far as Kar-Baniti (in the eastern Delta) to bring speedy relief to the kings and regents in Egypt, servants who belong to me. Tarqû, king of Egypt and Nubia, heard in Memphis of the coming of my expedition and he called up his warriors for a decisive battle with me . . . . I defeated the soldiers of his army in a great open battle. Tarqû heard in Memphis of the defeat of his army and the splendor of Ashur and Ishtar blinded him such that he became a madman . . . . He left Memphis and fled, to save his life, into the town of Thebes. This town I seized and led my army into it to stay.[134]

Egyptian allusions to this Assyrian incursion are to be found in an inscription of Montjuemhat at the Mut temple.[135] It speaks of an "overturning" of the whole land, and "re-pelling enemies from the southern nomes," the latter seemingly reflecting that the Assyrians then rapidly withdrew northward, without interfering with Montjuemhat himself or the Kushite-born High Priest and God's Wife. Similarly, in the north, Ashurbanipal relates that

[the] kings, governors and officials whom my own father had appointed in Egypt and who had left their offices in the face of the advance of Tarqû and had scattered into the countryside, I reinstalled in their offices and in their seats of office. I reor-ganized Egypt and Kush which my own father had conquered; I made the garrisons stronger than before and new regulations. With many prisoners and heavy booty I returned safely to Nineveh.

The Assyrians would seem to have arrived at Memphis after IV *prt* 23 in Taharqa's Year 24 (September 667).[136] This was the day on which the latest Apis bull had been buried[137] and, given the Assyrians' antipathy toward Taharqa, it seems highly unlikely that any event would have been dated to his reign if Ashurbanipal had seized the city by then. It would not be until 664 that a replacement for this Apis would be identified, however, and the dis-ordered state of the country is indicated by the fact that when the new bull's epitaph was composed in Year 20 of Psamtik I,[138] its actual birth date seems not to have been available.

Although Taharqa had retreated southward into his southern heartlands, it seems that the Delta rulers soon turned to the view that he might after all be preferable to the "stron-ger garrisons" and "more severe regulations" now imposed by the Assyrians. To once again quote Ashurbanipal:

Afterwards all the kings whom I appointed broke their oaths, did not keep the agreements sworn by the great gods. They forgot that I had treated them mildly and conceived evil. They talked of rebellion and came among themselves to an unholy

FIGURE 73 Relief showing the Assyrian capture of a fortress in Egypt, perhaps Memphis, during the campaign of 667 BC; from Room M of the North Palace at Nineveh (BM WA124928).

decision . . . . And they sent their mounted messengers to Tarqû, king of Kush, to establish a treaty: "Let there be peace between us and let us come to a mutual agreement; we will divide the country between us, no other lord will be ruler over us" . . . .

My officers heard about these matters, captured their mounted messengers with their messages and learned about their rebellious doings. They arrested these kings and put their hands and feet in iron cuffs and fetters . . . . These kings who had repeatedly schemed, they brought alive to me in Nineveh.[139]

There, all were killed, except for Nekau I of Sais, who was greatly honored, bound with even stronger oaths, while his son Psamtik, invested with the new Assyrian name Nabushazzibanni, was made ruler of Athribis in place of the previous (executed) prince, Bakennefi C. The occupants of the rebel towns were also put to the sword, with some victims flayed and their skins nailed to the city walls as a warning against further resistance. Taharqa never returned to Egypt, and died in 664. He was succeeded by his nephew Tanutamun.

Tanutamun

As already noted (page 57), contemporary Assyrian texts state both that Tanutamun (fig. 74) was a son of Shabaka, and a son of a sister of Taharqa. The latter was Qalhata, named on Tanutamun's Dream Stela (see just below) and buried in tomb Ku5 at El-Kurru (fig. 108). No wives of Tanutamun are known for certain, but a Queen Malaqaye, buried in pyramid Nu59 at Nuri (page 127), could have been one of his spouses.

Only parts of the king's titulary are known, all being new formulations:

H.		*wꜣḥ-mrwt*	Enduring of love
P.		*bꜣ-kꜣ-rꜥ*	Power(?) of the *ka* of Re
N.		*tꜣnwt-imn*	Tanutamun

The new king seems to have moved rapidly to claim the Egyptian part of his inheritance, prompted by a prophetic dream (fig. 75):

> In the first year of his appearance as king [. . .] His Person saw a dream in the night: two snakes, one on his right, the other on his left. His Person woke up but did not find them. His Person then said: "Why has this happened to me?" Then reply was made to him, saying: "The southland is yours; (now) seize the northland. The Two Ladies are upon your head, and the land will be given to you in its breadth and its length, there being none who will share it with you."[140]

Tanutamun, who was at the time somewhere in Upper Nubia, then proceeded to Napata. The text remarks that when he did so "there [were] none who stood [against] him." It is unclear whether this simply indicates unanimous approval of his intent to follow his dream, or implies the existence of substantive opposition that had to be overcome. This could conceivably have come from a son of Taharqa, if there is any basis for Jerome's tradition (pages 68–69) that Tanutamun's father Shabaka had been murdered, and thus that Tanutamun's succession had been delayed by a generation.

FIGURE 74 Statue of Tanutamun from the statue cache at Kerma–Dukki Gel (Kerma Museum).

FIGURE 75 The Dream Stela of Tanutamun; from Gebel Barkal (Nubian Museum ex-JE48863).

However, nothing more is said on this matter, and the king proceeded to the Amun temple at Gebel Barkal to make offerings. He then descended the Nile to Aswan, where he offered to Khnum at Elephantine, and proceeded onward to Thebes, before embarking for the north. When the king arrived at Memphis, "out came the children of rebellion to fight His Person. His Person made a great bloodbath among them, their number being unknown." The victorious king then made his way to the great temple of Ptah and offered to the god and his consort Sekhmet. He also decreed the celebratory erection of a new porch at the Amun temple at Barkal, the order being sent south to Nubia while Tanutamun remained in the north.

It is likely that the organizer of the Memphite resistance was the Saite king Nekau I, the trusted associate of the Assyrians, and that he was killed in the fighting, his son Psamtik escaping to Assyrian-held territory.[141] In retrospect at least, Psamtik immediately assumed the Saite crown, so that his and Tanutamun's regnal years ran in parallel. Now taking up residence in the palace at Memphis, the stela records that the Kushite king received a delegation of the northern Egyptian potentates, whose spokesman was Pakerer, the Mayor of Saft el-Henna.

> He said: "You kill whom you will; you let live whom you will; no one will reproach a lord for a deed in accordance with *maat*." They then replied to him as one, saying: "Grant us life, O lord of life: there is no life without you. Let us serve you like those who have nothing, as you said concerning it on the first time, on the day as you arose as king." His Person's heart was joyful after he heard this speech, and he gave them bread, beer and every good thing.
>
> Now when some days had passed after this, they placed themselves on their bellies and said: "Why are we here, O sovereign our lord?" Then His Person spoke saying, "Why (indeed)?" Then they said before His Person "Let us go to our cities, that we may command our subjects and bring our offerings to the Residence."
>
> So His Person <let> them go to their cities, and they were alive. The southerners have been sailing northwards, and the northerners southwards, to the place where His Person is, with every good thing of the southland and every foodstuff of the northland, to satisfy His Person's heart.

However, this state of affairs would be short-lived. As Ashurbanipal recounts:

> Afterwards, Tandamane, son of Shabaku/son of [Tarqû]'s sister,[142] sat down on the throne of his kingdom. He made the cities of Thebes and Heliopolis his fortresses and assembled his forces. He called upon his soldiers to attack my troops, the Assyrians stationed at Memphis. He surrounded these men and cut off all escape routes. A fast messenger came to Nineveh and told me about this.
>
> On this my second campaign I marched directly against Egypt and Nubia. Tandamane heard of the approach of my expedition and that I had set foot on Egyptian territory. He left the city of Memphis and fled into Thebes to save his life. The kings, governors and regents whom I had installed in Egypt came to meet me and kissed my feet. I followed Tandamane (and) went as far as Thebes, his fortress. He saw my battle array approaching, left Thebes and fled to Kipkipi[143] . . . . From Thebes I carried away booty, heavy and beyond counting. . . .[144] I made Egypt and Kush feel my weapons bitterly and celebrated my triumph. With full hands and safety, I returned to Nineveh.[145]

FIGURE 76 The chapel of
Osiris-Ptah-Nebankh at
Karnak, built by Taharqa
and Tanutamun.

Thus the northern Egyptian potentates once again changed sides and acknowledged
the Assyrian king as their overlord. Although not mentioned in the Assyrian text, it is
likely that Psamtik I was with the Assyrian forces: a passage in a second-century AD work
by the Greek author Polyaenus describes how "Psammetichus . . . took into his service a
large number of Carians, with whom he advanced against Memphis. Psammetichus defeated Tementhes in a battle near the temple of Isis, which is about five stades away from
the palace."[146] The use of Carian (and other Hellenic) mercenaries would be a feature of
Psamtik I's dynasty. In any case, it is clear that Psamtik was left as the Assyrians' principal
vassal in the north of Egypt, beginning a process that would lead, eight years later, to his
becoming the sole king of a reunified Egypt (pages 97–98, below).

FIGURE 77 Donation stela of Year 8 of Tanutamun; bought at Thebes (Cairo JE37888).

Although Tanutamun had been expelled from Egypt, with no evidence that he ever returned, the south of the country initially remained formally under his rule. Despite the devastation wrought by the Assyrians, the Theban hierarchy remained essentially intact, with Horemakhet (or perhaps now his son, Horkhebit) as High Priest, Shepenwepet II as God's Wife, Akhamenru as her steward, Amenirdis II as her heir apparent, and Montjuemhat as Fourth Prophet and Mayor.

The chapel of Osiris-Ptah-Nebankh, between the Amun and Mut precincts at Karnak (fig. 76),[147] seems to have been begun under Taharqa, and finished by Tanutamun. The decoration shows both monarchs, probably a consequence of Tanutamun wishing to link himself firmly with his illustrious predecessor.[148] Otherwise, Tanutamun's continuing recognition within Egypt proper is only evidenced by two texts of Year 3, one of Year 4, and one of Year 9 from Luxor temple relating to priestly inductions,[149] a Year 8 donation stela (fig. 77),[150] and a statue of the God's Wife's Steward, Akhamenru.[151]

In Nubia, work was undertaken in Tanutamun's name at Sanam,[152] Dukki Gel (fig. 74),[153] and the Gebel Barkal Amun temple (fig. 23).[154] The latter included a kiosk in the center of court B502,[155] perhaps the structure that the king decreed to be built in celebration of his Egyptian campaign. However, no data is available about how long the king ruled beyond his Year 9—the year when he lost the last part of the Kushite pharaohs' Egyptian possessions to his old rival Psamtik I.

4 OF SAIS, THEBES, NAPATA, AND MEROË

The Twilight of Kushite Thebes

Little is known of the individual events of the first years of the reign of Psamtik I, which nevertheless saw both the absorption of the territories of his northern rivals into the Saite monarchy,[1] and his extraction of Egypt from direct Assyrian hegemony. Egypt now became an ally, rather than a subject, and Egyptian forces were present during Assyria's terminal conflict with Babylon that led to the fall of Nineveh in 612 BC (see below, page 100). In particular, nothing is known about the negotiations that led to the reunification of Egypt in Psamtik's Year 9 (656 BC) through the adoption of a daughter of the Saite king as the next heir to the office of God's Wife of Amun—exactly mirroring the way in which the adoption of Amenirdis I had marked the absorption of Thebes into the Kushite king's domains nearly a century earlier. This parallelism was probably explicitly recognized by the reworking of the reliefs that seem originally to have been carved to mark the arrival of a Kushite princess (page 21, fig. 16).

On the stela erected at Karnak to commemorate the event, Psamtik states:

I have given to him (Amun) my daughter to be God's Wife . . . . Now, I have heard that a king's daughter is there (of) the Horus Qakhau, the good god, [Taharqa], true of voice, whom he gave to his sister (Shepenwepet II) to be her eldest daughter and is there as God's Adoratrix. I will not do what in fact should not be done and expel an heir from his seat . . . . I will give her (my daughter) to her (Taharqa's daughter) to be her eldest daughter just as she (Taharqa's daughter) was made over to the sister of her father.[2]

Thus, Neitiqerti (I), Psamtik's daughter, was to be the eventual heir to Amenirdis II, heir to the still-living Shepenwepet II, and thus unlikely to take office for some decades.

The Saite princess left the royal residence (whether at Sais, Memphis, or elsewhere is not recorded) on I *3ḥt* 28 of Psamtik I's Year 9 (2 March 656 BC), in a flotilla of boats commanded by the Nomarch of Herakleopolis, Sematawytefnakhte. Sixteen days later the convoy reached Thebes, and Neitiqerti was received by Shepenwepet II, who

> was pleased with her; she loved her more than anything and made over to her the testament which her father (Taharqa) and her mother (Amenirdis I) had executed for her; and her eldest daughter Amenirdis (II), daughter of King Ta[harqa], true of voice, did likewise. Their transfer-document was done in writing: "Herewith we give to you all our property in country and in town. You shall be established upon our throne firmly and enduringly till the end of eternity."

This formal incorporation of Neitiqerti into the sisterhood was witnessed by "all the prophets, priests, and friends of the temple." The stela also includes a listing of the daily rations to be paid to her by the great magnates of the region, headed by Montjuemhat, his son, Nesptah, and Montjuemhat's wife Wadjrenes, the High Priest Horkhebit, and the Third Prophet, Padiamennesuttawy. It is interesting that, even in the temple of Amun-Re itself, the Fourth Prophet, Montjuemhat, had precedence over his nominal seniors, the High Priest and Third Prophet, perhaps reflecting his further role of Governor of Upper Egypt. The office of Second Prophet was seemingly vacant, with Taharqa's son Nesishutefnut presumably dead. Further revenues were decreed by the king from temple estates throughout Egypt.

The continuation in office of the Nubian-born High Priest and God's Wife, and the guarantee of the succession of Amenirdis II, must clearly have been a key feature of the "deal" that would seem to have been made to persuade Tanutamun to give up his last Egyptian claims. However, it is possible that Psamtik later reneged on the agreement, as there is no unequivocal evidence that Amenirdis II ever became God's Wife: rather, it appears that Shepenwepet II was directly succeeded by Neitiqerti.

Various explanations as to the fate of Amenirdis II have been suggested. These range from an early death, through marriage with the Vizier Montjuhotep (who married *a* Princess Amenirdis), to a return to Kush, to become the mother of Nasalsa, mother of King Aspelta (cf. fig. 83).[3] Given that Nasalsa's mother is given the titles of "Adorer of the God of Amun-Re-nesunetjeru"—that is, Amun of Karnak—at a point in time after the Kushite withdrawal from Thebes, the latter option would seem to be the most likely. Amenirdis would have been sent back to Kush after the decision was taken to bypass her, presumably on the death of Shepenwepet II, and on arrival married the incumbent king, as the only fitting match for someone originally betrothed to Amun. It may also be noted that no High Priest is known after Horkhebit, and it may be that the Theban high priesthood was then subsumed into the office of the God's Wife—now the Saite Princess Neitiqerti.

The Anti-Kushite Reaction

Continuing—if perhaps grudging—acknowledgment of the Nubians as having been legitimate kings is to be seen through much of the reign of Psamtik I. However, while depictions of Neitiqerti alongside Shepenwepet II (e.g., fig. 78) continued to denote the latter as "daughter of Pi(ankh)y," the apparent non-succession of Amenirdis II may indicate that Egyptian attitudes toward the Kushites were hardening.

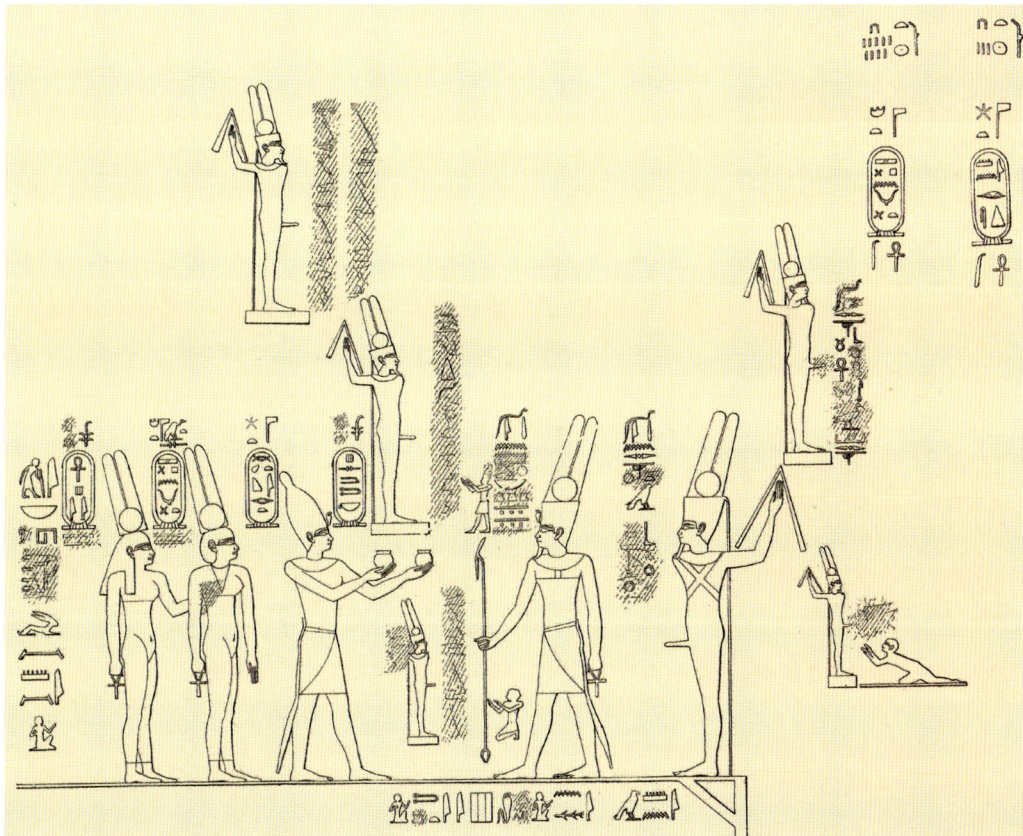

FIGURE 78 Graffiti in the Wadi Gasus. The principal scene shows Psamtik I, Neitiqerti I, and Shepenwepet II before Amun and Min. At the top right are two earlier, wholly separate, graffiti, associating a Shepenwepet with a Year 19 and Amenirdis I with a Year 13. These were once thought to have been made at the same time, representing a synchronization of two kings' reigns.

That this spilled over into physical conflict may be indicated by a fragmentary text from Edfu, describing a war in Lower Nubia, that has been dated by some to Psamtik I.[4] In addition, a second-century BC Greek letter speaks of Jewish mercenaries having fought "in the army of Psammetichus against the King of the Ethiopians," with the king identified by some scholars as the first ruler of the name (rather than the second, cf. just below).[5] Likewise, some have suggested that the passage from Polyaenus describing a battle between Psamtik and Tanutamun near Memphis (page 93) might refer to a final invasion by Tanutamun, following whose repulse the reunification occurred.

However, within two decades of Psamtik I's death, after a reign of fifty-four years, there was certainly violent conflict between the kings of the Saite dynasty and elements in Nubia. In the interim, military activity by Egypt had been concentrated in Syria-Palestine and farther east, where Psamtik I and his successor Nekau II supported the Assyrians in their final conflict with Babylon.[6] Then, under Nekau II, we find a fragmentary stela relating to a "rebellion" south of Aswan that resulted in the dispatch of troops, with a mention of "Kush," but in an uncertain context.[7] From the reign of his successor, Psamtik II, survive accounts of an unequivocal campaign against an enemy in the far south—although exactly who this was, as well as the objectives and extent of the campaign, remain a matter for discussion.[8] Aspects of the operation undertaken under Psamtik II are related on three surviving stelae.[9] The fullest version (fig. 79 left)[10] is unfortunately badly damaged, with much of the end lost.

> His Person had been passing his time restoring temples that had fallen into ruin . . . . One came to His Person in Year 3, saying "The land of Nubians [are thinking of] fighting [against you]. His Person marched an army towards the land of *š3s*, the nobles of the palace being with it. They reached [*t*]*rgb*, which is the residence of the *kw3r* (Nubian leader), as well as a place called *t3-dhn*. So the army of His Person slaughtered and made a great carnage among them [. . .] . We cut down their trees [. . .] .

The other two stelae (fig. 79 center and right) share a rather different text, the best preserved of them bearing the specific date of II *šmw* 10 in Year 3 (8 October 592 BC), indicating that the expedition was undertaken at the highest point of the Nile flood, to make the passage across the Nile cataracts easier. This text picks up the story some time after the expedition had departed.

> His Person had been bird-hunting . . . when one came to say to His Person: "The troops that Your Person sent to Kush reached the area around *pnbs*, a land that has no flat ground, a grave for horses. Nubians of every land were waiting, their hearts

filled with misery . . . and when His Person made every fighter join fighter, the enemies showed their back, without firing a single arrow; they were prisoners without the scratching of a hand. One waded in their blood as if in water. Not one escaped and the survivors were brought as prisoners: 4,200 men."

Further information is provided by graffiti left at Abu Simbel by Greek, Carian, and Phoenician[11] mercenaries[12] who took part in the campaign (fig. 80). These indicate that they were led by General "Potsameto" (Padiamennesuttawy),[13] the Egyptian part of the force being led by a General Ahmose.

These two official Egyptian versions of the campaign[14] seem to differ over how far the expedition got: *pnbs* or *trgb*. The former can be identified with Kerma-Dukki Gel, while the latter would seem to be at Soniyat, 150 kilometers farther upstream. It is most likely that the texts mentioning *pnbs* were specific commemorations of a key battle (especially given its specific date), while the other text, which also includes the background to the war, concerns the overall campaign, which went farther south. Certainly, a victory at Kerma, the ancient heart of Nubian civilization, would have been an event worthy of specific commemoration, while the presence of a large palace at Soniyat would support it as a further objective.[15]

FIGURE 79 Stelae of Psamtik II, relating his Nubian campaign (left: from Tanis [Cairo JE37488]; middle: Sehel [now at New Kalabsha]; right: Karnak).

FIGURE 80 Greek graffiti on the leg of a colossus on the façade of the Great Temple at Abu Simbel.

It has also been suggested, however, that the palace referred to was at Gebel Barkal, with the holy mountain referred to dismissively as "the cliff" (*t3-dhn*), and the cutting down of trees connected with the burning of Level II of palace B1200 at Barkal.[16] Also linked into this idea has been the attribution to the Egyptian invaders of erasures of the names and figures of Pi(ankh)y (see fig. 19), and the presence at Dukki Gel (fig. 129)[17] and Gebel Barkal of caches of broken statues of Taharqa, Tanutamun, and their successors (see page 168) down to Aspelta,[18] perhaps the Kushite contemporary of Psamtik II. The erasure of all the names in the genealogy of Aspelta on his Enthronement Stela (page 104, fig. 83) has also been folded into this scenario.

However, while Pi(ankh)y might have been a credible target for Egyptian invaders, the details of Aspelta's ancestry would seem unlikely to have been of interest to them. Indeed, the damage at Gebel Barkal has also been suggested as being the outcome of a civil conflict within the Kushite ruling family (see page 104). This view may be supported by yet another deposit of broken statues, in this case including Taharqa, Senkamenisken, and Aspelta, at Dangeil, above the Fifth Cataract, and far beyond any conceivable Egyptian penetration. That this deposit is also much later is indicated by a Meroitic graffito on the statue of Taharqa, and an additional late-Kushite sculpture.[19] Accordingly, it would seem most likely that the forces of Psamtik II did not get beyond the Dongola Reach. It should also be pointed out that it is by no means certain that the Egyptians' foe was actually the kingdom of Kush, rather than local elements in northern Nubia who were regarded as hostile by the Egyptians.[20]

Back in Egypt, the reign of Psamtik II saw a widespread erasure of the names of Kushite kings, and often their replacement by cartouches of Psamtik himself. This has generally been regarded as a systematic attack on the legitimacy of the Twenty-fifth Dynasty kings, but it has also been pointed out that Psamtik II was a prolific appropriator of predecessors' monuments,[21] so that the erasures may not actually have been carried out primarily through malice. Such a view may be supported by the state of cartouches that had been erased, but not actually surcharged with a new royal name. In such cases, the removal of the old signs is careful, leaving a smooth surface for recarving (e.g., figs. 31, 33 bottom, 41, 45, 46, 47, 49, 81), and in some cases the sun sign in the prenomen is also left for reuse (although possibly also as an act of respect for the divine name). Likewise the *nfr*-sign in the prenomen of Shabaka (shared with that of Psamtik II, who was Nefer*ib*re to Shabaka's Nefer*ka*re) was also often left alone. Malicious defacement tends to be more violent and less nuanced.

The actual figures of the Kushite kings are generally left untouched, apart from the removal of their distinctive second uraeus (although there are exceptions—e.g., one scene on fig. 47). The evidence as to the Egyptian treatment of the memory of the Twenty-fifth Dynasty kings is thus to a degree equivocal, and while there may well have been a lack of affection for the Kushites under the heirs of their erstwhile opponent Psamtik I, it may have been manifested more in a willingness to usurp, with occasional acts of vandalism, rather than a systematic campaign such as waged against Hatshepsut by Thutmose III, against the god Amun by Akhenaten, and against Akhenaten by Horemheb and later kings.

There are what are clearly "malicious" erasures of the names of Kushite kings in the filiations of the God's Wives of Amun, but it is possible that these did not occur until after the death of Neitiqerti I in Year 4 of Wahibre.[22] This is because the (undamaged) cartouche Pi(ankh)y appears in an inscription on Neitiqerti's sarcophagus,[23] which would seem odd if the Kushite kings had been outlawed under Psamtik II.

FIGURE 81 Erased cartouche of Shabaka on the chapel of Osiris-Nebankh at Karnak-North.

It is not impossible that these latter erasures were linked with a potential Egyptian incursion into Nubia in Year 41 of Ahmose II (529 BC), again comprising a mixture of Egyptians and foreign mercenaries.[24] In any case, by this time, the border between the Egyptian and Kushite control lay somewhere around the Second Cataract, with the fortress at Dorginarti there controlled from Egypt into the fifth century. By then, Egypt had long been absorbed into the Persian Empire following the conquest by Cambyses in 525 BC, and would not regain her independence until 404. Cambyses is stated by Herodotus to have launched a campaign into Upper Nubia, but then turned back, allegedly owing to a lack of food supplies. Thus, while "Kush" would be listed as among those making tribute to the Persian king, this seems simply to have reflected a nominal Kushite presence in Lower Nubia. There is certainly little evidence for further conflict between those ruling Egypt and Kush until the third century BC (pages 106–107).

A degree of continued official Egyptian regard for at least some of the Kushite kings is to be seen during the reign of the Twenty-ninth Dynasty king Pasherenmut. Then, a text in praise of Taharqa was included on the façade of a bark shrine that was erected just to the southeast of that king's ramp on the Karnak river wall (fig. 82).[25]

Events of the time of the Kushites also survived in folk tales that are preserved in some Demotic texts. The extant copies date to the first centuries AD, but their content seems to have its origin back in the fifth century BC.[26] These recount fabulous stories featuring characters based on individuals who lived during the Assyrian conquest of Egypt, and are clearly intended as Egyptian nationalist propaganda. Taharqa appears in one story, as a far-off king in Meroë, whose lands are being ravaged by a griffon.[27] This fabulous beast is later defeated by the principal protagonist of the story cycle, Inaros, depicted as a son of a Bakennefi of Athribis—presumably the Bakennefi C who was deported and executed by the Assyrians.

Napata and Meroë

Documentation for the internal history of Nubia after the withdrawal from Egypt is often scanty, with much of the reconstruction of the royal succession depending heavily on analyses of the topography of the royal cemeteries and the typology of individual tombs (see chapter 5).[28]

It seems clear that Tanutamun was followed on the throne successively by Atlanersa, Senkamanisken, Anlamani, and Aspelta. It has often been suggested that the last-named was king at the time of Psamtik II's attack, but this is by no means certain. The erasure of not only Aspelta's own names, but those of his female ancestors, from his Enthronement Stela (fig. 83)[29] hints at disputes over his legitimacy. These may have led to civil conflict, including the destruction by fire of palace B1200 at Gebel Barkal, something that has also been attributed to Egyptian invaders under Psamtik II (see pages 100–102).

FIGURE 82 The Twenty-ninth Dynasty chapel of Pasherenmut (usurped by Hagar) at Karnak, with detail of a doorjamb with a text mentioning Taharqa.

Whether these erasures took place at the same time as the removal of the names *and figures* of Pi(ankh)y on his stelae is unknown, but the different approach taken could argue against it. Likewise, the later crude restorations of Pi(ankh)y's names and figure are not paralleled as far as the Aspelta names are concerned.

After Aspelta, the reconstructed succession becomes entirely reliant on tomb position and typology, until a text from Kawa confirms that Malawiebamani, Talakhamani, and Arikeamanote ruled in succession, probably in the mid/late fifth century BC. Kings Horsiyotef and Nastasen have been placed during the very late fifth and fourth centuries on account of their operations in Lower Nubia, probably in the wake of renewed Egyptian independence between 404 and the return of the Persians in 343.

The capital appears to have moved south from Napata to Meroë (fig. 84) in the middle of the fifth century, although the royal cemetery remained at Nuri in the north until the time of Arqamaniqo, when it shifted to Begarawiya, just west of the city of Meroë (figs. 109, 117). Arqamaniqo has been equated with the "Ergamenes" stated by the first-century BC writer Diodorus Siculus to have been a contemporary of Ptolemy II of Egypt (285–246 BC).

Estimates of the royal succession based on pyramid location/typology continue after the move to Meroë. A few additional chronological "hooks" are provided by building work by Arqamani and Adikhalamani in Lower Nubia (figs. 85, 86), which is almost

FIGURE 83 Enthronement Stela of Aspelta; the erasures of the names of the king's female ancestors can be seen in the lower part of the text; from Gebel Barkal (Nubian Museum ex-JE48866).

certainly to be dated to the period of the 207–186 BC Upper Egyptian revolt against the Ptolemies (see just below). These two kings, as well as Amanitekha and Arnekhamani, incorporated epithets within their names that were also used by Ptolemy IV (221–205 BC), reinforcing the idea that this group of kings should be placed in the late third/early second centuries. Also dating to this same time is the great complex of buildings at Musawwarat el-Sufra (fig. 87), whose purpose remains obscure, but attests to the power and wealth of the contemporary Kushite state.

The Egyptian language and its hieroglyphs continued to be the Kushite kings' monumental mode of discourse down to the early third century. However, we then find Amqamaniqo

FIGURE 84 The temple of Amun at Meroë.

FIGURE 85 The temple of Dakka, with detail of the decoration by Arqamani.

FIGURE 86 The temple from Debod, with detail of the decoration by Adikhalamani; in Madrid, Spain.

employing a prenomen written in the Meroitic language, but using Egyptian hieroglyphs, and during the second century King Tanyidamani and the ruling Queen Shanakdakhete were apparently the first rulers to write their names using Meroitic hieroglyphs, which had recently emerged, alongside the cursive Meroitic script. Although Meroitic would then become the dominant language and writing systems, Egyptian continued to be used on occasion.

FIGURE 87 Monuments at Musawwarat el-Sufra, including a sculpture of an elephant.

Control of Lower Nubia ebbed and flowed between Egypt and Nubia during Greco-Roman times. In 24 BC Kushite armies pushed through the area and sacked Aswan, en route destroying Roman imperial statues at Philae (fig. 88). Reaction was swift: the Prefect of Egypt pushed the Nubians back to Dakka, and then to Qasr Ibrim, before driving south as far as Napata, which the Roman forces sacked. They then retired, fixing the Roman Empire's southern frontier at Qasr Ibrim in the following year. The border was pulled back to Maharaqqa under the Peace of Samos of 21/20 BC.

FIGURE 88 Bronze head of Augustus, and its finding place at Meroë (BM 1911,0901.1).

Around the same time (late first century BC) is probably to be dated the joint rule of King Natakamani and Queen Amanitore. This seems to have been an era of particular prosperity, with increased imports and major building projects in Upper Nubia (fig. 89), probably facilitated by the more stable conditions in the wake of the Peace of Samos. Interestingly, the use of Egyptian writing is extensively revived on the monuments of Natakamani and Amanitore (although Meroitic was still employed on many occasions), including in the writing of the rulers' names (fig. 117).[30] This may have been done, in part, through desire to link the regime with the prosperity of the reigns of Arnekhamani and Arqamani, and/or perhaps even back to the glory days of the Twenty-fifth Dynasty.

Absolute chronology becomes less exact as we move into the second century AD. Even the names of kings are often now difficult to identify, although a sequence of tombs based on topography and typology can still be constructed down to pyramid BegN25 (Queen Amanipilade?) at Meroë (c. AD 350: fig. 117). This is seemingly the last Kushite royal funerary monument of the sequence that had begun a millennium earlier at El-Kurru.

The story of the final years of the Meroitic regime has been the subject of much debate.[31] The Romans withdrew from Lower Nubia in AD 298, and the name of the late fourth/early fifth century Meroite king Yesbokhamani has been found at Philae and Qasr Ibrim, although other groups, the Nobidae and the Blemmyes, were also present in the region.

Farther south, a campaign by King Ezana of Axum in Ethiopia in the mid-fourth century may have contributed to a clear trajectory of decline that can be observed in

FIGURE 89 The temple of Amun, and the Lion Temple, at Naga, built by King Natakamani and Queen Amanitore.

Meroitic material culture. In Upper Nubia there is a transition to the successor X-Group, characterized by a shift of high-status burials from pyramids to tumuli. These are to be found throughout the region, from the Second Cataract to south of the Sixth, suggesting the existence of a number of separate polities. The tombs at Ballana and Qustul, near the Second Cataract (pages 136–37; fig. 119), contained both local and imported material, the former including royal regalia that incorporated adaptations of Egyptian and Kushite symbolism (fig. 90), indicating some degree of conceptual continuity. On the other hand, the extensive human sacrifices found in the cemeteries recall the much more remote parallels at Kerma two millennia earlier (page 3, above). But Christianization of Nubia during the sixth century AD marked the definitive break with the past and the very last links with the Kushite pharaohs of Egypt.

FIGURE 90 An inlaid silver crown from X-Group tomb 118 at Ballana (Nubian Museum ex-JE70455).

5 THE WORLD OF THE KUSHITE ROYAL DEAD

The Tombs of the First Kushite Kings of Egypt

As already noted, the necropolis of El-Kurru (figs. 91, 92) contains a series of tombs that appear "ancestral" to those of Kushite rulers of Egypt. The cemetery would ultimately hold the burials of all but one of these latter kings. While the likely tomb of Kashta (Ku8—fig. 93)[1] has been attributed solely on typological grounds, the later tombs there all contained inscribed material, making their ownership certain. Although the super-structure has entirely vanished at the tomb of Pi(ankh)y, whose tomb is now numbered Ku17,[2] it was almost certainly a pyramid, albeit only eight meters square, and with a high angle of elevation, as in earlier and later Nubian pyramids (figs. 94 top, 100a).

FIGURE 91 The site of El-Kurru, from the south. The large pyramid Ku1, to the left, dates to the fourth century BC, with the seventh century and earlier tombs behind.

FIGURE 92 Map of
the El-Kurru cemetery.

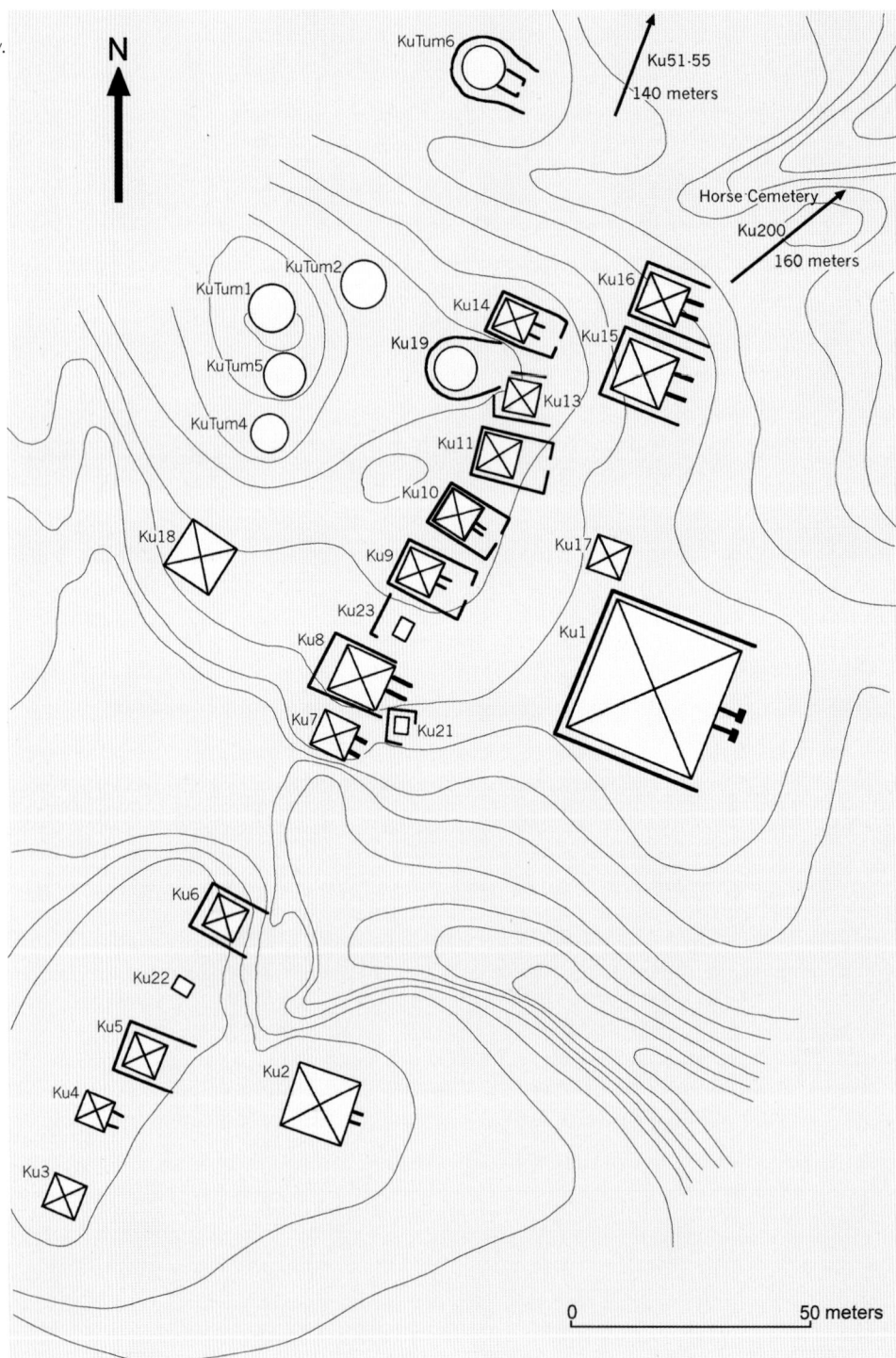

FIGURE 93 El-Kurru Ku8, probably the tomb of Kashta.

FIGURE 94 Tombs Ku17 and Ku18, the burial places of Pi(ankh)y and Shabataka.

The substructure was approached by a stairway, once covered by a chapel (as would be the case in all subsequent Kushite royal tombs), the burial chamber being a corbel-roofed room, built in an open pit. Sets of dummy[3] canopic jars (fig. 95) and shabtis (fig. 96) were provided, together with a wide range of other items, but instead of a sarcophagus a rock-cut rectangular bench lay in the middle of the burial chamber. The bench had a cutout in each corner, to receive the legs of a bed: interment on a bier has been characterized as a typical feature of Nubian burials since at least the middle of the second millennium.[4] Such small pyramids, with chapels on their east sides, built above the stairway entrance to the substructure, became the standard form of tomb for Kushite kings, soon extended to queens and later to other royal family members as well.

In addition to constructing his own tomb, Pi(ankh)y probably initiated the horse cemetery that lies some two hundred meters to the northeast.[5] Here, twenty-two equine interments (Ku201–222) have been found, four of which are definitely attributable to the reign of Shabataka, with the rest probably to be distributed among the other kings buried at El-Kurru. These burials underline the importance of horses to the Kushites, as indicated by Pi(ankh)y's reaction following the siege of Hermopolis (page 33).

The tomb of Shabataka (Ku18—figs. 94 bottom, 100b)[6] was very similar to that of Pi(ankh)y, just slightly larger and with a right-angle turn at the top of the longer descending stair. The latter resulted from the tomb's somewhat awkward position, among some of the more ancient tombs in the cemetery, which blocked an axial approach. Surviving contents included dummy canopic jars (fig. 97 left), some two hundred shabtis, an offering table, and fragments of carved ivory (fig. 97 right). A fragmentary skull and a few bones were also found, possibly representing remains of the king.[7]

FIGURE 95 The dummy canopic jars of Pi(ankh)y (MFA 19-3-261, 19-3-726).

Shabaka's tomb at el-Kurru (Ku15—figs. 98, 100c)[8] marks an architectural and decorative advance over those of his predecessors. Rather than a corbeled chamber built in an open cutting, the sepulcher had a wholly rock-cut substructure, incorporating a plastered and painted vaulted burial chamber. The decoration seems to have comprised scenes from the New Kingdom books of the underworld, as employed in later Kushite royal tombs (e.g., figs. 104–106). A considerable quantity of the burial equipment was recovered (fig. 99), including two canopic jar lids, at least 183 shabtis, inscribed gold foil, amulets and beads from jewelry, and a wide range of other material.

Taharqa and Tanutamun

The reign of Taharqa saw radical changes in the royal tomb. First, rather than building at El-Kurru, he inaugurated a new royal cemetery at Nuri, some twenty-six kilometers upstream, and on the opposite bank of the river. The reasons for this are not fully clear, especially as his successor Tanutamun was buried at El-Kurru, before the royal cemetery was relocated at Nuri, where it stayed until the late fourth century.[9]

There may have been purely practical reasons: Taharqa's pyramid was far larger than those of his predecessors, and it

FIGURE 96 Two of the 60+ shabtis from the tomb of Pi(ankh)y, and a gilded bronze offering stand from the same monument (MFA 19.1974, 21.3112, 21.3238).

FIGURE 97 Dummy canopic jars and an ivory relief from the tomb of Shabataka (MFA 21.2814, 21.2813, 21.308a).

FIGURE 98 The foundations of the superstructures and the entrances to the tombs of Shabaka (Ku15) and Tanutamun (Ku16—entrance staircase covered by modern vaulted structure).

will have been difficult to fit into the space remaining at El-Kurru. It is also possible that Taharqa may have had issues regarding Shabaka (pages 68–69). Concerning the choice of Nuri as a site, it has been suggested that the pyramid of Taharqa was sited there to align with the uraeus-form pinnacle over his temple B300 (fig. 24 bottom) at Gebel Barkal.

The superstructure of Taharqa's sepulcher (Nu1—figs. 100d, 101 top, 123)[10] was built in two phases. The first comprised the construction of a sandstone pyramid 28.5 meters square and 30 meters high; the second involved an enlargement to make the structure 51.7 meters square and 65 meters high. This phase added more masonry to the west and south sides than the north and east, leaving the entrance to the substructure no longer in the middle of the east face of the pyramid. The pyramid's final base size approached that of the smaller Old Kingdom and Middle Kingdom monuments, and by virtue of its 69° slope made it as tall as Menkaure's Fourth Dynasty pyramid at Giza.

It is likely that the first phase of the superstructure was accompanied by a substructure of the same simple form seen in the immediately preceding kings' tombs at El-Kurru. However, as completed it included a unique six-pillared burial hall with vaulted aisles and a sunken central coffin cut (rather than the usual bed support) (fig. 101 bottom), surrounded by a corridor. This form is highly reminiscent of the Osireion cenotaph behind the Nineteenth Dynasty temple of Sethy I at Abydos,[11] and also found in other tombs of the Twenty-fifth/sixth Dynasties.[12]

Large quantities of material deriving from the king's burial have been recovered, including inlays from the royal coffin(s), parts of the canopic outfit (fig. 102), a huge number of shabtis (fig. 103), amulets and jewelry, and fragments of a human skull and leg bone. The canopic jars, of which two survive complete, with fragments of the others, are

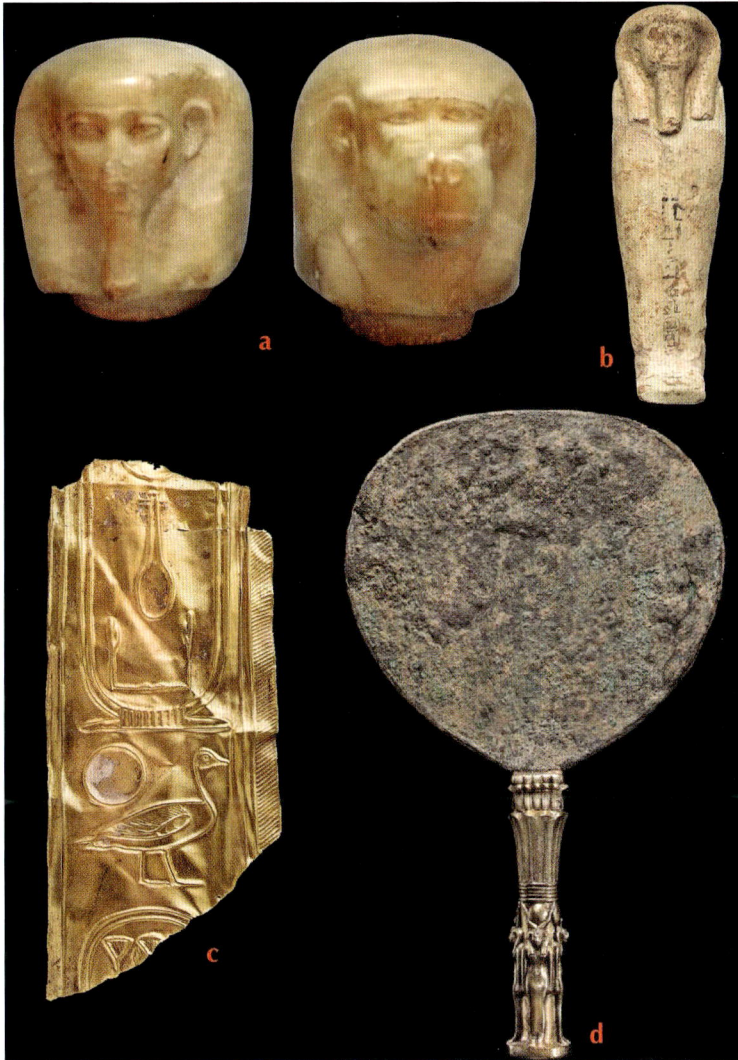

FIGURE 99 Objects from
the tomb of Shabaka:
a. canopic jar lids (SNM);
b. shabti (MFA 21.11707);
c. inscribed gold foil (MFA
21.303); d. bronze mirror
with silver-gilt handle (MFA
21.318).

interesting in a number of ways. First, rather than being solid dummies, as in the case of
Pi(ankh)y and Shabataka, they are "proper" hollowed-out jars. They also seem to be the
very first examples with a completely new textual formulation, which gives a distinctive
formula for each jar, rather than just differing in the deities invoked.[13] Both these features would become standard during the Twenty-sixth Dynasty.

Unlike the burials of his predecessors, whose shabtis were simple faience pieces
numbering no more than two hundred (figs. 96, 99b), the shabtis of Taharqa were not
only exceptionally numerous (around 1,070), but also of very different designs and sizes
(with some up to sixty centimeters tall), in calcite, serpentine, and granite. The figures

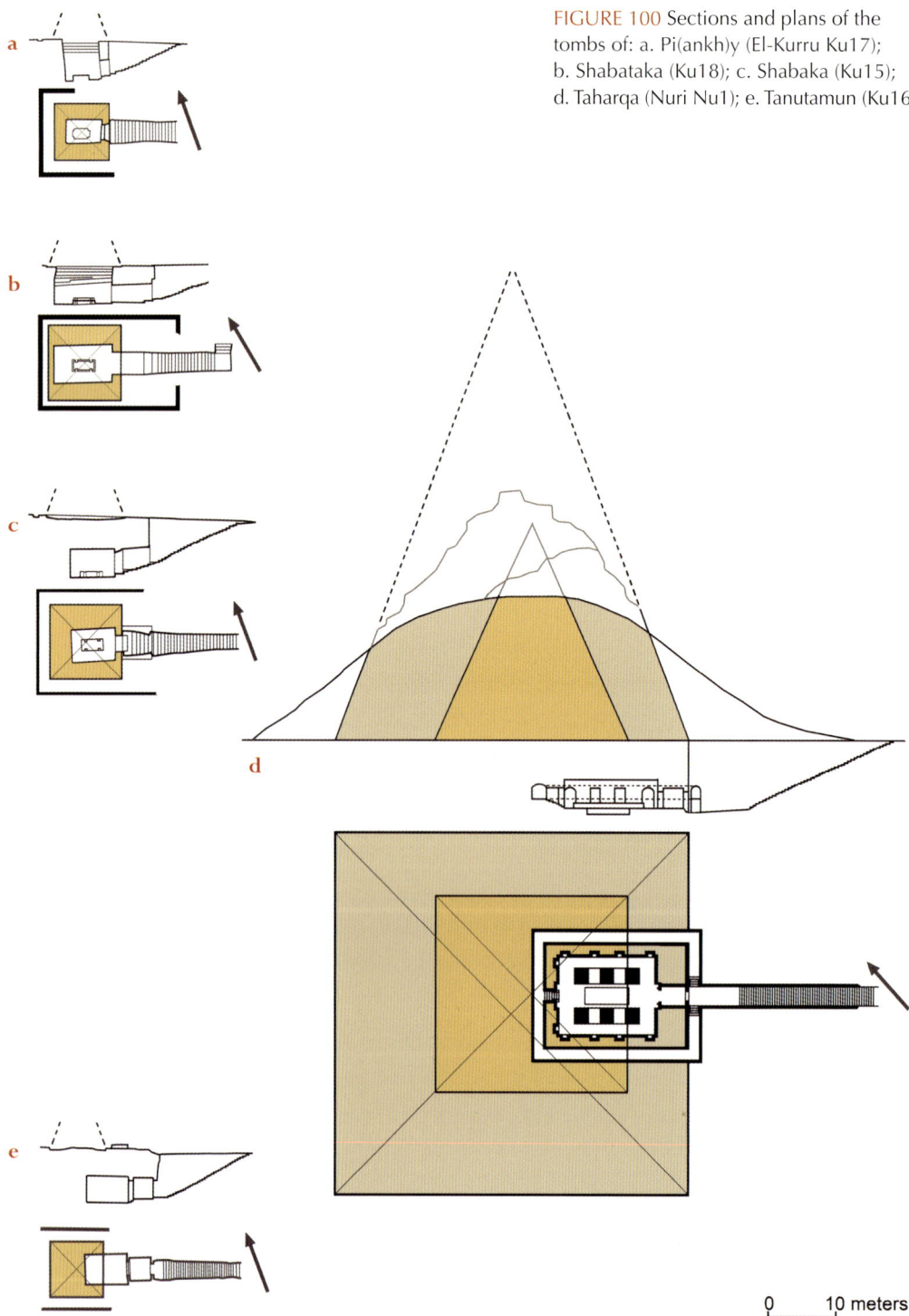

FIGURE 100 Sections and plans of the tombs of: a. Pi(ankh)y (El-Kurru Ku17); b. Shabataka (Ku18); c. Shabaka (Ku15); d. Taharqa (Nuri Nu1); e. Tanutamun (Ku16).

0   10 meters

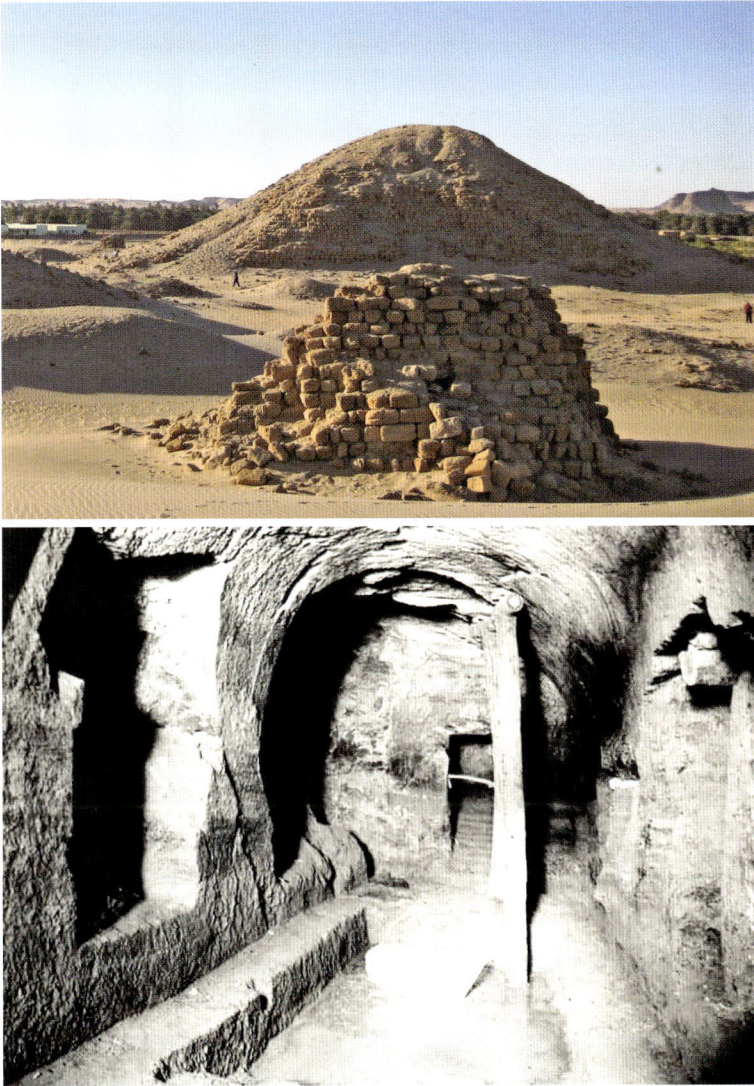

FIGURE 101 Top: the pyramid of Taharqa at Nuri (Nu1), with the pyramid of Nasakhma (Nu19, early fifth century) in the foreground. Bottom: the burial chamber of Taharqa.

had originally been arranged in three or more rows around the burial chamber, and were inscribed with a special version of the shabti formula. The interment of Taharqa can thus be seen to have incorporated a range of physical and textual innovations, some of which would endure into the future.[14]

As already noted, Tanutamun returned to El-Kurru for his burial, placing his pyramid (Ku16—figs. 98, 100d)[15] directly next to that of his father Shabaka. It closely followed the design of the latter, differing principally in omitting the raised bed support, already eliminated in Taharqa's tomb. Although the lower parts of the walls were damaged by

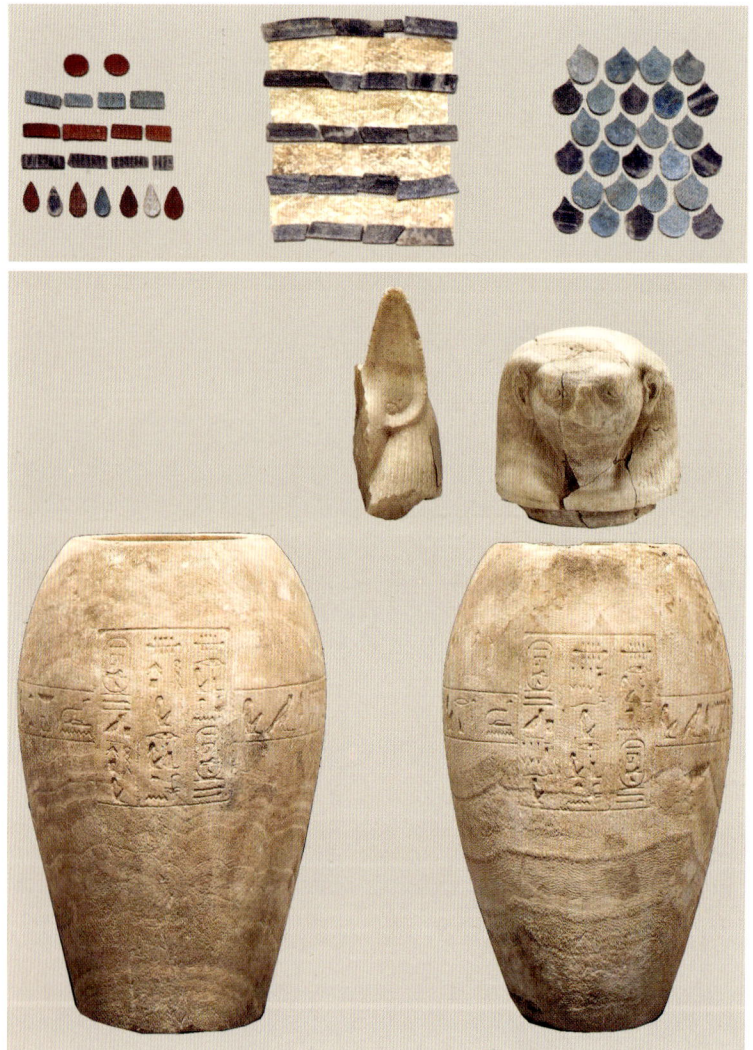

FIGURE 102 Top: coffin inlays from the tomb of Taharqa (MFA). Bottom: canopic jars of Taharqa (MFA 23.739; 17-3-69; 23.738).

flooding, much of the decoration of the substructure of the pyramid of Tanutamun remains intact. The side walls of the antechamber show the dead king led to the beyond by the Four Sons of Horus, Imseti and Duamutef on the south, and Hapy and Qebehsenuef on the north (fig. 104). It is notable that all four are shown with human heads, possibly an archaizing feature, reversing the shift to differentiated heads that had occurred during the Ramesside Period. The western wall features figures of Isis and Nephthys, flanking the door into the burial chamber, above which pairs of apes adore the sun bark, a motif that is repeated on the other side of the arch (fig. 105). The goddesses each hold two strips of red cloth, alluding to mummification.

FIGURE 103 Shabtis of Taharqa.
a. BM EA55491; b. BM EA55486;
c. BM EA55489; d. BM EA55483;
e. BM EA55485; f. BM EA55487;
g. BM EA55482; h. BM EA55488;
i. BM EA55484; j. BM EA55490.

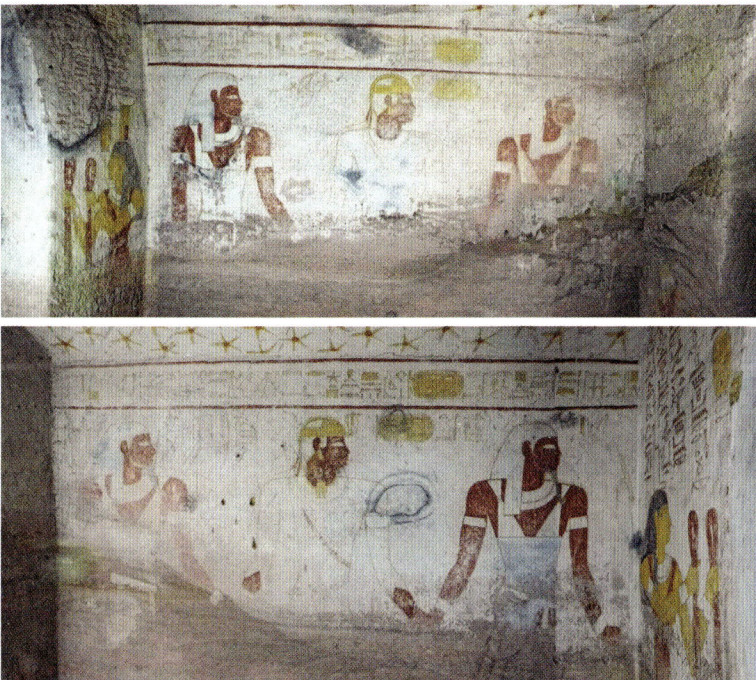

FIGURE 104 The long walls of
the antechamber of Tanutamun
in El-Kurru Ku16.

FIGURE 105 The east wall of the burial chamber of Tanutamun.

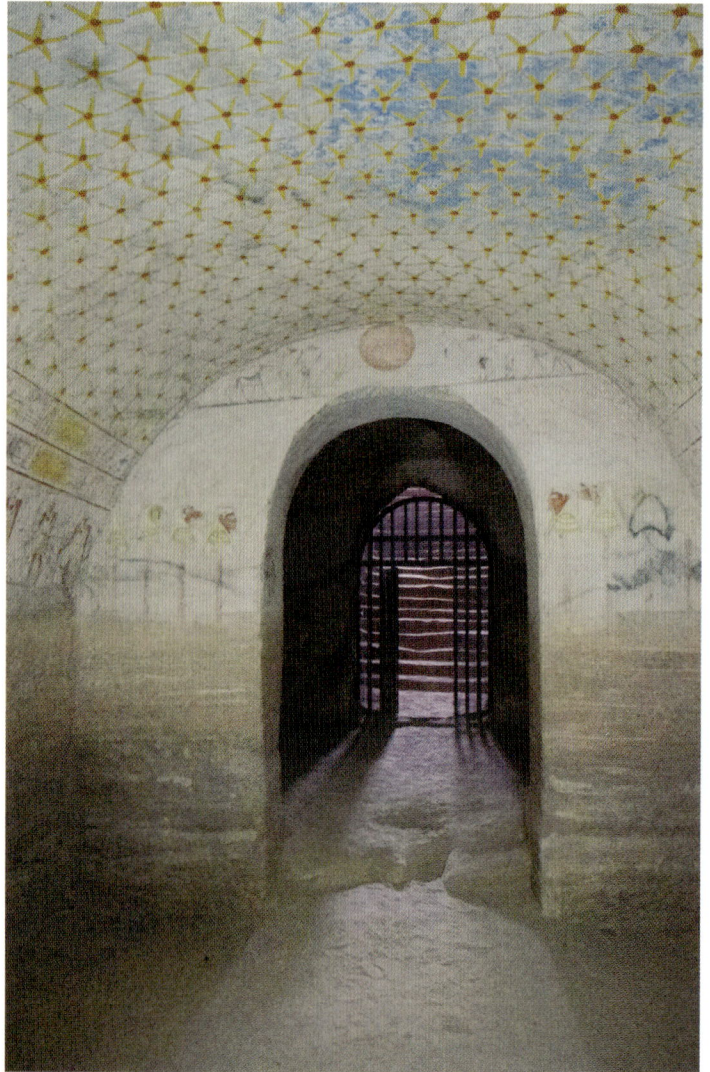

Apart from the apes and sun bark, the entrance (east) wall of the burial chamber has standards of the Four Sons of Horus on each side of the doorway—in this case with the normal differentiated heads. The remaining walls of the room have decoration grounded in Chapters 27, 28, and 30 of the Book of the Dead, with some text unfinished. The north and south walls are dominated by an image of the catafalque of the dead king (of which only the upper part survives; for a complete example, see fig. 108), flanked by genii. The principal difference between these two walls is that the northern has the figure of a deity holding a *w3s*-scepter toward the face of the reviving mummy (fig. 106 top).

FIGURE 106 The north and west walls of the burial chamber of Tanutamun.

The west wall (fig. 106 bottom) has three surviving registers. The vaulted upper section is occupied by a sun disk and supporting figures of apes and jackals. The middle register is divided in two, the left-hand portion having a figure of the king himself, kneeling before his heart, placed upon a standard-pole, his *ba*, and two/three standing divine figures. The right-hand part of the register has a standing image of the king, before his heart-on-a-pole and a squatting figure, over part of which a sun disk may have been superimposed. Below is inscribed Chapter 28 of the Book of the Dead, arranged over twenty-five columns, the middle pair of which extend upward into the middle register, serving as its division point.

FIGURE 107 Canopic jar lids of Tanutamun (MFA 21.2801; 21.2797).

Three fragments of the Imseti canopic jar were recovered from the tomb, with an unusual formula, together with three lids (fig. 107). Also recovered were some 180 shabtis, two heart scarabs—one perhaps a "stray" from the adjacent tomb of Shabaka, since Tanutamun would only have had one—and a range of other items, including an offering table.

The Tombs of the Royal Family of the Twenty-fifth Dynasty

The burial places of the family members of the Twenty-fifth Dynasty kings are to be found in both Egypt and Nubia, as far south as Meroë, although the senior women, the wives of the kings, were generally buried close to their husbands, at El-Kurru[16] and Nuri.

Pi(ankh)y's wives, Khensa and Tabiry, were buried at the former site, in Ku4 and Ku53 respectively, the latter being much the smaller of the two. Adjacent were four other similar tombs, one belonging to Neferukakashta (Ku52), who was possibly another of Pi(ankh)y's spouses. Three other definite royal ladies' tombs have also been identified at El-Kurru: Arty (Ku6), Naparaye (Ku3), and Qalhata (Ku5). The substructure of Ku5 contains well-preserved decoration, following the same basic scheme as found both in the tomb of Qalhata's son, Tanutamun, and in later sepulchers (fig. 108).

The presence of the tomb of Naparaye at El-Kurru is interesting in that her husband, Taharqa, was buried at Nuri. Meanwhile, another wife of that king, Atakhebasken, was interred in Nuri Nu36,[17] where many subsequent queens' pyramids were erected. The

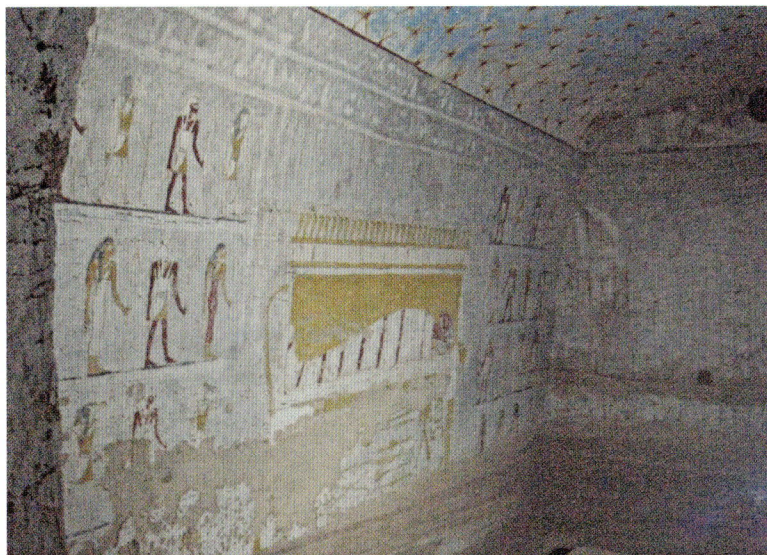

FIGURE 108 The north and south walls of the burial chamber of Queen Qalhata (Ku5).

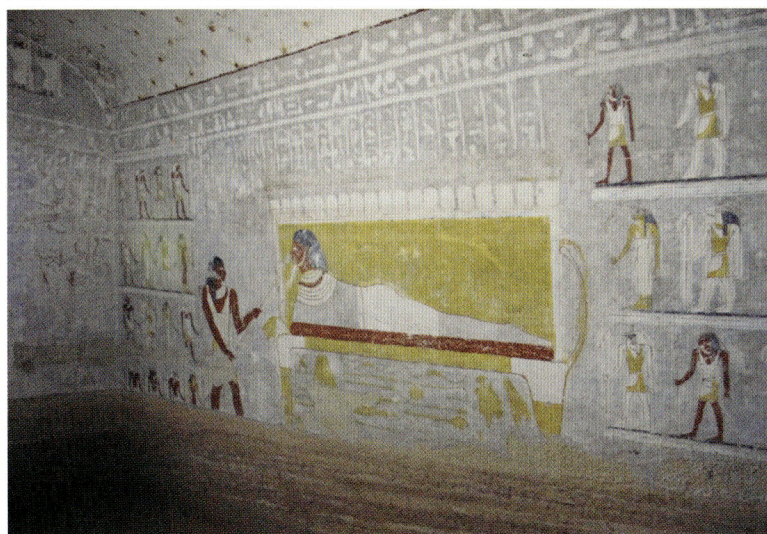

tombs of Taharqa's other wives have not been positively identified, although the anonymous Nu35, Nu74, Nu77, and Nu80 may have belonged to some of them. Nu59, belonging to Malaqaye, may be datable to the reign of Tanutamun, and is notable in that its current form is an enlargement of an earlier tomb. The remains of the displaced owner of this original sepulcher were placed in a cutting in the floor of what had now become the antechamber.[18] Much of the burial of Malaqaye remained in situ when found, including the mummy mask and other mummy trappings, the queen's bones, the heart scarab, other amulets, and some two hundred shabtis.

It is likely that some members of the royal family were interred in the West and South Cemeteries at Meroë.[19] These interments go back to at least the time of Pi(ankh)y, and include one royal wife (Mernua, in BegS85), buried there during the decades immediately following Tanutamun's reign (fig. 109).[20]

In addition to the members of the Kushite royal family interred in their home cemeteries, a number were buried in Egypt. At the ancient necropolis of Abydos, the Kushites used Cemetery D, in the northern part of the site.[21] This had been employed for high-status burials since the Twenty-first/second Dynasties, when the Theban High Priests Menkheperre and Iuput found rest there, as did senior officials of the Twenty-fifth Dynasty (e.g., pages 74–79). Royalty now buried there included Pi(ankh)y's wife Peksater (unnumbered),[22] Shabaka's daughter (and probably wife of Tanutamun) Isetemkheb H (D3),[23] and Paabtameri, apparently the wife of a king of the dynasty (D9).[24] The Lady

FIGURE 109 The South Cemetery at Meroë. Although the pyramids in the center and right date to the late third century BC (the largest two belonging to Kings Amqamaniqo and Amanislo [BegS6 and BegS5]), parts of it (together with the West Cemetery) were employed for much earlier burials of members of the royal family, including Mernua of around the end of the seventh century in tomb BegS85. Her tomb was found intact, with the mummy equipped with trappings of the kind found in contemporary Egyptian burials (MFA 23.1396).

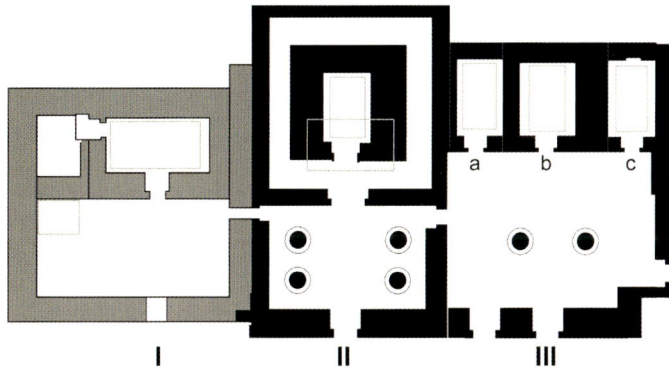

FIGURE 110 Top: Medinet Habu, showing the small temple, the tomb-chapels of the God's Wives of Amun, and memorial temple of Rameses III. Bottom: plans of the tomb-chapels of the God's Wives of Amun. I: Shepenwepet I(?); II: Amenirdis I; IIIa: Neitiqerti I; IIIb: Shepenwepet II; IIIc: Mehytenweskhet C.

Taniy, a senior member of the household of a Kushite queen, was also interred in the area,[25] as was a Prince Ptahmaakeru (D19).[26] Also probably buried there was Princess Meryetamun G, of unknown parentage, but definitely of this time, and whose stela almost certainly came from Abydos.[27] It is interesting to see royal wives apparently being buried at Abydos, far away from their husbands in Nubia, as there is no evidence to suggest that the monuments at Abydos were cenotaphs. Perhaps it was regarded as more straightforward for those who died in Egypt to be buried in the time-hallowed sands of the city of Osiris, rather than shipping their mummies all the way back to Upper Nubia.

The other significant group of royal family tombs of the Twenty-fifth Dynasty are those of the God's Wives of Amun at Medinet Habu (fig. 110).[28] This complex had become a royal burial ground in the ninth century with the interment there of the local king Horsieset I, and it is probable that a now-destroyed brick structure (MH17) opposite Horsieset's sepulcher was the tomb of Shepenwepet I. A similar building, with an underground crypt and a brick chapel, may have been constructed for Amenirdis I, but if so, it was soon replaced by a stone version (figs. 111, 112 top), as evidenced by a dedicatory inscription by Shepenwepet II.[29] The plan was essentially that of a miniature temple, fronted by a colonnade or porch, and followed by a pylon, a peristyle court, and an inner sanctuary, surrounded by a corridor. All surfaces were decorated with scenes of Amenirdis and Shepenwepet II interacting with the gods, except for the interior of the sanctuary, which included offering lists and images of priests. Below the floor of the sanctuary was the burial chamber, with stone walls, but a plain dirt floor, which was just large enough to contain the encoffined mummy.[30] The sanctuary lay partly above a transverse brick-lined compartment, which would seem to have been the burial chamber of the original brick chapel, but was then reused as the embalming cache of the final tomb. A number of items from the burial of Amenirdis I are known (fig. 112 bottom), including five shabtis that were found some distance from the tomb, along with two canopic jar lids, perhaps also from her burial; her heart scarab was acquired before any excavations were undertaken.

FIGURE 111 The façade of the tomb-chapel of Amenirdis I.

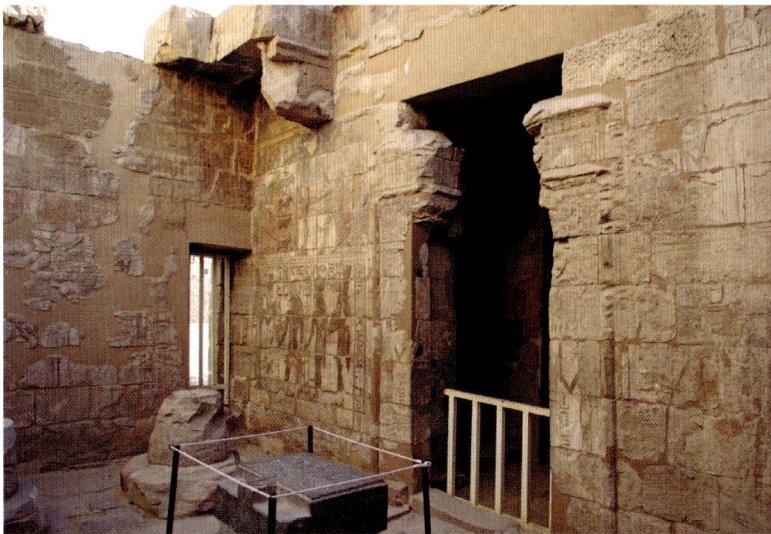

FIGURE 112 The entrance to the inner chapel of Amenirdis I, one of her shabtis (ISACM 14198), and her heart scarab (MMA 15.6.38).

Shepenwepet II had begun a very similar adjoining tomb-chapel (fig. 113) while that of Amenirdis was still in the process of decoration. However, only the façade and the sanctuary (with the subterranean burial chamber) had been erected by Shepenwepet's death. After this, Neitiqerti added a sanctuary of her own between Shepenwepet's and the west wall of Amenirdis's monument and, somewhat later, another for her mother, Queen Mehytenweskhet C, to the west of Shepenwepet's. Neitiqerti seems to have been responsible for all the decoration of the monument. Well over sixty shabtis of Shepenwepet II, or fragments thereof, were found in the area to the west of the tomb.

FIGURE 113 The tomb-chapel of Shepenwepet II, flanked by those of Neitiqerti I and Mehytenweskhet C.

Nuri, Meroë, and Beyond

With the interment of Tanutamun, the royal cemetery moved back to Nuri, where it would remain until the fourth century BC.[31] Atlanersa's pyramid (Nu20) followed the small and simple design of that of his predecessor Tanutamun (with the coffin bench reinstated), rather than the large and elaborate scheme of Taharqa, southeast of which it was erected.

Atlanera's successor, Senkamanisken, built his much larger Nu3 directly to the north of Nu20 (fig. 114 top). Internally, it was much more elaborate than the preceding tomb, with two antechambers added, all chambers decorated in relief, with carved architectural detailing, and the coffin bench made of granite. The next ruler, Anlamani, placed his very similar monument (Nu6) around a hundred meters to the east, beginning what would become a long line of pyramids along the eastern edge of the cemetery (fig. 114 bottom). Senkamenisken's readoption of a granite coffin bench was taken a step further by the provision of the first stone sarcophagus to be placed in a Kushite royal tomb (fig. 115 top). It was based on contemporary Egyptian sarcophagi, and an even finer example (fig. 115 bottom) was provided in the pyramid of Aspelta (Nu8), built a little to the north, to a very similar design.

However, while the same basic design of tomb was employed for the succeeding king Amtalqa (Nu9), no sarcophagus (or coffin bench) was provided, although the coffin bench was reinstated under Karakamani (Nu7). The latter tomb provided a template for the remaining kings' pyramids at Nuri, ending with Nastasen's Nu15. Large numbers of smaller pyramids, principally belonging to royal wives, lay to the west of the kings' monuments.

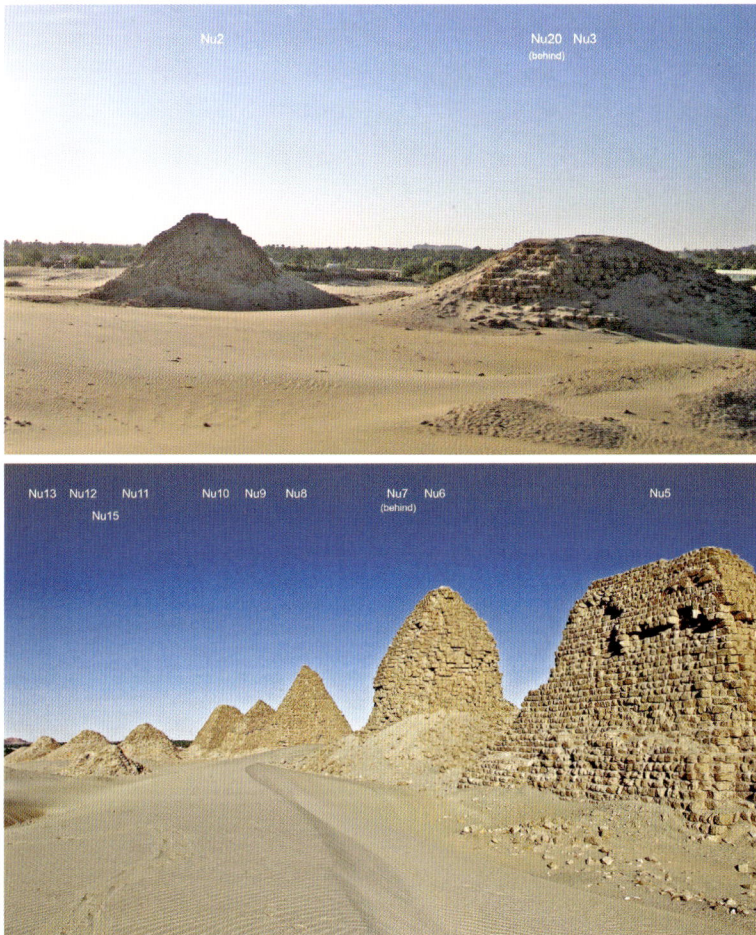

FIGURE 114 The principal post-Taharqa kings' pyramids at Nuri. Nu2: Amaniastabarqa (late sixth century BC); Nu3: Senkamanisken (late seventh century); Nu20: Atlanersa? (late seventh century); Nu5: Malenaqen (early sixth century); Nu6: Anlamani (late seventh century); Nu7: Karakamani (late sixth century); Nu8: Aspelta (early sixth century); Nu9: Amtalqa (late sixth century); Nu10: Amaninatakilebte (late sixth century); Nu11: Malawiebamani (mid-fifth century); Nu12: Amanneteyerike (late fifth century); Nu13: Horsiyotef (early fourth century); Nu15: Nastasen (late fourth century).

It seems that the royal cemetery then shifted briefly to a location directly south of the mountain at Gebel Barkal, where pyramid Bar11 (fig. 116 top)[32] seems on typological grounds to belong to a king of the same period as these Nuri pyramids. There then came the shift to the south, with the royal tombs henceforth placed close to the now-capital of Meroë, with the exception of a short return to Barkal during the first century BC (fig. 116 bottom).[33]

The first two kingly burials at Meroë were placed on the eastern edge of the old South Cemetery (fig. 109), but during the third century a whole new cemetery was established to the north (fig. 117). This would continue in use until the end of the Kushite kingdom. Unlike the earlier cemeteries, including those of the Kushite kings who ruled in Egypt, the chapels of many of the Meroë pyramids are quite well preserved (fig. 118). This has allowed their decoration—mainly concerned with offering activities—to be

FIGURE 115 Sarcophagi of Anlamani, from Nu6 (SNM 1868) and Aspelta, from Nu8 (MFA 23.729).

studied.[34] Interestingly, the most elaborate preserved texts are those in the chapels of Natakamani (BegN22) and Amanitore (BegN1), whose era has already been noted for its archaism and revival of Egyptian hieroglyphs, and after which a number of changes may be seen in the general decorative schemes of royal funerary chapels. It is also interesting to note that the pyramids of Natakamani and Amanitore stand respectively at the eastern and western extremes of the cemetery.

FIGURE 116 Barkal pyramids Bar11 (top), Bar14, Bar15, and Bar25.

FIGURE 117 The North Cemetery at Meroë, the principal burial place of the kings of Kush from the late third century BC to the fourth century AD.

FIGURE 118 The chapel of Meroë pyramid BegN12, of an unknown king of the late second century BC.

By now, substructures had changed significantly in configuration, having reverted to just two rooms, with the antechamber now equipped with two (three in a few examples, including BegN1 and BegN22) niches in the north and south walls. Later, however, this element reverted to a simple form, with the underground rooms becoming increasingly summary in their cutting. In parallel, there was a shift from stone to brick in the material used for the superstructure, now often built directly above the descending stairway, rather than the chambers.

As already noted (page 110), the sequence of royal tombs at Meroë seems to come to an end around AD 350. After this, the most prominent funerary monuments of the successor polities to the Kushite kingdom are to be found in the tumuli at Ballana and Qustul (fig. 119), with their extensive human sacrifices and other features recalling Kerman practice of two millennia earlier.[35] With this, the story of pagan burial in Nubia is essentially over, with the region increasingly embracing Christianity.

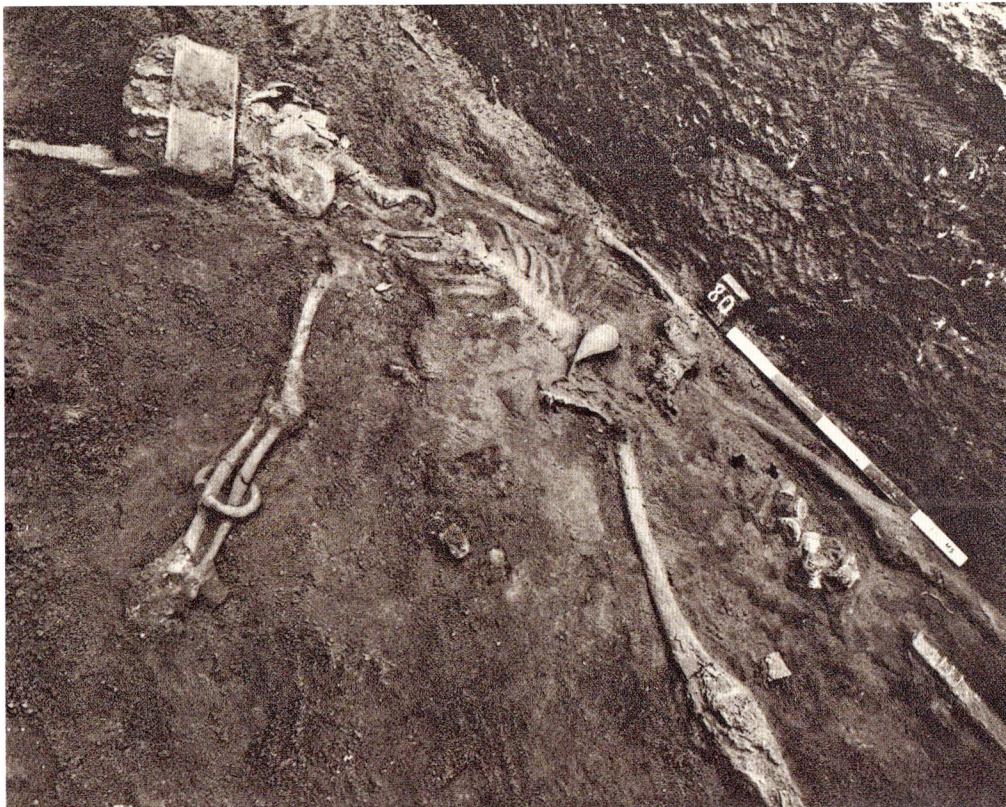

FIGURE 119 Model of Ballana tomb 80 (Nubian Museum), and the burial of the king found in it.

6 LIMBO

The Kushites in the Greek and Latin Literature

Herodotus

Although there had been some attacks on the memory of the Kushite kings of Egypt, there is no indication of any formal attempt to write them out of history. Something of what was popularly known of them during the fifth century BC (two centuries after their departure from Egypt) may be gleaned from the tales recorded by Herodotus[1] during his visit to Egypt at that time.

The narrative of Egyptian history that Herodotus culled from the stories told by his guides is distinctly confused. It places the builders of the Giza pyramids after "Rhampsinitus"—probably Rameses II or III—and following them with "Asuchis" (alleged to be the builder of a brick pyramid) and then "a blind man called Anysis." The Greek historian states that during the latter's reign, "Egypt was invaded by Sabacos king of Ethiopia and a great army of Ethiopians . . . [who] ruled Egypt for fifty years."

Of "Sabacos," Herodotus states that "it is recorded that in the history of his reign he would never put to death any Egyptian wrongdoer, but sentenced all, according to the greatness of their offense, to raise embankments in the town of which each was a native." The end of the king's rule in Egypt is ascribed by the Greek writer to his reaction to a troubling dream, combined with the memory of an oracle that had foretold for him a fifty-year reign in Egypt.

Interestingly, this half-century corresponds closely to the actual duration of Kushite rule in Egypt, counting from the accession of Shabataka to the flight of Tanutamun. While this might indicate that some memories of the Nubian era were fairly clear, Herodotus' narrative then ascribes to an implicitly non-"Ethiopian" king an event that clearly belongs to the time of Kushite rule in Egypt.

The Herodotan story follows the departure of Sabacon with the return of Anysis to the throne, and then the succession of "a priest of Hephaestus, whose name was Sethos." To his time is ascribed a campaign of Sennacherib against Egypt, which failed when "one night a multitude of fieldmice swarmed over the Assyrian camp and devoured their quivers and their bows and the handles of their quivers and their bows and the handles of their shields likewise." This tale has been seen as a counterpoint to the Old Testament narrative that ascribed the failure of Assyria to capture Jerusalem during Sennacherib's 701 BC campaign (pages 65–68) to a death-dealing "angel of the Lord," and is surely an echo of Egypt's part in the campaign.[2] After the reign of "Sethos," Herodotus writes of the division of Egypt into twelve kingdoms (clearly a reflection of the multiple local rulers installed by Ashurbanipal), and the emergence of Psamtik I. The latter is described as having fled to Syria "from Sabacos the Ethiopian, who killed his father Necos," returning after Sabacos' departure.

From Psamtik I onward, Herodotus provides a historical narrative for Egypt which, although leavened with much material derived from folklore, can be shown to be essentially accurate. This makes the confusion regarding the preceding decades rather curious, although possibly explicable in light of the damage suffered by Kushite monuments during the Twenty-sixth Dynasty (pages 99–104), which might have been accompanied by a suppression of accurate knowledge of the events of the reigns of the Twenty-fifth Dynasty kings. In such a case, the mix of sound underlying history (the fact of the rule of Kushite kings and their involvement in conflict with Assyria) with folk tales would not, perhaps, be unexpected.

The names "Sabacon" and "Sethos" presumably conceal those of Shabataka and Shabaka, respectively, with the latter's quite extensive work at Memphis conceivably contributing to his equation with a "priest of Hephaestus" (i.e., Ptah). On the other hand, the story of "Sabacon" also incorporates, as killer of "Necos" (Nekau I), aspects of the reign of Tanutamun. He may thus be seen as a conflation of several of the Kushite kings of Egypt (especially given the similarities of the names of Shabataka and Shabaka). It is perhaps odd that no one with a name resembling that of Taharqa is to be found in Herodotus' narrative, given the survival of his name in the Old Testament.

Manetho

The next glimpse we have of the Kushite kings is in the surviving epitomes (in the works of the chroniclers Sextus Julius Africanus [c. AD 160–c. 240] and Eusebius of Caesarea [c. AD 260/265–339]) of the third-century BC Egyptian historian Manetho.[3] These are all consistent in listing just three kings, characterized as "Ethiopian:"

- Sabacôn, who, taking Bochchôris captive, burned him alive, and reigned for

8 (Africanus)/12 (Eusebius) years.
- Sebichôs, his son, for 14/12 years.
- Tarcus, for 18 years/Taracus, for 20 years.

The omission of Pi(ankh)y clearly reflects the fact that he never ruled in Egypt in the way that Shabataka, Shabaka, and Taharqa did, while the reign of Tanutamun ran in parallel with that of Psamtik I, who was certainly regarded by posterity as the sole legitimate king from the death of Nekau I.

While "Tar(a)cus" is transparently Taharqa, the transmogrification of the names of Shabataka and Shabaka into the first two names on the Manethonic list is less so—and would cause modern historians major headaches (see chapter 7). The name "Sabacôn" of course goes back to Herodotus, and both it and "Sebichôs" clearly conceal the syllables *š3* and *b3* that begin the names of both Shabataka and Shabaka. While the "s" of "Sebichôs" is certainly a straightforward Greek ending (as applied to a wide range of Hellenized Egyptian royal names in Manetho), the "n" that ends "Sabacôn" is more intriguing. One suggestion is that it may have been a result of a misreading (perhaps in the hieratic) of the ⸺ (*t3*)-sign in the name of Shabataka as an ⁓⁓⁓ (*n*)-sign,[4] and while there is no way of proving this, it provides at least some potential explanation.

The first-century BC account of Kushite rule in Egypt by Diodorus Siculus[5] largely follows Herodotus in its presentation and characterization of "Sabaco," but with Bakenrenef mentioned before him, albeit as one who reigned "many years" previously. Diodorus also places the appearance of the "twelve kings" two years after the retirement of Sabaco (years occupied by "fratricidal murder and strife"), and the triumph of Psamtik a full fifteen years after that.

As already noted (pages 68–69), a further ancient twist on the memory of the Twenty-fifth Dynasty is provided in the early fifth century AD, when St. Jerome (d. 420) added a gloss to Eusebius' quotation from Manetho, alleging Taharqa's murder of his predecessor. Apart from Diodorus' claims of "fratricidal murder and strife," this thread is not found in any extant earlier source. It is therefore difficult to suggest where this tradition originated, and still more problematic to assess whether it may have contained any element of fact. Nevertheless, this marks the last appearance of the Nubian pharaohs of Egypt in literature for a millennium and a half—albeit occurring only a few decades after the extinction of the Kushite monarchy of which they had been part.

7 RESURRECTION

The closure of the last pagan temples at the end of the fourth century AD soon spelled the final demise of the hieroglyphic writing system in Egypt, and thus all chance of engaging with the pre-Ptolemaic history of the country. Henceforth, any enquiries were constrained by the remaining available sources: the Bible, the Classical authors, and their excerptors. An extensive discussion of the Twenty-fifth Dynasty was undertaken on these bases in 1711 by Jakob Perizonius (1651–1715),[1] the discrepancies between them resulting in his conclusion that

> Sabacus and Taracus were the same king, but were wrongly divided by Manetho into two. I have many reasons. In other words, because the difference between the names of Sabacon and the Taracones is quite small; for they are related to the time of Sennacherib or Hezekiah; because they are likewise said to have been the Ethiopians and very powerful kings, who not only held Egypt, but also subjected other nations to themselves; because, finally, none of them, as far as I know, except Manetho, are both at the same time, as if two different persons who name one but do not know the other. Sacred Scripture and Strabo celebrate Tararacus or Tiracus, but do not acknowledge Sabicus or Sabaco; Herodotus, on the other hand, and Diodorus Siculus make no mention of Taracus in these times, but in like manner they praise Sabaco, and in the times of Hezekiah, nor even to the age of Psammetichus.[2]

This well illustrates the difficulties under which scholars labored without the ability to cross-check their sources with original Egyptian data.

Regarding the broader question of the place of Nubia (or "Ethiopia" as it was generally referred to down to the nineteenth century) in the history of the Nile valley, the Classical writers encouraged a view that Egyptian civilization owed much to the land to the south, and this chronological priority of Nubia and its monuments continued to be maintained by some even after the decipherment of the ancient Egyptian language allowed monuments to be properly placed on the historical timeline.[3] In the interim, the first European travelers in Nubia perceived the monuments they saw there as cruder than those in Egypt itself, and regarded this as a proof of their exceptional age. Thus, George Waddington* (1793–1869) and Barnard Hanbury* (1793–1833), who visited Gebel Barkal and its environs in 1820 (see pages 149–52), wrote of Taharqa's temple B300 that

> From the simplicity of the masonry, from the rudeness and decay of the remaining sculptures, and from the raggedness and decomposition of the walls, though they had been sheltered probably for ages by the solid rock from the sun and wind, I am inclined to believe that this is older than any of the temples of Egypt, or even Nubia.[4]

And further that:

> A people little removed from the Deluge, and living in dread of its return, sought the sides of the mountains, and built their habitations in the solid rock: such were the oldest dwelling places of men, the places of their labours, their studies, and their worship; and when they began in aftertimes to build temples for their gods, would they not naturally make for them some larger excavation in the rock, that had so long afforded shelter to themselves? If so, and I think it indisputable, the sculptured caverns of Gyrshe [Gerf Hussein], of Derr, and Ebsambal, are of higher antiquity than the columns of Thebes, and have received the gods of Ethiopia in their progress towards the North. I believed at the time, and do still believe, as far as can be judged from rudeness of masonry and sculpture, and from the mere effect of time on colours, figures, and even the surface of the hard and solid rock, that the smaller of the two excavated temples at Djebel el Berkel is much the oldest that I ever saw; older by centuries than those of Nubia, or than the temple of Bacchus by its side: now the few figures and hieroglyphics yet visible there are exactly such as are found in greater perfection in Egypt.[5]

The Kushites and the First Egyptologists

It was not until the later 1820s that the first phases of the decipherment of the ancient Egyptian language and its scripts allowed original sources to be brought into the process of reconstructing the history of pharaonic Egypt. However, although the way ahead had been set out by Jean-François Champollion* (1790–1832) in 1822, it would be two decades before texts could be read with any degree of fluency. In the interim, the first attempts at historical reconstructions were based on melding what had hitherto been extracted from the biblical and Classical sources with the new ability to transliterate royal names, and to translate various key words and phrases to gain the gist of some inscriptions.

The first step in this process was to try to identify the hieroglyphic originals of the names to be found in the biblical and Classical sources. As far as the Twenty-fifth Dynasty was concerned, it was immediately recognized that the biblical "Tirhakah" and the Manethonic "Tar(a)cus" were represented by the name we now transliterate as *t3hrq*. John Gardner Wilkinson* (1797–1875), combining the hieroglyphic, Classical, and biblical data available to him, thus felt able to state in his pioneering *Materia hieroglyphica* of 1828:

> While Sethos ruled lower Egypt, Tirhaka possessed, perhaps by right of succession from the first of these [Twenty-fifth Dynasty] kings, the dominion of the upper country, and hearing of the aggressions of Sennacherib in the North, marched to the defence of the lower provinces, and defeated the Assyrians; which he commemorated in the temple of Medeenet Haboo at Thebes. He also added, if not the columns, in the front court of Karnak, at least the sculptures on them, afterwards erased by Psamaticus I.[6]

However, "Sabacôn" and "Sebichôs" presented more problems. The first was rapidly equated with *š3b3k3*, but the rarer *š3b3t3k3* was not initially recognized as a separate king, the *t3*-sign not being noticed, and the different prenomina seen simply as a part of variant titulary.[7]

The idea that the two names might be a dittography in the transmission of Manetho was nevertheless rejected by Wilkinson:

> I am obliged to admit two kings bearing the name of Sabaco, which indeed seems required, to keep up a harmony in the events recorded by ancient authors.
>
> First—How otherwise could the Sabaco who dethroned Anysis be the same from whom Psamaticus fled on the death of his father Nechos, as mentioned by Herodotus; the former reigned fifty years; Anysis on his return, seven; Sethos, forty; and Psamaticus, fifty four.

Secondly—This Sabaco never put any one to death, according to the same historian.[8]

Accordingly, in searching for an Egyptian equivalent for the "other Sabaco," Wilkinson lit upon the name *sbk-ḥtp*,[9] an equivalency that had been put forward for "Sabacon" by Henry Salt* (1780–1827) in 1825.[10] Wilkinson further proposed that the prenomina Ankhkhare and/or Khaneferre belonged to this king. However, here he and Salt (and also their contemporary, Orlando Felix* [1790–1860])[11] went badly astray: the Sobekhoteps actually belonged to the Thirteenth Dynasty, a millennium before the Twenty-fifth Dynasty. As regards the order of his two kings, Wilkinson wrote that he was "still doubtful as to which of these two Sabacos should be placed first."[12] He maintained this position, and also that concerning the identification of one of the "Sabacos" as a Sobekhotep, when he published his first extensive account of Egyptian history in 1835:[13]

XXV. DYNASTY OF ETHIOPIANS.

Sabaco, So of S.S.	Sabakoftep or Sabakoph	1. 2	778	Rome founded 753. Captivity of the ten tribes of Israel, 721. Herodotus mentions Anysis expelled by Sabaco.
Sebechon or Sevechus (his son)	Shebek	3. 4	728	I am not quite certain if Sabakoftep should be before or after Shebek. Sethos of Herodotus was the contemporary of Tirhakah, and ruled at Memphis.
Teraces or Tarchus	Tehrak	5. 6	714 to 690	Date of his 12th year on the monuments. Sennacherib attacks Judah 268 years after the death of Solomon, 710. Tearchon of Strabo, Tirhaka of S. S.

Wilkinson retained this arrangement in his seminal *Manners and Customs of the Ancient Egyptians* in 1837.[14] He would continue to do so for the rest of his career, this fact doubtless contributing to the identification appearing in the sixth edition of the popular *History of Egypt* by Samuel Sharpe* (1799–1881), published as late as 1876.[15] Edward Lane* (1801–76) followed his friend Wilkinson in his basic scheme for the Twenty-fifth Dynasty that was included in his *Description of Egypt*, completed in 1833, but not published until nearly a century and three-quarters later.[16]

However, Ippolito Rosellini* (1800–43—fig. 120) had already (in 1833) noted in print the existence of Shabataka, and that he was clearly the "other" king at the beginning of Manetho's list. This was based on the discovery by him and Champollion of the chapel of Shabataka south of the Sacred Lake at Karnak (pages 47–48, above), while leading the Franco-Tuscan expedition to Egypt during 1828–29. Rosellini concluded that "it is clear that this is the name of Sabbakon's successor, called in the lists Sevechus, or Sebichus"; he also equated him with Herodotus' "Sethos" and the biblical "So" (now regarded as most likely Osorkon IV [cf. page 36]).[17] No reasons were given for this ordering of the kings, other than an implicit assumption that the first of Manetho's

Twenty-fifth Dynasty kings was Shabaka. Despite the lack of any rationale for this conclusion, the Shabaka–Shabataka sequence would remain an apparently unchallenged "fact" of Egyptology down to the twenty-first century. It was only then revealed to be a "zombie fact" that had come to significantly hinder study of Kushite rule in Egypt (pages 170–73, below).

Although Rosellini's identification of Shabataka was accepted by George Hoskins in 1835,[18] in the historical appendix to his account of his Nubian travels (see page 152), it was not more generally accepted for some time. We have already noted Wilkinson's retention of the idea of a Sobekhotep lurking behind one of the first two Manethonian kings of the Twenty-fifth Dynasty, while Richard Lepsius* (1810–84) at first explicitly rejected Rosellini's reading.[19] He changed his view following his leadership of the great Prussian expedition to Egypt during 1842–45. During this sojourn his team copied and dismantled, for transport to Berlin, the Shabataka chapel found by Rosellini and Champollion, allowing the reading of the name to be verified (cf. fig. 30). Lepsius's examination of the temples at Gebel Barkal in May 1844[20] not only yielded one of the rams from the front of temple B500 (page 37, fig. 24 bottom), together with other items, for the Berlin collection, but also additional names of Kushite kings.

FIGURE 120 Marble bust of Ippolito Rosellini (Florence).

FIGURE 121
Sarcophagus and coffin of Tjesraperet, nurse of a daughter of Taharqa, found by the Franco-Tuscan expedition, probably in front of Sheikh Abd el-Qurna (Florence 2161, 2159).

Thus, Lepsius's *Königsbuch*, eventually published in 1858, not only placed Shabataka as Shabaka's successor (again without any discussion),[21] but also included Kashta and Pi(ankh)y as members of a "Dynastie XXIVbis," alongside the God's Wives Amenirdis I and Shepenwepet II.[22] The book also listed many of the later "Äthiopische Könige."[23] Lepsius was also aware of Tanutamun, but as this was on the basis of a re-used block from Luxor,[24] he could only place the king (whose name he read as "Amen-not") among his "unordered names."[25] The *Königsbuch* also set out Lepsius's absolute chronology, which placed the accession of Shabaka in 716 BC and that of Shabataka in 704, with the reign of Taharqa running from 692 to 664.[26] Subject to some relatively minor adjustments (cf. pages 163–64), this would remain the working hypothesis for the arrangement and dating of the Twenty-fifth Dynasty for a century and a half.

This basic scheme was also employed in the first edition of the influential history of ancient Egypt produced by Heinrich Brugsch* (1827–94) in 1859, with Kashta and Pi(ankh)y viewed as descendants of Bakenrenef, ruling in parallel with the "Ethiopians," the pre–Psamtik I members of the Twenty-sixth Dynasty, and perhaps "still other collateral branches in the different parts of Egypt which at the end formed the twelve regencies that the ancients designated by the name of dodecarchy and from which Psammetichus I emerged as sole and unique sovereign over the whole country."[27]

The Monuments of the Kushites

By this time, a significant number of the key Egyptian monuments of the Nubian kings had been acquired by museums or had been copied in situ. The "Shabaka Stone" (page 59, fig. 41) had been presented to the British Museum by Earl Spencer (1758–1834) in 1805. It had come from Alexandria to the United Kingdom as ballast in a Royal Navy warship[28] (Spencer had been First Lord of the Admiralty [Navy Minister] from 1794 to 1801, and was also a keen antiquarian and a Trustee of the Museum). Many of the buildings erected or embellished by the Twenty-fifth Dynasty kings at Thebes had been noted by Wilkinson, Champollion, Rosellini, and others, as well as in the more recent work of Lepsius, which had not only produced the best copies to date of the Egyptian corpus, but had extended coverage into Sudan (fig. 53).

In doing so, Lepsius's great Prussian expedition was following in the footsteps of the handful of pioneering travelers who had previously penetrated beyond the First Cataract. In 1772 James Bruce* (1730–94), returning from his search for the source of the Nile, had observed remains that he (correctly) surmised to be those of Meroë. However, as his journey northward then proceeded across the desert, only rejoining the Nile at Kom Ombo, he missed almost all the other monuments of Nubia.

Johann Ludwig Burckhardt* (1784–1817) traveled up the Nile as far as Soleb in 1813, but for his journey into Upper Nubia the following year, he went across the desert from Kom Ombo to the area of the Fifth Cataract. Thus, like Bruce, he saw only the remains of Meroë.

During the early nineteenth century, many more individuals investigated Lower Nubia, but rather fewer made it beyond the Second Cataract. These included the aforementioned Waddington and Hanbury, and Frédéric Cailliaud* (1787–1869), who accompanied Ismail Pasha, son of the governor of Egypt, Mehmet Ali, on his 1820–21 military expedition against Dongola. Their publications,[29] especially that of Cailliaud, who went beyond the Fourth Cataract, where the other two were turned back, provided the first detailed accounts and depictions of the monuments of Upper Nubia.

Waddington and Hanbury made a number of visits to Gebel Barkal in late December 1820, making a sketch map of the site and plans of the principal monuments.

The remains of antiquity which lie at the foot of Djebel el Berkel are of two kinds—temples, or other public buildings, and pyramids; the former, which have ornamented the city of the living, are situated towards the river, on the S.E. side of the mountain, and all the ground about them, for several acres, is scattered over with broken pottery; the latter, which have been the receptacles and monuments of the dead, are on the W. and N.W. side, farther from the Nile, among the sands and rocks of the Desert . . . .

About a hundred yards West of [temple B900] stands the temple [B300], of which the two first chambers are of masonry, and the four interior are ex-cavated in the solid rock, resembling in this respect the temples of Gyrshe, Seboua, and Derr, in Nubia.

The first chamber is forty-five feet wide, and about forty in length; it con-tains four rows of pillars with four in each row; those of the two inner rows are square on round bases, those nearer the wall are round; their diameter is four feet, and that of the base five, and before them stand figures of the bearded Bacchus, as represented in the annexed Plate [fig. 122c]; the monster, there very imperfectly delineated, measures four feet two inches across the hips . . . .

The third chamber is in the solid rock, and the roof is sustained by two square columns, before which Bacchus again presented himself to us, in ruder sculpture than before . . . . The kind of architrave above is covered with hiero-glyphics, and the colours remain very fresh on the plaster here, as well as in other parts of the temple.

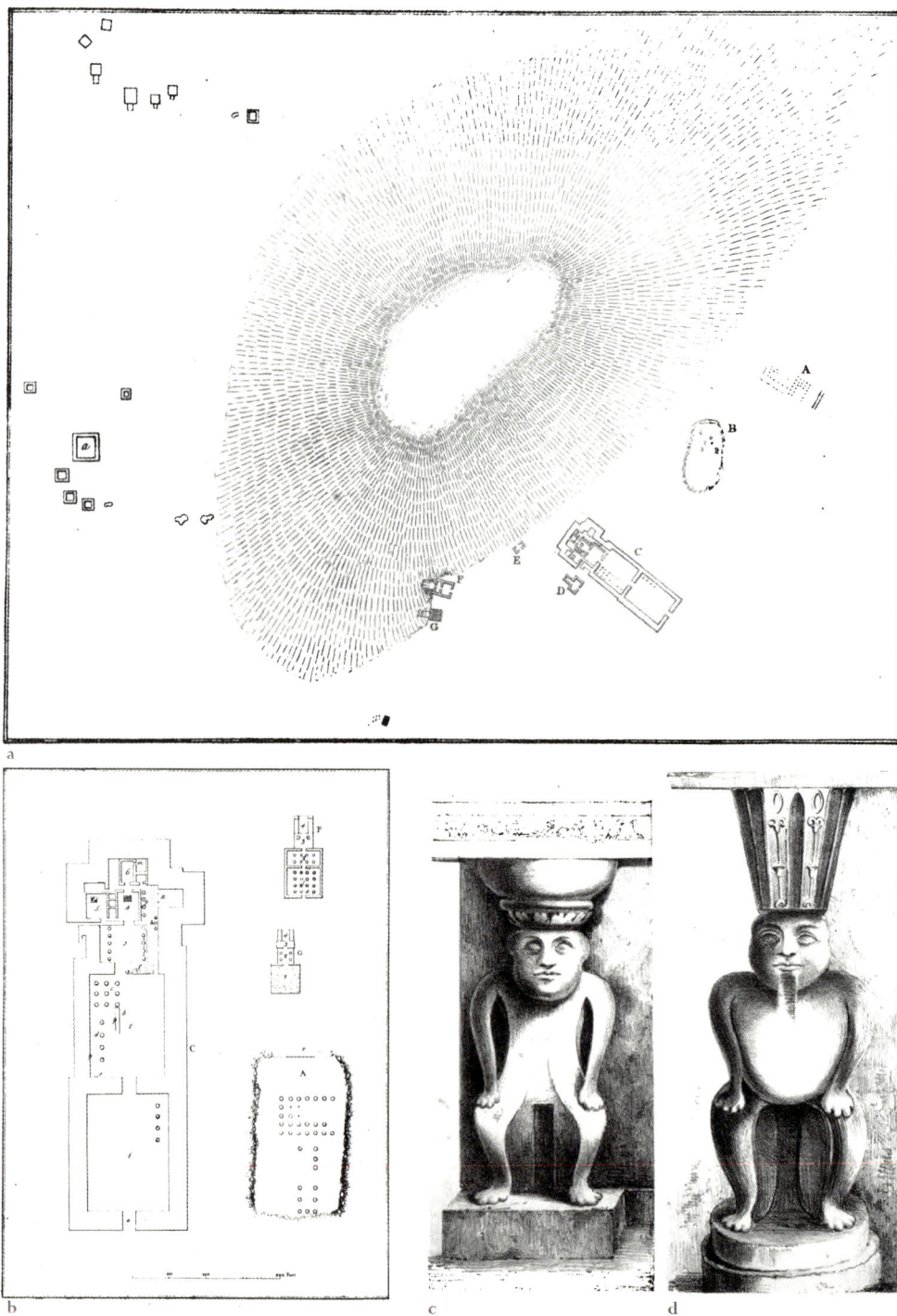

FIGURE 122 Waddington and Hanbury's map and plans of Gebel Barkal and its temples, and their sketches of the Bes figures of temple B300 (cf. fig. 70).

The walls are ornamented with sculptures; on the right side Jupiter Ammon is seated, and Horus on the left; a figure of Isis is represented standing behind each of those divinities . . . .

On the right side of the adytum appear Jupiter Ammon, Isis, Apis, and Osiris, with the heads of the hawk and ibis; Horus (the young divinity with the long thin beard) and Isis; the cloaked figure with offerings, Mendes, and a warrior with the ornamented corn-measure, are sculptured on the left—the first figure on each side is a man presenting offerings; and in the far corner, on the right, is a horned animal, with the ball on his head, reposing on a kind of pedestal, with a branch growing up before it, of which the leaves most nearly resemble those of the doum-tree.[30]

Waddington and Hanbury also examined and mapped the pyramids at Barkal and Nuri;[31] at the latter

[t]here are remains of nearly forty, of different sizes; eleven of them are larger than any of the perfect ones of Djebel el Berkel, and the greater part of the rest are reduced to a mere mound of decomposed stone and gravel and sand. That of most importance in size and interest [has] its base . . . one hundred and fifty-two feet square, and its height one hundred and three feet seven inches [fig. 123]. It has been built in stories, but is most curious from its containing within itself another pyramid of a different age, stone, and architecture. This interior building, which the other has enclosed like a case, seems to form about two-thirds of the whole structure; it is of neat workmanship, and is composed of a hard light-coloured sandstone, more durable than that which, after sheltering it for ages, has at last decayed and fallen off; and left it once more exposed to the eyes of men. May it have happened, that some king of Ethiopia, jealous of the glory of one of his predecessors, and wishing to conceal what he was unable to surpass, has enveloped with his own monument the monument of his rival, in his thirst for the exclusive possession of that immortality, which was to be the destiny of neither? . . .

These pyramids appear to be of higher antiquity than those of Djebel el Berkel, and present in general a more ruinous appearance than the most ruined of those at Saccara; the softer quality of the material may partly account for this.[32]

The first post-decipherment travelers to examine the Upper Nubian monuments were Lord Prudhoe* (1792–1865, later fourth Duke of Northumberland) and George

FIGURE 123 The pyramid of Taharqa (Nuri Nu1), as drawn by Waddington and Hanbury in December 1820.

Hoskins* (1802–63). Prudhoe reached Gebel Barkal in 1829, whence he removed to the United Kingdom two granite lions,[33] while Hoskins proceeded as far as Meroë and Musawwarat in 1833, and published a detailed account.[34] His book included both extensive illustrations and a discussion of the history of the region. In doing so, he was able to correctly identify the true owners, and thus dates, of those monuments he examined that retained identifiable cartouches. Having identified the owner of Barkal B300 as Taharqa (who he argued was the "Sethos" of Herodotus),[35] Hoskins comments,

> The sculpture of this temple has not the striking characteristics of the true Ethiopian style; it more resembles the Egyptian, and is good, though by no means the best. It is not improbable that this Ethiopian dynasty, being possessed also of Egypt, introduced into their own country a taste for the improved style of Egyptian sculpture.[36]

However, where he was unable to find helpful texts, he found it difficult to break from the tradition of the exceptional age of the Nubian monuments. Speaking of the pyramids at Barkal, he remarks:

> As to the antiquity of these structures, I conceive it to be very great. Some of them appear more ancient than any that exist in the valley of the Nile, with the exception, perhaps, of the pyramids of Meroe and Nouri.[37]

Besides the more remote Nubian monuments, ongoing examination of those of Thebes was revealing further data, with parts of the decoration of the Edifice of Taharqa at Karnak published for the first time by Émile Prisse d'Avennes* (1807–79) in 1847.[38] New data was now also becoming available via the discovery and the beginning of the translation of Assyrian texts that covered the final years of Kushite rule in Egypt, and also informed some of the biblical links.

Mariette and the Kushites

There was, however, still much more to be found and published. A stela that would (but not quite yet) place the relative chronology of the reign of Taharqa on an unassailable basis by linking it directly to that of Psamtik I was found by Auguste Mariette* (1821–81) in the Serapeum on 22 February 1852. However, the discoverer was hindered in his assessment of this data by an assumption that Taharqa was already a reigning king when mentioned in the Old Testament as the opponent of Sennacherib in 701 BC. This required the introduction of not only an interregnum between the death of Taharqa and the accession of Psamtik I, but also positing a major ancient error in citing the age at death quoted for the Apis bull that died in Year 20 of Psamtik.[39]

Mariette became the first head of the resurrected Egyptian antiquities service in June 1858.[40] He immediately began excavations at key locations in Egypt, including Karnak. There, in July, his workmen found, in the remains of the chapel of Osiris-Nebankh in the temenos of Montju (fig. 124), a calcite statue of Amenirdis I (fig. 48 right). For many years this was regarded as one of the masterpieces of Egyptian art, although its status would diminish over time. Its texts, and others from the same chapel, linked Amenirdis I with Shabaka, and gave her the title *snt-nsw*, which was long regarded as proving that she and the king were siblings, and thus both children of Kashta (cf. pages 24–25).

FIGURE 124 The remains of the chapels Osiris-Nebankh-dihebsed and Osiris-Nebankh at Karnak-North; the calcite statue of Amenirdis I (fig. 47 right) was found in the latter by Mariette.

The most spectacular discovery occurred, however, in 1862, when an Egyptian of-ficer stationed across the river from Gebel Barkal reported finding five granite stelae at that site.[41] Arrangements were immediately made by Mariette for their transport to the Bulaq Museum in Cairo. There, they proved to be the Victory Stela of Pi(ankh)y (fig. 19), the Excommunication Stela (fig. 17 top), the Dream Stela of Tanutamun (fig. 75), the Enthronement Stela of Aspelta (fig. 83), and a stela of Horsiyotef. As published for the first time in 1863[42] and 1865,[43] the stelae from the group revealed whole new episodes of Kushite history. The Dream Stela also allowed Tanutamun, whose name had been noted, but not placed, by Lepsius, to be recognized as a Kushite king.

The reconstruction of the Kushite succession in Egypt, beyond the three kings list-ed by Manetho, nevertheless remained problematic. Mariette placed Tanutamun and Pi(ankh)y (in that order) within the seventeen years' anarchy (of the "Twelve Kings" of Herodotus) that he interposed between the death of Taharqa and the accession of Psamtik I.[44] He also mistook the nature of the office of God's Wives of Amun. He thus saw Amenirdis I as a wife of Pi(ankh)y, with Shepenwepet II as their daughter, who became a wife of Psamtik I. For Mariette, this made the latter "by marriage and by the expulsion of his eleven competitors the undisputed sovereign of all Egypt." This miscon-ception would endure for some time.

The Kushites in the Late Nineteenth Century AD

The 1870s saw the publication of two histories of ancient Egypt: by Samuel Birch* (1813–85) in 1875; and an entirely recast version of that of Brugsch in 1877.[45] These volumes' treatment of the Twenty-fifth Dynasty[46] demonstrated not only the greatly increased amount of material that had become available since Brugsch's first edition of 1859, especially the Gebel Barkal stelae and the Assyrian texts, but also the continuing lack of certainty and/or agreement over key points. For example, while minded to place Pi(ankh)y before Bakenrenef, Birch regarded a reversal of their order "within the verge of probability."[47]

A fundamental difference between the reconstructions of the two scholars was over the position of Tanutamun. Brugsch placed him directly after Pi(ankh)y, while Birch made him the second successor of a king whose name was then read as "Urdamane" in the Assyrian texts (actually "Tandamane," i.e., Tanutamun). Edward Hincks* (1792–1866) had argued in 1866 that this was an Assyrian writing of the Egyptian name Rudamun.[48]

Although not yet admitting the correct reading of the name as that of Tanutamun, the identification of "Urdamane" with the king of the Dream Stela was argued by Daniel Haigh* (1819–79) in 1868.[49] However, as he was working only from a preliminary translation of Ashurbanipal's text, he also understood that Taharqa had abdicated and that Tanutamun had been captured and executed by the Assyrians. This misunderstanding was corrected by the Assyriologist George Smith (1840–76) later the same year,[50] who nevertheless preferred to keep "Urdamane" as a Rudamun, also identifying the Assyrian "Mantimanhe" (i.e., Montjuemhat) with Pi(ankh)y. The latter conclusion was speedily refuted by Haigh,[51] while the correct reading of the name on the Dream Stela (by recognizing that a sign hitherto misread as *mr* was actually a *t3*-sign) was finally noted by Lepsius in 1871 (transliterating "Amon-to-nut").[52]

Birch seemed confident of the placement of Shabaka and Shabataka as predecessors of Taharqa, and he used the seal impression of the Shabaka found at Nineveh (fig. 54) as evidence for a treaty between Shabaka and the Assyrians. On the other hand, Brugsch's narrative jumps from his pairing of Pi(ankh)y and Tanutamun to Taharqa, remarking that

> [a] thick veil covers the ensuing times, in which the Ethiopians place themselves in the foreground of Egyptian history. Taharaqa, Pi-ankhi, (with his oft-named wife, Ameniritis), Shabak and Shabatak—all appear as contemporary, and are frequently introduced in connection with each other . . . . If we might give credit to the lists of Manetho, they would seem to have reigned in succession over Patoris, whose capital, Thebes, retains manifold evidences of their presence; but we are unable to find anything in the monuments to confirm this succession.[53]

In Brugsch's listing, "Pi-ankhi" is a different king from the author of the Victory Stela, whom Brugsch places two generations earlier, as a separate "Meri-Amen Piankhi." This Egyptological multiplication of Kings Pi(ankh)y—a result of Pi(ankh)y's serial use of alternate prenomina (pages 27–28)—would get worse before it got better.

Birch makes no remarks about the background of the Kushite kings who ruled Egypt, simply stating that "[i]t would appear that after Sheshanka [V], Egypt had fallen into the power of the Ethiopians, having previously, from some unexplained causes, broken up into a number of small states. These were under the protection or government of Piankhi, an Ethiopian monarch residing at Noph or Napata." However, Brugsch sets out an origin story that would influence scholars and writers for a long time to come.

> Towards the end of the eleventh century . . . the whole South from the boundary line at the city of Syene, recovered their freedom, and the tribes of Ethiopia begin to enjoy a state of independence . . . . Nothing could have appeared more opportune to the priests of Amon, who had now become unpopular in order to

make their profit out of the favourable opportunity of the moment, than this state of things in Nubia and Ethiopia, where the minds of an imperfectly developed people must needs, under skilful guidance, soon show themselves pliable and submissive to the dominant priestly caste . . . It is difficult to say which it was of the chief-priests of Amon of the race of Hirhor, that first entered Napata and made preparations for the foundation of that Ethiopian kingdom which became afterwards so dangerous to the Egyptians.[54]

The underlying assumption made here is that the Nubians themselves were too "imperfectly developed" to have evolved the culture that would later take over Egypt. As a consequence, it was held that only a ruling family of ultimately Egyptian blood would have had the ability to do so.[55]

This reflected a clear trend during the latter part of the nineteenth century toward negative assessments of both the Nubians as a people and the competence of their rulers.[56] This seems likely to be rooted (consciously or unconsciously) in attitudes about African people that derived from the European colonization of most of the continent during the nineteenth century.[57]

That this tendency included twisting actual evidence to fit such a preconceived negative picture is seen from published treatments of the Twenty-fifth Dynasty kings' involvement in Palestine.[58] While the Assyrian and Old Testament accounts speak solely of Judah's appeals for Kushite alliance and aid (with indications of a degree of reluctance on the part of the Kushite kings to provide this—page 64), many historians from the early twentieth century onward came to accuse the Kushites of having "seduced" Judah into rebelling. As late as the end of the twentieth century, Kenneth Kitchen (b. 1932) felt able to combine this with more general anti-Kushite invective by accusing them of "meddling . . . incompetent interference in Palestinian affairs . . . disastrous for Egypt and Palestine alike," and of being "most certainly the 'bruised reed' of the Assyrian king's jibe" (pages 66–67).[59]

As regards the detailed history of the time, during 1863–64 Emmanuel de Rougé* (1811–72) had copied at Tanis fragments of a stela that preserved an incomplete version of Taharqa's autobiographical account quoted on page 47.[60] De Rougé's treatment of the text was not published, however, until shortly after his death, as part of an important paper on the monuments of Taharqa.[61] Alfred Wiedemann* (1856–1936) combined what the stela seemed to be saying with Jerome's gloss to Eusebius (pages 68–69) to conclude that "[a]fter Shabataka had ruled over Egypt for 12 years, he was attacked, dethroned and executed by his former ally against the Assyrians, Taharka. To celebrate this victory, and to consecrate his usurpation of the Egyptian empire, Taharka summoned his mother, through whose intermediary he probably had claims to the crown of Egypt, to come from Ethiopia."[62]

In his broader comments on the Twenty-fifth Dynasty, Wiedemann clearly distinguished between the "temporary raid and levying of tribute" by Pi(ankh)y and the formal takeover of Egypt by the later Kushite kings. In this connection, he remarks: "Of course, Shabako was not a barbarian, as the first Hyksos kings had once been, but a monarch educated entirely in the Egyptian way, who also exercised his rule in the manner of the native pharaohs."[63] Wiedemann perpetuated the equation of Shabaka with the "So" of the Old Testament (page 36), also confidently making Herodotus' "Sethos" a reference to Shabataka—in contrast to de Rougé, who made him a "Séti III,"[64] and identified him with the problematic king Menkheperre [. . .]y (page 28).

The lack of understanding of the institution of God's Wife persisted in Wiedemann's work, with Amenirdis I seen again as a wife of Pi(ankh)y, and Shepenwepet II their daughter and wife of Psamtik I: "All the claims of the 26th dynasty to the throne of Egypt rested on the marriage with this daughter of Ameneritis, and on her the legitimacy of the Psammetichids."[65] Similarly, Gaston Maspero* (1846–1916), writing in 1889, made Kashta the husband of Shepenwepet I, and Amenirdis I the wife of a Pi(ankh)y, but in his case a "Pi(ankh)y II": for him, Usermaatre and Seneferre were separate kings.[66] For Maspero, "Pi(ankh)y I" was the king of the Victory Stela, and the father of Kashta; "Pi(ankh)y II" was viewed as a grandson of "Pi(ankh)y I."[67]

The same study also demonstrated that a stela, which showed Shabaka and Shabataka together in a manner implying coregency,[68] and had been published in 1876 by Willem Pleyte* (1836–1903), was a fake.[69] Nevertheless, the idea that there might have been some form of co-rule between the kings would be revived on more than one occasion over the coming century (cf. page 171). However, in his treatment of Taharqa's accession to power, Maspero perpetuated the conflation of the incomplete Tanis stela text with the work of Jerome to conclude that Taharqa's northern expedition had been to overthrow his predecessor.[70] It would be over three decades before the discovery of a complete copy of the stela text (page 164) would allow this misunderstanding to be resolved.

Nevertheless, Flinders Petrie* (1853–1942) showed a degree of skepticism regarding this point in his 1905 history, although viewing the circumstances as conducive to such a scenario.[71] Petrie had actually found more of the Tanis stela of Taharqa during his excavations at the site in 1884 (fig. 125), publishing the first full facsimile in 1888, but the additional fragments were not sufficient to clarify matters. Petrie's narrative of the dynasty basically followed Maspero's scheme, seeing Kashta and "Pankhy II." as ruling in Thebes in parallel with the overarching rule of Shabaka and Shabataka.[72]

FIGURE 125 Tanis during Petrie's excavations, following a storm, and his drawing of the Tanis stela of Taharqa.

The year 1905 also saw the first edition of the hugely influential *History of Egypt* by James H. Breasted* (1865–1935). This was built on the extensive digest of Egyptian historical texts that Breasted was publishing in parallel. He confidently placed Kashta at the head of the sequence of Kushite rulers in Egypt, viewing the Pi(ankh)y of the Victory Stela as the brother of Amenirdis I. However, he accepted the existence of no fewer than *three* kings of the name, although unwilling to place the "spares."[73] In the *History*, he gives an expansive account of the period of Kushite rule in Egypt.[74] In his narrative, Breasted included a number of gratuitous comments regarding the performance of the Kushites on the world stage, expanding significantly on the negativity toward the Kushites as Africans that had already become established during the latter part of the nineteenth century (page 156). Thus, Breasted writes of a "motley army gathered by the tardy Shabaka among his northern vassals" fighting at Eltekeh, "inglorious Ethiopians," and that it was "now patent that the Ethiopians were quite unfitted for the imperial task before them. The southern strain with which their blood was tinctured began to appear as the reign of Shabataka drew to a close."

In assessing the performance of Taharqa and Tanutamun in their defense of Egypt against the Assyrians, Breasted laments that "[t]o this great task the Ethiopians were appointed; but there was never a line of kings so ill suited to their high destiny." The importance of this crude, racially tinged invective lies in the fact that Breasted's book would long be the "standard" history of ancient Egypt, especially for non-Egyptologists, and thus his prejudices would become solidified into "fact."

Legrain's Karnak

As far as actual facts are concerned, important new data was revealed during the last years of the nineteenth century and the first of the twentieth through the extensive work being carried out at the temples of Karnak by Georges Legrain* (1865–1917). Among the first finds relating to the Kushite epoch was the Neitiqerti Adoption Stela, which not only revealed the events of March 656 BC, but also indicated the adoptive nature of the succession of the God's Wives.[75] It would nevertheless still be some time before it was recognized that the incumbents of this period were not also royal wives. During 1899 and the years immediately following, the chapel of Osiris-Heqadjet was finally cleared, revealing the reliefs of Shabataka, Shepenwepet I, and Amenirdis I, as were the chapels of the God's Wives, and the eastern colonnade of Taharqa. The discovery and clearance of the so-called Karnak *cachette* between 1903 and 1907 (fig. 126) revealed a considerable number of sculptures belonging to the time of the Twenty-fifth Dynasty (e.g., figs. 36, 48 left, 59 top left) among the many thousands of items discovered there.[76]

FIGURE 126 The excavation of the Karnak *cachette*, as seen on 27 February 1906.

Meroë, Faras, and Sanam

Although not bearing on the period of Kushite rule in Egypt, important information on the later phases of the monarchy was gathered between 1909 and 1914. This was when John Garstang* (1876–1956) undertook the first work at the site of the city of Meroë. Its location had been identified by James Bruce in 1772, but had since been forgotten, and the site was not formally re-identified (by Archibald Sayce* [1845–1933]) as the Kushite capital until 1909. Although preliminary reports on the work were issued as it progressed, full publication did not occur until 1997.[77]

Francis Llewellyn Griffith* (1862–1934; fig. 128) spent the winter of 1912–13 at Sanam, where the temple of Taharqa was cleared, together with a nearby cemetery.[78] Further work in the area proved impossible owing to the First World War, and the concession for the area surrounding Gebel Barkal was transferred to the team led by George Reisner* (1867–1942) on behalf of the Museum of Fine Arts, Boston (MFA) and Harvard University.

Reisner's Excavations

The results of its work would be of fundamental importance to the study of the Kushite monarchy. Excavations began in January 1916 at Gebel Barkal itself, covering principally the temples, but also the nearby pyramids. Investigations of the latter structures were finished in February, and initial work at Nuri was carried out during March–April. This included the identification of one pyramid as that of Aspelta, and the speculation that the largest pyramid at the site (Nu1) might be "the tomb of one of the five kings of Ethiopia who ruled over Egypt."[79]

On Thursday, October 26, 1916, the work of clearing the "western" front of the large pyramid (Pyramid I) was begun with a force of Egyptians and of men and boys from the local tribe of the Shagiah. The mass of debris was enormous, consisting of drift sand and debris fallen from the pyramid. It was not until a month later, November 26, that this mass was cleared away. The chapel was found to be utterly destroyed; but on that day we opened the stairway leading down to the burial chambers. On December 5 the men found in the debris filling the stairway a fragment of a stone figure on which was written the name of Tirhaqa. It was at once concluded that Pyramid I was in fact the tomb of that Tirhaqa who was one of the five kings of Ethiopia who ruled over Egypt, and this conclusion was fully borne out by later finds. The excavation of the stairway and the chambers met with great difficulties owing to the dangerous condition of the cracked walls and the half fallen roofs, to the water which covered the floors, and to the

unexampled heat of the interior. Several times, after propping overhanging mass-
es of rock we waited a few days to see what would happen. Once we had to wait
three days to allow the interior to cool, and a month we waited for the water
to fall; but in vain. The chambers were cut in the solid rock, a sort of micacious
schist which deteriorates under the action of water . . . . A large part of the work
of removing the debris and the water was carried out through this corridor in
order to avoid risking the lives of the workmen under the threatening roof of the
hall. Our architect, Mr. Robert Williams, experienced in more civilized methods
of propping, was inclined to smile at our rough use of dom-logs; but Said Ahmed,
the chief Egyptian foreman, vowed to sacrifice a sheep if we finished the work
without accident; and whether because of this vow or because the place was
not so dangerous as it looked, the excavation was finished in safety on March 6
[1917]. About a month earlier, on February 12, we had reached the watertable
and had begun to remove the earth which lay under the surface of the water. On
that day, one of the Egyptians feeling about with his feet in the "western" end of
the "southern" aisle[80] discovered that a number of stone figures lay embedded
in the floor debris of the aisle. A great effort was then made with the bailing,—a
hard struggle, as the water never ceased running in as from some great spring.
Finally we got the tomb temporarily dry and saw the floors of the two side aisles
covered with over a thousand beautifully carved stone figures varying in height
from 18 to 64 cm. Many of them had been ruined by soaking in water, but about
600 were in good condition. The coffin which had been made of wood, the mummy cases, and the mummy had been torn to pieces by thieves looking for gold,
and had decayed except for a few fragments of bones, three pairs of inlaid eyes,
and some bronze trappings. These remains were found partly in the antechamber and partly just outside the main entrance. We found along with them two
canopic jars, several stone vessels, and a number of gold ornaments, the latter
dropped unintentionally by the thieves.[81]

The completion of the excavation of the Nuri pyramids was undertaken between
November 1916 and May 1917 and then December 1917 and April 1918, when some
preliminary work was also undertaken at El-Kurru.

The large fourth-century BC pyramid Ku1 was investigated, and the small tombs behind it tentatively identified as those of the queens of its owner. However,

during these preliminary works at Pyramid I, three or four fragments of the small
blue faience figures called shawwabti were found, and these were inscribed with

the words: "King of Upper and Lower Egypt, Piankhy." At that time historians believed there were two or even more kings called Piankhy, and I thought these figures might have come from the tomb of Piankhy II (so-called). But the season of 1917–1918 was at an end.

When we returned to the Sudan for the season of 1918–1919, I planned to resume the excavation of the great temple of Amon at Gebel Barkal, the Napata of the ancients, and meanwhile, as a secondary undertaking, I began a search for the pyramid of the Piankhy whose funerary figures in blue faience had been found at El-Kur'uw. Following the plan of the royal cemetery at Nuri, the tombs of the kings should have been in the forefield. This was searched with trenches cut to bed-rock over an area about half a mile square, with the idea that a large pyramid, or even several pyramids, might have been carried away as building stone, leaving only the stairway. But it was in vain. There were no pyramids at El-Kur'uw except the miserable little heaps of ruins behind and beside the large pyramid of the late king. Left without any alternative, I gave the apparently hopeless order to excavate the stairways of these . . . .

[T]he preliminary work was begun by attacking the stairway of a ruined pyramid which I numbered Ku XV. To my surprise the stairway proved un-usually large for the size of the pyramid, which was only twelve meters square; but our men have had long practice in clearing such places, and after three days were close to the doorway, where the greater part of the objects thrown away by the plunderers lay scattered. On February 2 a fragment of a blue faience figure was found on which, written in ink, I read: "The king of Upper and Lower Egypt, Shabaka." In amazement I suddenly realized that these poor ruined pyramids at El-Kur'uw must be the tombs of the Twenty-fifth Dynasty of Egypt, the first Dynasty of Ethiopia. I ordered the whole force of workmen to the pyramids of El-Kur'uw. The excavation of the pyramids, Ku XVII, XVI, XVIII, and VIII was begun at almost the same time. On the 9th of February, Ku XVIII was identified, again by a broken shawwabti-figure found in the thieves' hole, as the tomb of Shabataka, the son of Shabaka. On the 15th, Ku XVII was found to be the tomb of the long-sought Piankhy, and on the 17th, Ku XVI, the tomb of Tanutaman. But Ku VIII was never identified by an inscription, and it was not until the end of the season that I realized that Ku VIII must be the burial-place of King Kashta, the father of Piankhy. The identification of the tombs of four kings of Egypt in fifteen days was one of the most amazing series of discoveries which has ever fallen to the lot of any expedition.[82]

Thus, from January to May 1919 the tombs at El-Kurru were cleared, focus moving back to the Barkal temples from December 1919 to April 1920. Excavations then transitioned to the cemeteries of Meroë, where full-scale work was undertaken between January and April 1921, November 1921 and April 1922, and December 1922 and March 1923.

The finds from these excavations were divided between the MFA and the Sudanese authorities, some being housed in a museum at Merowe, opposite Gebel Barkal, until the opening of the new Sudan National Museum (fig. 127) in 1971. Publication of the results was much delayed; Reisner having died in 1942, the preparation of the material from the Kushite temples and cemeteries fell to Dows Dunham* (1890–1984). The publication of El-Kurru appeared in 1950, followed by the pyramid-chapels at Meroë in 1952, Nuri in 1955, the pyramids at Meroë and Barkal in 1957, the West and South Cemeteries at Meroë in 1963, and, finally, the Barkal temples in 1970. In the time since the original excavation, documentation had gone astray (although some later turned up),[83] and Dunham's Barkal temples publication is particularly flawed, being incomplete and on occasion simply referring the reader to preliminary reports published at the time of the excavation, rather than reproducing or amplifying them.

The Kushites in the 1920s

On the basis of the new material revealed by the Harvard–Boston excavations, Reisner produced some initial new historical sketches. The idea that the stem of the Kushite monarchy was to be found other than in Nubia itself was still strong. Thus, in Reisner's view, Kashta was probably the son of Prince Pashedbast B, whom he saw as a governor of Kush under his father, Shoshenq III:[84] "[t]hus it came about that Egypt passed from the hands of the Libyan Twenty-third Dynasty into those of the Libyan Twenty-fifth Dynasty, which was called Ethiopian by the ancients simply because it seized Egypt after having first established a monarchy in Ethiopia."[85] Reisner further opined that Kashta had displaced Osorkon III from Thebes, who had then retreated to Bubastis to become the Osorkon (today IV) encountered by Pi(ankh)y.[86]

Reisner's basic scheme for the chronology and succession of the period was essentially that which would be current down to the 2010s. Thus, Kashta was followed in direct succession by Pi(ankh)y, Shabaka, Shabataka, Taharqa, and Tanutamun, placing the Victory Stela campaign in 721 BC and the definitive conquest of Egypt by Shabaka in 715. He rejected the interpretation of the Tanis stela that saw it as recording the overthrow of Shabataka by Taharqa, rather taking the view that he had "come away from Napata as a young man of twenty in attendance on the king, that is, his uncle Shabaka."[87] The idea of multiple Pi(ankh)ys still endured, however. A "Piankhy II" was thus inserted as the successor of Tanutamun in the post-Taharqa king list that Reisner was now compiling on the basis of the typology and topography of the tombs he was excavating at the royal cemetery of Nuri.[88] "Piankhy II" was firstly assigned one of the tombs at El-Kurru, where initial work had revealed shabtis bearing the name of a Pi(ankh)y, but the full excavation of the site meant that, by 1921, Reisner had realized that

> [t]he scholars who have endeavored to arrange the list of kings of Egypt have been led astray by the unexpected use of a multiplicity of names by Piankhy, and have set forth as many as four different Piankhys and three Kashtas . . . . Piankhy, whose knowledge of Egyptian traditions was gained from life in Napata, a provincial town lying beyond the borders of Egypt proper, and from a corps of servile scribes to whom his merest nod was life or death, appears to have indulged himself with two names for the "Son of Ra" title, and his example was followed by Shabaka and Shabataka. Piankhy, indeed, had two full sets of five names, except that the name Piankhy was common to each; and one set he had adopted from the older stelae of Thothmes III, which he found in the temple of Amon at Barkal, and set up again in the outer court when he rebuilt the temple. The solution is now quite clear. Kashta, Piankhy, Shabaka, Shabataka, Tirhaqa, and Tanutaman are all to be reckoned as kings of the Egyptian Twenty-fifth Dynasty in this order.
>   There was no other Kashta and no other Piankhy.[89]

Reisner's work was well timed for its conclusions to be embedded in the account of the Twenty-fifth Dynasty included in the first edition of the monumental *Cambridge Ancient History*.[90] That the casual and gratuitous racism of Breasted was still flourishing can be seen in a comment by the author of the relevant chapters, Henry Hall* (1873–1930), regarding the inherent wealth of the Nubian lands: the Kushites "at least received the adherence to which gold-masters are accustomed, even if they are black or, at any rate, chocolate-coloured."[91]

Kawa

The next set of "history-rewriting" excavations were carried out by Griffith at Kawa during 1929–31 (figs. 67, 128). Not only was Taharqa's Temple T uncovered, with its five granite stelae of the king himself (figs. 54, 67 bottom) and others of Anlamani and Aspelta, but also Temples A and B, the former with the stela of Iry (figs. 8, 67 top).[92]

In addition to the stelae, Temple T yielded various other material. These included four granite rams (now in the Ashmolean Museum, the British Museum [fig. 68 bottom],

FIGURE 127 The Sudan National Museum in Khartoum. Rams of Taharqa from Kawa flank the entrance to the building, and a colossus of the same king, from Gebel Barkal (SNM 1841), can be seen in the bottom right of the interior view.

and the Sudan National Museum [two]), a sphinx (British Museum—fig. 68 top), and a statue of Taharqa (Ny Carlsberg). A complete shrine of Taharqa was transported to the Ashmolean Museum (fig. 67 bottom left).

Sadly, Griffith died in 1934, having issued short notes only regarding his work at Kawa,[93] and drafted only a small part of the prospective final publication. While its drawings were being prepared, there was a need for their collation with the originals on site, and accordingly a third season began in October 1935 under Lawrence Kirwan* (1907–99). Unfortunately, the death of Nora Griffith* (1870–1937), under whose direction the

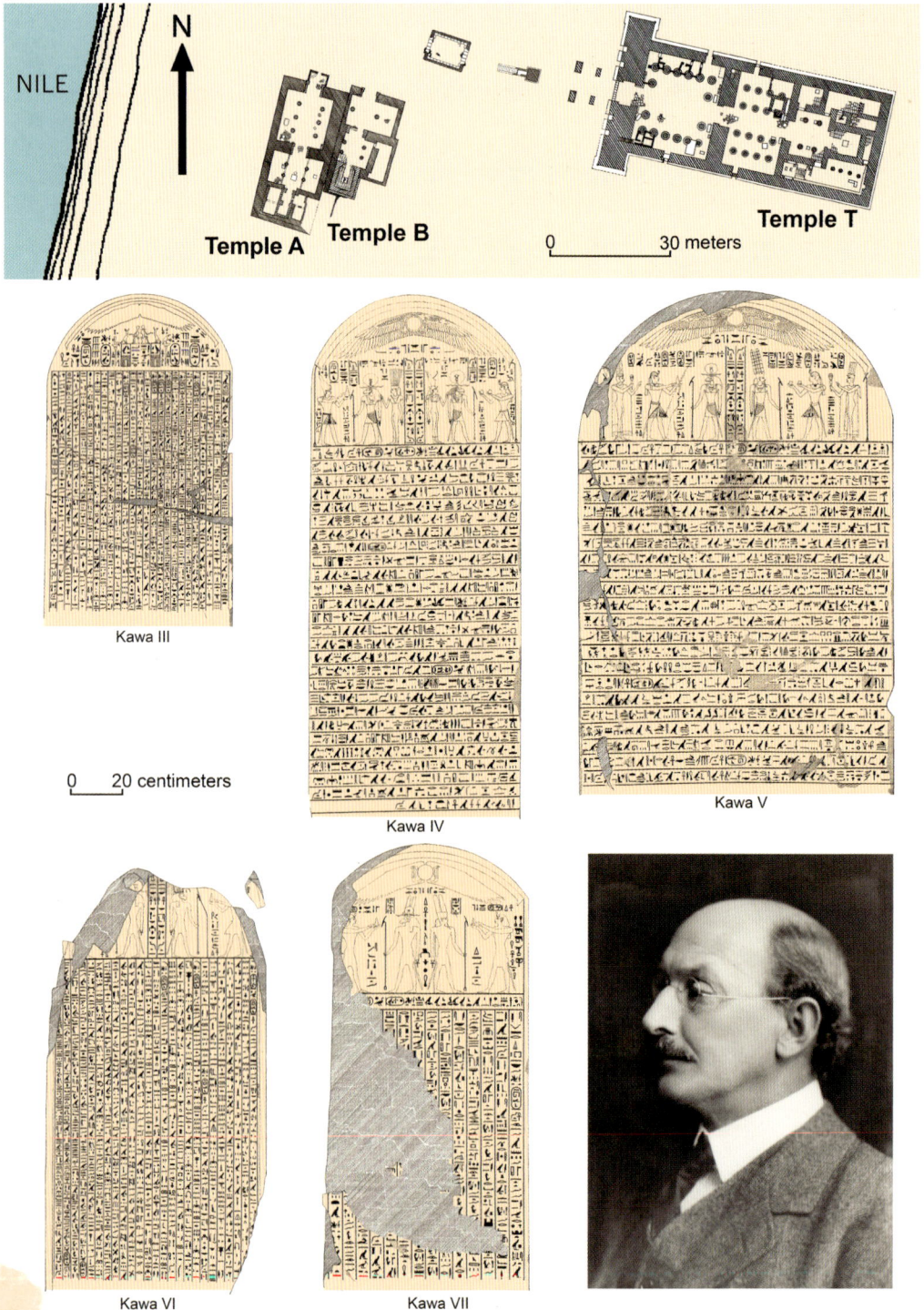

FIGURE 128 Map of Kawa, the stelae of Taharqa from the site, and the site's excavator, Francis Llewellyn Griffith.

publication was being carried on, further delayed its appearance, although a posthumous paper by Professor Griffith publishing one of the Kawa stelae (Kawa V) was issued during 1935–38.[94] This was important for the writing of history, as it included in its final section a complete version of the long-problematic text of Taharqa preserved on the fragmentary Tanis stela.[95] The work at Kawa was finally published in two volumes by M.F. Laming Macadam (1909–97) in 1949 and 1955.

Griffith had been minded to date Iry broadly to the Ramesside Period, but Macadam moved the king into the Meroitic Period, remarking of Griffith that "had he lived to consider the matter further he would probably have altered his decision."[96] Macadam's grounds for this dating were on an alleged similarity of style to that seen in "earlier Meroitic pyramids," and the poor quality of the Egyptian language used on the stela. He failed, however, to consider whether the latter factor might also be valid for work carried out during the period following the end of the Egyptian presence in Nubia (cf. pages 11–12).

Accordingly, Macadam placed Iry at a point following the reign of Nastasen, possibly as an occupant of one of the pyramids at Barkal, where he would become classified as one of a group of so-called "Neo-Ramesside" kings, alongside ⌜Qa⌝tiaa⌜t⌝, with whom Iry shared a Nineteenth/Twentieth Dynasty–type prenomen, and three others with names that were unusual for the post-Nastasen period.[97] This placement has been widely accepted, and it has only been more recently that the placement of Iry and ⌜Qa⌝tiaa⌜t⌝ in the immediate post-Ramesside age has been reconsidered by some scholars.[98] The older dating is, however, still maintained by others, for example in the major exhibition of Kushite royal material that was held at the Louvre Museum in Paris in 2022.

The Succession Question

Macadam took the opportunity of his Kawa publication to discuss the genealogy of the Kushite royal family.[99] He also collaborated with Dows Dunham—then engaged on the publication of Reisner's work—on a paper covering the same broad issues.[100] Many of their conclusions formed the basis for understandings of the history of the Twenty-fifth Dynasty and the broader Kushite monarchy down to the end of the twentieth century, and beyond.[101]

A key conclusion was that, rather than by father–son succession, as generally practiced in Egypt, Kushite kingship was passed from brother to brother, before reverting to the offspring of the eldest brother.[102] To help make this work, Macadam "corrected" the Assyrian statement (page 57) that Tanutamun was a son of Shabaka to make it say that his father was Shabataka. At no point did he question the time-hallowed assumption of the relative order of the latter two kings. In addition, Macadam extended the principle of adoption that underpinned the succession of God's Wives at Thebes to the broader royal family.[103] He took this even further by asserting that *mwt.s* ("her mother") *only* referred to an adoptive relationship at this time, and also arguing for a matrilineal element in the royal succession. The latter built on long-standing assumptions about Egyptian royal succession as well, only finally demolished in the 1980s,[104] but also on the exclusively female ancestry given for Aspelta on his Enthronement Stela (page 69, fig. 83).

When dealing with Kawa stela V,[105] Macadam misinterpreted its contents to provide a chronology for Taharqa's life that included coregencies between Shabaka and Shabataka, and Shabataka and Taharqa. The latter became widely accepted among Old Testament scholars, who were particularly interested in Taharqa in the context of Sennacherib's attack on Jerusalem, although much less so among Egyptologists. A comprehensive rebuttal of Macadam's arguments was published by Kitchen in his 1973 book on the Third Intermediate Period;[106] this volume, with updates in 1986 and 1996, would until the end of the twentieth century AD enshrine a "standard" account of the history of the eleventh though seventh centuries BC.

Ongoing Archaeology

A large corpus of material relating to the Twenty-fifth Dynasty kings had been assembled by the 1960s, when Jean Leclant* (1920–2011) produced a monumental documentation of their Theban monuments.[107] However, much still remained to be examined, an important new site being that of Dukki Gel, part of the broader site of Kerma, which would be excavated by a team led by Charles Bonnet between 1997 and 2017. In January 2003, excavations there uncovered a cache of broken statues, very similar to one found nearly nine decades earlier by Reisner at Gebel Barkal, comprising images of Taharqa, Tanutamun, Senkamanisken, Anlamani, and Aspelta (fig. 129).[108] The fact that all had inscriptions invoking Amun-of-Pnubs confirmed the identification of Pnubs and Dukki Gel, rather than at Tabo on Argo Island, as had once been believed.[109]

In 2006, excavation and conservation work (still ongoing) began at the long-neglected early Twenty-fifth Dynasty necropolis of the South Asasif (pages 51–53) under the direction of Elena Pischikova. Across the river, work at Karnak from 2008 by the Franco-Egyptian Center revealed the extensive precinct laid out around the area of the temple of Ptah by Shabaka (pages 58–59). Furthermore, the recording and conservation of the Taharqa/Tanutamun chapel of Osiris-Ptah-Nebankh has been underway by the eponymous research project (OPNRP) since 2018.

FIGURE 129 The cache of royal statues from Kerma-Dukki Gel, comprising images of Taharqa, Tanutamun, Senkamanisken, Anlamani, and Aspelta (Kerma Museum).

The "Black Pharaohs"

The Kushite kings' undisputed "African" status has made them of particular interest to proponents of Africanist readings of history.[110] A prominent writer in this genre, Ivan Van Sertima (1935–2009), provided a treatment of the Twenty-fifth Dynasty in his 1976 attempt to demonstrate an early African presence in the Americas. While including a generally sound overview of the history of the Kushites in Egypt, the book provides a good example of the failure of a non-specialist author to grasp the magnitude of the changes in scholarly working hypotheses over time. We thus read of "dreams . . . described in the stelae of King Nut and King Tanutamon,"[111] Van Sertima not realizing that they were the same person (with just one stela).[112] The Africanist agenda is, however, highlighted by a statement that Montjuemhat was "a black Sudanese High Priest,"[113] in spite of all indications that his ancestry was wholly Egyptian, albeit married to a Kushite princess (page 74).

That agenda is taken much further, however, in Van Sertima's claim that the Twenty-fifth Dynasty kings sent out an expedition that reached Mesoamerica, and founded the Olmec civilization—whose works of art are asserted to show people of African origin.[114]

Thus, we find once again an attempt to employ the Kushite kings' backgrounds to infer aspects of their careers that have no grounding in any objective data.

Fresh Looks

More mainstream re-examinations of the Kushite kings began around the end of the twentieth century. These included a fresh look at their genealogy and chronology in a paper published in 1999 by Robert Morkot (b. 1957)—who would issue a book on Kushite history the following year.[115] His paper critically examined all the various current proposals and noted the jumps of logic and internal contradictions that were present in many of them.[116] In particular, he underlined that "the direct evidence for the relationship between rulers renders any attempt at explaining the succession within a set of rules virtually impossible."[117] However, while forensically dissecting and querying many of the accepted relationships of the Kushite kings, he accepted without citations or analysis that the Shabaka–Shabataka succession was "not explicitly stated in any Egyptian or Kushite text, but is certain from a large number of monuments and other criteria."[118] This long-standing assumption regarding the succession of the two kings, going back to the 1820s, would, however, finally be challenged in the new century.

Kushites as saviors

In 2002 appeared a book, *The Rescue of Jerusalem*, by Henry T. Aubin,[119] that investigated the role of the Egypto-Nubian army during Sennacherib's campaign of 701 BC. Arguing that the army had played a crucial role in the Assyrian king's withdrawal from Jerusalem, contrary to the negative assessments of its capabilities and of the Kushite kings themselves found in most publications since the late nineteenth century, it also provided a useful review of scholarly attitudes toward Nubia and its kings, as did a volume of retrospective studies issued two decades later.[120]

Tang-i Var and beyond

The idea of an association or coregency between Shabaka and Shabataka had continued to be supported by some scholars on broader chronological grounds,[121] and this approach would receive a significant boost in 1999. This was a result of the first publication of an Assyrian text from Tang-i Var in Iran (pages 54–56), which showed that Shabataka was in a position of authority before the death of Sargon II in 705 BC. This was at least three years earlier than the generally accepted date for his accession to the throne.

Although only a relatively short period of time, this would stretch Shabataka's reign to fifteen years at the very least—well beyond his highest known regnal year (3), or even the 12/14 years assumed to be attributed to him by Manetho. Such a change also had knock-on effects on the dates of earlier rulers in the Nile valley. These included further complicating a number of emerging chronological and historical issues within the current working hypotheses for the later part of the Third Intermediate Period.

As a result, a number of scholars sought to avoid some of the problems by arguing that the text should be interpreted as indicating that, at the time in question, Shabaka and Shabataka were ruling together, either as formal coregents[122] or with the latter as some form of "viceroy," ruling Kush while Shabaka was in Egypt.[123] Both options allowed the hitherto generally accepted basic chronological structure to remain undisturbed, with the "coregency" version followed in Aubin's aforementioned 2002 study of Sennacherib's Jerusalem campaign.[124] Unfortunately, both of these "explanations" lack any independent verification and are replete with problems. Taking the second first, we have no evidence for any office of the kind implied by the "viceroy" theory. Such an explanation also begs the questions of how/why an Assyrian king would have direct dealings with such a subordinate of Shabaka's, given that Shabaka was now based in Egypt, which lay between Assyrian territory and that of the alleged "viceroy" Shabataka.[125] As for the question of a formal coregency, there survives no material with double dates of Shabaka and Shabataka, nor any representations of them acting together. Indeed, it is by no means clear that coregencies were as common as has often been asserted in Egyptology.[126]

By the beginning of the twenty-first century, the question of how to deal with the new data from Tang-i Var was not the only issue concerning the Twenty-fifth Dynasty that was exercising scholarly minds. Various "minor" issues made the then-current reconstruction of the period problematic. The possibly excessive length of the reign of Shabataka, given the relative paucity of his contemporary attestations (with or without Tang-i Var) was one; another was the question of the number and identity of the Apis bulls of the period.[127] A further issue arose from the fact that the inscription on a statue of the High Priest of Amun Horemakhet (fig. 48 left) mentions Shabaka (his father), Taharqa, and Tanutamun as the kings he served—with no sign of Shabataka. Likewise, at the Small Temple at Medinet Habu, the Twenty-fifth Dynasty pylon (fig. 46) bears the names of Shabaka and Taharqa, arranged in such a way as to suggest that decoration began under Shabaka and was continued under Taharqa: there is no indication of any hiatus covering an intervening reign of Shabataka.

In the temple of Osiris-Heqadjet at Karnak (fig. 31), Shepenwepet I appears in a portion of the temple decorated under Shabataka, on a wall also showing her successor, Amenirdis I (fig. 32). Under the normal ordering of kings, Shepenwepet I would have been long dead when these scenes were carved, as Amenirdis I is known to have been in office as God's Wife in Year 12 of Shabaka (page 73). While posthumous depictions are not unknown, it would seem odd for Shepenwepet to be depicted as though alive half a decade or more after her death. Also at Karnak, the surviving Nile Level text of Shabataka is placed in such a position as to appear to have been carved before those of Shabaka.[128]

At El-Kurru, the tombs of Pi(ankh)y and Shabataka are very similar in design, constructed using a "cut and cover" method found only among the earliest Kushite royal tombs (figs. 94, 100), with neither showing any trace of decoration. Yet the tomb of Shabaka, on the conventional order of kings allegedly built between the tombs of Pi(ankh)y and Shabataka, has a tunneled substructure of the kind found in later Kushite royal tombs—and was decorated with mythological texts, also a feature found in later royal tombs.

It was against this background that in 2013 Michael Bányai (b. 1963) produced a paper that made some radical proposals regarding the chronology and structure of the Twenty-fifth Dynasty.[129] These included the reversal of the conventional ordering of Shabaka and Shabataka, and a shortening of the dynasty (and a lowering of earlier Third Intermediate dates). This truncation was achieved in part by overlapping the reigns of

FIGURE 130 The 2022 Louvre exhibition regarding the Napatan kings, including a replica of a statue of Taharqa from Dukki Gel, with restored gilding.

Shabataka and Shabaka by two years, and of Shabaka and Taharqa by six. This parallel rule was posited in the context of a long-running dispute over the royal succession, bringing into play both Jerome's statement that Taharqa had killed his predecessor, and some of Macadam's interpretations of the Kawa texts.

While most of Bányai's ideas received little support,[130] a number of participants at a seminar that took place in Münster, Germany, in May 2014 found the reversal of the order of Shabaka and Shabataka attractive, with the implications further explored in a number of papers published over the immediately following years.[131] Egyptology is generally a very conservative field, in which changes in paradigm tend to take decades to gain something approaching general acceptance. However, the Shabaka/Shabataka re-configuration has come to be adopted remarkably rapidly as the new working hypothesis by a significant proportion of those who have made this period a specialization.[132]

Study of the kings of Kush continues apace, both in their Nubian heartlands and at sites that saw the activities of those who ruled in Egypt. Interest in the region of Nubia and its rulers has been underlined by major exhibitions, for example at the British Museum in 2004, and at the Louvre, Paris, from April to July 2022 (fig. 130). The role of the Nubian kings of Egypt as a bridge between ancient Africa and the ancient Levant—especially their fleeting appearance in the Old Testament—continues to make them a perennial subject of interest to a range of constituencies. The latter include some involved in the racial politics, polemics, and prejudices of modern times, marking not only the lives of the Nubian pharaohs of Egypt, but also their afterlives, as fruitful topics of enquiry.

CHRONOLOGY OF ANCIENT EGYPT

LE = Lower Egypt only; UE = Upper Egypt.

All dates are more or less uncertain prior to 690 BC.

Parentheses around a name and date indicate a co-ruler.

Only kings mentioned in the text are included.

EARLY DYNASTIC PERIOD

Dynasty 1		3050–2800 BC
Dynasty 2		2800–2660

OLD KINGDOM

Dynasty 3		2660–2600
Dynasty 4		2600–2470
Menkaure	2493–2475	
Dynasty 5		2470–2360
Dynasty 6		2360–2200
Pepy II	2270–2195	

FIRST INTERMEDIATE PERIOD

Dynasties 7/8	2200–2100
Dynasties 9/10 (LE)	2100–2000
Dynasty 11a (UE)	2080–2010

MIDDLE KINGDOM

Dynasty 11b		2014–1943
Montjuhotep II	2014–1962	
Dynasty 12		1943–1780
Senwosret I	1923–1878	
Senwosret III	1838–1797	
Dynasty 13		1780–1650
Neferhotep I		

SECOND INTERMEDIATE PERIOD

Dynasty 14 (LE)		1700–1650
Dynasty 15 (LE)		1650–1535
Dynasty 16 (UE)		1660–1590
Dynasty 17 (UE)		1585–1540
Kamose	1544–1540	

NEW KINGDOM

Dynasty 18		1540–1278
Ahmose I	1540–1516	
Thutmose I	1496–1481	
Thutmose III	1468–1415	
(Hatshepsut	1462–1447)	
Amenhotep III	1377–1337	
Akhenaten	1337–1321	
Tutankhamun	1321–1312	
Horemheb	1308–1278	
Dynasty 19		1278–1176
Sethy I	1276–1265	
Rameses II	1265–1200	
Dynasty 20		1176–1078
Rameses VI	1132–1125	
Rameses IX	1116–1098	

THIRD INTERMEDIATE PERIOD

Dynasty 21		1078–941
Herihor	1078–1065	
Dynasty 22		943–666
Shoshenq I	943–922	
Osorkon II	872–831	
Shoshenq III	831–791	
Shoshenq IV	791–779	
Shoshenq V	773–736	
Osorkon IV	736–716+	
Gemenefkhonsubak		
Padubast III	–666	
Dynasty 23 (Thebes)		834–755
Takelot II	834–810	
Osorkon III	791–762	
Takelot III	768–755	
Dynasty 23 (Herakleopolis)		
Peftjauawybast	fl. 730	
Dynasty 23 (Hermopolis)		
Nimlot	fl. 730	
Dynasty 23 (Leontopolis)		
Iuput II	fl. 730	
Dynasty 24 (LE)		
Tefnakhte	728–718	
Bakenrenef	718–712	
Dynasty 25		755–656
Kashta	755–750	
Pi(ankh)y	750–713	
Shabataka	713–705	
Shabaka	705–690	
Taharqa	690–664	
Tanutamun	664–656+	

SAITE PERIOD
Dynasty 26

Nekau I (LE)	672–664	
Psamtik I	664–610	
Nekau II	610–595	
Psamtik II	595–589	
Wahibre	589–570	
Ahmose II	570–526	
Psamtik III	526–525	

LATE PERIOD

Dynasty 27 (Persians)		525–404
Cambyses	525–522	
Dynasty 28		404–398
Dynasty 29		398–379
Pasherenmut	392–391	
Dynasty 30		379–340
Dynasty 31 (Persians)		340–332

HELLENISTIC PERIOD

Dynasty of Macedonia		332–310
Dynasty of Ptolemy		310–30
Ptolemy II	284–246	
Ptolemy IV	221–204	

ROMAN PERIOD   30 BC–AD 395

NOTES

Notes to Introduction

1 For which see Hafsaas 2021.
2 For a discussion of the early political geography of Nubia, see O'Connor 1986.
3 Stela Berlin ÄM14753, from Semna.
4 Stelae Berlin ÄM1157 (from Semna), SNM 451 (from Uronarti).
5 Ryholt 1997: 346[32, 33].
6 Bonnet 2014.
7 Bonnet 2000.
8 Davies 2003a; 2003b.
9 Kamose stela I, lines 3–5.
10 Kamose stela II, lines 19–24.
11 Weigall 1907: 127, pl. lxv[4]; Simpson 1962: 42–45; cf. Krauss 1993.
12 Habachi 1959.
13 Davies 2001: 46–53.
14 Porter and Moss 1952: 203–23; for an overview of the temples at the site, incorporating the latest research, see Kendall and Mohamed 2016.
15 Kendall 2009.
16 Simpson 1963: 2–18.
17 Dodson 1997.
18 Müller 2009: 257 n. 33.
19 Titles on her coffins, from TT320.

Notes to Chapter 1

1 Kawa XIV [Ny Carlsberg ÆIN1709], Kawa XV [BM EA1777 + left in situ] (Porter and Moss 1952: 181[3–4], with latter number misquoted as 1708; Eide et al. 1994–2000: II, 522–28[91]; 528–32[92]).
2 The correct reading of the nomen is unclear: cf. Morkot 2000: 147.
3 SNM 5225, 5227 (Porter and Moss 1952: 216[18], 222); Dunham 1970: 34, pl. xxxvii.
4 Priese 1977, from an unpublished Lepsius expedition copy.
5 Morkot 2000: 145–50.
6 Or possibly Karimala—see Darnell 2006: 12–14.
7 Caminos 1998: 1:pls. 15, 18–19; Darnell 2006; Eide et al. 1994–2000: I, 35–41.
8 Darnell 2006: 45–48; cf. Morkot 2000: 153.
9 Horton 1991: 264–65.
10 Dunham 1950; there are also a pair of pyramids of uncertain, but probably fourth-century, date.
11 Formerly thought to be mastabas.

12 Plus the fourth-century BC Ku1 and 2.

13 Dunham 1950: 1–3.

14 Kendall 1982: 22–23, a view later recanted; Hakem 1988: 253–55; Török 1995. Cf. Lull 2002: 197–210.

15 Cf. Morkot 2000: 140–44.

16 Cf. Morkot 2000: 143.

17 For an overview of the episode, see Cline 2021.

18 Contrary to what has long been an implicit assumption: see chapter 7 n.126.

19 Morkot 2007; 2014.

20 Indeed, some of these productions were misidentified as genuine works of the Old Kingdom when first examined by Egyptologists: see Dodson 2021: 129–30.

Notes to Chapter 2

1 Cairo JE41013 (Jansen-Winkeln 2007–14: II, 336[34.1]; Eide et al. 1994–2000: I, 45–47[4]).

2 Jansen-Winkeln 2007–14: II, 336[34.4].

3 Filiation on coffin of his descendant Padiamenet (Jansen-Winkeln 2007–14: II, 399[44.38]).

4 Stelae Kawa IV [SNM 2678] (Jansen-Winkeln 2007–14: III, 132–35[48.74]; Eide et al. 1994–2000: I, 140–51): l.16–17; Kawa VI [SNM 2679] (Jansen-Winkeln 2007–14: III, 138–41[48.76]; Eide et al. 1994–2000: I, 173–74): l.23–24; Kawa IX (Eide et al. 1994–2000: II, 400–28[71]): l.54.

5 Stela SNM 1901, from her tomb, El-Kurru Ku53 (Jansen-Winkeln 2007–14: II, 358–59; Eide et al. 1994–2000: I, 119–20[11]). This names her mother as Kasaqa.

6 Kendall (1999: 64) and Morkot (2000: 149, 157) have raised the possibility that Alara might be equated with the aforementioned Iry, but this seems unlikely on chronological grounds; also, as Morkot points out, Alara is never given a prenomen in these sources.

7 Jansen-Winkeln 2007–14: II, 336[34.2–3].

8 Filiation on statue Cairo CG42498 (Jansen-Winkeln 2007–14: III, 259[51.2]).

9 MFA exc. 19-3-537, found in pyramid Ku1 (Dunham 1950: 23–24, pl. xxxiic); cf. Lull 2002: 180–82.

10 Cf. Morkot 1999: 194–96.

11 Cairo JE31886 (Jansen-Winkeln 2007–14: II, 354–57[35.17]).

12 Jansen-Winkeln 2007–14: II, 355; Broekman 2009: 100–101, a view opposed in Perdu 2010; 2011; 2022a.

13 Museo Barracco, Rome (Jansen-Winkeln 2007–14: II, 366[36.1]).

14 For an overview of her career and monuments, see Coulon 2022.

15 Cairo JE32022–3, from Peksater's tomb at Abydos (Jansen-Winkeln 2007–14: II, 360[35.29]).

16 Cf. Leahy 1994: 182–87; Morkot 2000: 159–61.

17 Respectively buried in tombs D48 and D9 at Abydos (Jansen-Winkeln 2007–14: III, 352–53[52.12–13]; see Leahy 1994: 182–87).

18 According to Paabtameri's stela, her son was only twenty when she died.

19 Cf. Dodson 1990: 88–89.

20 Given that Shepenwepet II held an office for some six and a half decades, she may indeed have been born to a younger wife of Pi(ankh)y who could still have been of childbearing age following that king's death.

21 Cf. Leahy 1994: 187.

22 Jansen-Winkeln 2007–14: III, 11–12[46.24].

23 As it does in many languages, in which the term can embrace cousins.

24 As was long ago demonstrated by Maspero (1892: 177–80), in the context of the debate whether Thutmose III was the nephew or brother of Hatshepsut.

25 E.g., on statue BM EA1131 (Porter and Moss 1960–64: 788).

26 Porter and Moss 1972: 14–15.

27 Farrulla 2013: 64–75.

28 Cairo JE48865 (Porter and Moss 1952: 218; Grimal 1981: 36–39; Eide et al. 1994–2000: 252–58[38]).

29 Farrulla 2013: 75–78.

30 Vittmann 1974.

31 Jansen-Winkeln 2007–14: II, 353[35.7].

32 Jansen-Winkeln 2007–14: II, 352[4], 353[35.7], 357–58[35.19].

33 Jansen-Winkeln 2007–14: II, 354[35.12], 363[35.33].

34 Louvre C100 (Jansen-Winkeln 2007–14: II, 382–83[42.1]; Rondot 2022: 100–101[48]).

35 SNM 1851 (Jansen-Winkeln 2007–14: II, 350–51[35.2]; Ritner 2009: 461–64[143]; Rondot 2022: 187, fig. 63).

36 SNM 462 (Jansen-Winkeln 2007–14: II, 365[35.11]).

37 Berlin ÄM1068+Cairo JE47085 (Jansen-Winkeln 2007–14: II, 351–52[35.3]; Ritner 2009: 464–65[144]).

38 Cairo JE48862+47086–9 (Jansen-Winkeln 2007–14: II, 337–50[35.1]); all further quotations in this chapter are from this document, unless otherwise stated. Morkot suggests (2000: 171–72) that the Year 21 stela may actually be a retelling of the Year 4 campaign, but it seems unlikely that the date of the stela would have been so far removed from the events related.

39 II Kings 17:4; "So" is a credible contraction of (O)so(rkon).

40 Sargon's Annals and Display Inscriptions at Khorsabad (Frame 2021: 57–58[53–57]).

41 Botta and Flandin 1849–50: 2:pl. 87.

42 Cf. Kahn 2001: 12.

43 Sargon's Annals; prism Berlin VA8424 (Frame 2021: 267[ii′ 8′–11′]).

44 Jansen-Winkeln 2007–14: III, 252–55[50.11–14, 16]; also of this group may be a king Neferkare (Jansen-Winkeln 2007–14: III, 256[50.17–19a]).

45 Jansen-Winkeln 2007–14: III, 255[50.15].

46 For reconstructions of the scheme, see Kendall and Mohamed 2016: 53–62.

47 Jansen-Winkeln 2007–14: II, 353[35.7], 357[35.19].

48 BM EA6640 (Jansen-Winkeln 2007–14: II, 363[35.33]). This prenomen is also used on slab SNM 5220 (Jansen-Winkeln 2007–14: II, 354[35.12]).

49 Cf. Parkinson 1999: 97[21].

50 Ashmolean 1894.107b (Jansen-Winkeln 2007–14: II, 36365[35.34]; Ritner 2009: 492–94[146].

51 Louvre statuette E3915 (Jansen-Winkeln 2007–14: II, 357–58[35.19]; Rondot 2022: 90–91[39]).

52 Cairo JE32022–3, from Peksater's tomb at Abydos (Jansen-Winkeln 2007–14: II, 360[35.29]).

53 Known from a stela of the reign of Aspelta in the approach to temple Barkal B500, which established a mortuary cult for him (Porter and Moss 1952: 216; Eide et al. 1994–2000: I, 268–78[40]).

54 Known from an inscription of his daughter, Wadjrenes, in the tomb of her husband, Montjuemhat (TT34—Jansen-Winkeln 2007–14: III, 483[52.238]).

55 Jansen-Winkeln 2007–14: III, 301–22.

56 Named on statue Cairo JE49157 of the High Priest Horemakhet, who probably served during the reigns of Shabaka through Tanutamun (Jansen-Winkeln 2007–14: III, 348[52.5]). Cf. Morkot 2000: 205.

57 Jansen-Winkeln 2007–14: II, 372–73[40.1–2].

58 Priese 1970: 19–20; von Beckerath 1997: 93; Perdu 2002; Gombert-Meurice 2022.

59   See the discussion of Kahn 2009.

60   Diodorus Siculus i, 45, 65, 69.

61   Cf. Moret 1903; Hölbl 1981; Janssen 1954; Gill and Vickers 1996; Ridgway 1999.

62   Manetho, all versions; cf. Waddell 1940: 164–65.

63   Jansen-Winkeln 2007–14: II, 375[41.1], 376–81[41.11–24].

64   Hamm 5770 (Jansen-Winkeln 2007–14: II, 381[41.25]).

65   Jansen-Winkeln 2007–14: II, 375[41.2].

66   Cf. Gill and Vickers 1996; Ridgway 1999.

Notes to Chapter 3

1   For an alleged alternate Wahibre, cf. Kitchen 1996: 152.

2   Jansen-Winkeln 2007–14: III, 353[52.14]).

3   Jansen-Winkeln 2007–14: III, 250[50.1].

4   Jansen-Winkeln 2007–14: III, 40[47.5]; Eide et al. 1994–2000: I, 128[17].

5   Broekman 2017b: 31.

6   Stela Kawa V [Ny Carlsberg ÆIN 1712] (Jansen-Winkeln 2007–14: III, 135–38[48.75]): l.17.

7   Kawa stela IV [SNM 2678] (Jansen-Winkeln 2007–14: III, 132–35[48.74]): l.7–10.

8   Jansen-Winkeln 2007–14: III, 39[47.1].

9   Parts now Berlin ÄM1480 (Jansen-Winkeln 2007–14: III, 46–50[47.7]; Rondot 2022: 258–59[104]).

10   Jansen-Winkeln 2007–14: III, 40–46[47.6]; since Shepenwepet I had been in office since the 780s (if not before), she cannot have lived much beyond 710, even if appointed God's Wife as a child.

11   Jansen-Winkeln 2007–14: III, 50[47.8].

12   Hourdin 2013–15.

13   MMA 65.45 (Jansen-Winkeln 2007–14: III, 53[47.21]).

14   Cairo CG655 (Jansen-Winkeln 2007–14: III, 39[47.2]).

15   One now Cairo JE46195 (Jansen-Winkeln 2007–14: III, 40[47.3–4].

16   For this and the nearby tomb of Karakhamun, see Pischikova 2014; 2017; 2021.

17   Eigner 1984.

18   Dodson and Ikram 2008: 270–75.

19   Pischikova 2008.

20   Titles that by this time did not denote a functional role, but indicated a position in the overall hierarchy (e.g., *iry-pʿt*).

21   Naunton 2014 suggests a military role.

22   Einaudi 2014.

23   Yoyotte 1961: 159–60.

24   On whom, see Howley and Creasman 2021.

25   BM K.1668.b [Prism A] (Frame 2021: 368[vii 30″]).

26   Display Inscriptions in Sargon II's palace at Khorsabad (Frame 2021: 147[100–104]; 157[11b–14]); inscription from Tang-i Var in Iran (Frame 1999: 40; Frame 2021: 441[19–21]).

27   Khorsabad Display Inscriptions (Frame 2021: 147[109b–112a]).

28   Tang-i Var inscription (Frame 2021: 441[22–24]).

29   While earlier absolute dates have been put forward on the bases of astronomical observations and synchronisms with other cultures (especially Assyria), all are subject to margins of error or broader doubts as to their validity (cf. Dodson 2019: 181–89).

30   Statue Cairo CG42204 and coffin lid Cairo JE55194 (Jansen-Winkeln 2007–14: III, 347[52.4], 350[52.8]).

31   Stela Cairo JE48863 (Jansen-Winkeln 2007–14: III, 236[49.8]).

32   Rassam Cylinder (BM WA91026—fig. 71 right; Novotny and Jeffers 2018–23: 235[ii 22–27]).

33   Coffin fragments Cairo JE34431=TR
      9/2/15/11, from Abydos tomb D3
      (Jansen-Winkeln 2007–14: III, 351[52.10]).

34   This has generally been taken to have been
      written in the same room as that contain-
      ing an Apis burial of Year 6 of Bakenrenef
      and, on the traditional order of Shabaka
      and Shabataka, used to argue for the de-
      feat of Bakenrenef by Shabaka while the
      bull of Bakenrenef was still in the process
      of burial (cf. Vercoutter 1960: 65–67).
      With the reversal of the order of Shabaka
      and Shabataka, this no longer becomes an
      option—and in any case it seems likely
      that the text was in a different room from
      that used for the Bakenrenef Apis burial
      (Jansen-Winkeln 2007–14: III, 2[4]).

35   Louvre IM3019 (Jansen-Winkeln 2007–
      14: III, 193[48.128]); for the others,
      see Brunet 2005: 33 n. 32. A bull dying
      in Year 4 of Shabaka would have been
      around twelve years old, and so half the
      usual age of a bull at death. The next bull,
      which died in Year 14 of Taharqa (see
      page 75,) would, however, have been of
      an appropriate age. It may be noted that
      the problems of Twenty-fifth Dynasty Apis
      bulls discussed by Brunet 2005 and Thijs
      2015: 45–50 are essentially resolved by
      the reversal of the reigns of Shabaka and
      Shabataka (for which see pages 170–73).
      On the general question of Twenty-fifth
      Dynasty Apis burials, see Ibrahim Ali and
      Devauchelle 2022.

36   Jansen-Winkeln 2007–14: III, 4[46.11].

37   Louvre E10571 (Jansen-Winkeln 2007–
      14: III, 29[46.72]).

38   From near Bubastis (Jansen-Winkeln
      2007–14: III, 28[46.71]).

39   Moscow I.1.a.5646=4118 (Jansen-
      Winkeln 2007–14: III, 28[46.69]).

40   From Tell Farain (MMA 55.144.6—
      Jansen-Winkeln 2007–14: III, 28[46.70]).

41   Jansen-Winkeln 2007–14: III, 1[46.1–3],
      inc. Berlin ÄM31235 (Rondot 2022:
      208[96]).

42   Louvre N2541; Cairo CG38020; Berlin
      ÄM7742 (Jansen-Winkeln 2007–14:
      III, 2–3[46.5, 8–3]; Rondot 2022:
      200–201[90]).

43   BM EA498 (Jansen-Winkeln
      2007–14: III, 2[46.6]; Rondot 2022:
      206–207[95]).

44   Jansen-Winkeln 2007–14: III,
      4–12[46.11–25].

45   Licitra, Thiers, and Zignani 2014; Licitra
      2018.

46   Jansen-Winkeln 2007–14: III, 12–
      14[46.26]; Hourdin 2018: 263–66.

47   Jansen-Winkeln 2007–14: III,
      14–17[46.27].

48   Jansen-Winkeln 2007–14: III,
      17–19[46.28].

49   Jansen-Winkeln 2007–14: III,
      20–21[46.34].

50   Jansen-Winkeln 2007–14: III, 21[46.35].

51   Jansen-Winkeln 2007–14: III,
      21–22[46.37].

52   Bonnet, Valbelle, and Marchi 2020;
      Valbelle and Bonnet 2022; for the New
      Kingdom phase of temple building at the
      site, see Bonnet and Valbelle 2018.

53   Jansen-Winkeln 2007–14: III,
      347–51[52.4–8].

54   Jansen-Winkeln 2007–14: III, 38[46.83].

55   As has frequently been claimed by mod-
      ern writers without any direct evidence:
      see discussion in Aubin 2002: 226–32.

56   By virtue of the plural presumably in-
      cluding the Tanite and other northern
      monarchs as well as Shabaka.

57   Chicago Prism of Sennacherib and Taylor
      Prism (Grayson and Novotny 2012–14: I,
      175–76).

58   II Kings 18:19–21; Isaiah 36:4–6.

59   Aubin 2002: 180–86.

60   II Kings 19:9; Isaiah 37:9.

61   II Kings 19:36; Isaiah 37:37.

62   Aubin 2002: 132–38.

63   As argued by Aubin 2002: 13, 226–65. This contrasts with the usual scholarly dismissal of the Kushite efforts in 701 as a failure. For discussions of Aubin's thesis from a number of perspectives, see Bellis 2020.

64   Arguments for each option are summarized in Kitchen 1996: 158–61, 552–54, but coming down firmly in favor of the second.

65   BM WA84527 and WA84884 (Jansen-Winkeln 2007–14: III, 24[46.50]).

66   Block statue of Iti (BM EA24429—Jansen-Winkeln 2007–14: III, 30[46.76]).

67   In Africanus's version of Manetho (cf. pages 140–41), "Sebichôs" is given fourteen years, although Eusebius gives only twelve (as he does to "Sabacôn").

68   Depuydt 2001: 33–34 (making the victim Shabataka, this paper having been written before reversal of the order of him and Shabaka).

69   Kawa stela V (Jansen-Winkeln 2007–14: III, 135–38[48.75]): l.14–15.

70   See Morkot 1999 and Broekman 2017a for overviews and discussions.

71   Cf. Dodson 2009.

72   For whom in general, see Dallibor 2005; Pope 2014.

73   Cf. Morkot 1999; 2000: 156.

74   Porter and Moss 1952: 209[5].

75   Nuri Nu36 (Dunham 1955: 19–24).

76   ElKurru Ku3 (Dunham 1950: 27–29).

77   Other children have been identified on the basis of assumptions concerning the antecedents of the later king Atlanersa: cf. Morkot 2000: 290–91.

78   Kawa stela V (Jansen-Winkeln 2007–14: III, 135–38[48.75]): l.16–21.

79   Alluding to Horus taking refuge in the marshes of Khemmis when threatened by Seth after the murder of Osiris.

80   Goedicke 1962: 27; it is recorded on a stela found six kilometers along the road (Jansen-Winkeln 2007–14: III, 59–61[48.12]).

81   Bell 1971; 1975; Hassan 1997; 2007.

82   Gabolde 2022.

83   Kawa stela V (Jansen-Winkeln 2007–14: III, 135–38[48.75]): l.11–13; the same basic account is also to be found on stelae from Koptos (Cairo JE48400) and Mataana (north of Esna; Cairo JE38269) and Tanis (fig. 122) (Jansen-Winkeln 2007–14: III, 61–63[48.13], 121–23[48.60], 54–55[48.1]).

84   Jansen-Winkeln 2007–14: III, 81–82[48.23–27]).

85   Boraik 2010; 2017; Boraik, Gabolde, and Graham 2017.

86   Bunbury, Graham, and Hunter 2008.

87   Lichtheim 1948.

88   Cairo CG42203 (Jansen-Winkeln 2007–14: III, 192[48.126]); the name of the prince's mother has been erased, but her title of King's Great Wife remains, suggesting that she may have been either Tekahatamun or Atakhebasken.

89   Leclant 1961; Perdu 2022b.

90   Russman 1997.

91   Jansen-Winkeln 2007–14: III, 395–96[52.102].

92   Jansen-Winkeln 2007–14: III, 366–97[52.103], 491–92[52.25556].

93   Jansen-Winkeln 2007–14: III, 55–56[48.3].

94   Jansen-Winkeln 2007–14: III, 54–55[48.1–2].

95   Jansen-Winkeln 2007–14: III, 58–59[48.8–10].

96   Cf. Spencer 1989: 70.

97   Florence 7655 (Russman 1974: 54[31]).

98   Brunet 2005: 29, quoting Ibrahim Ali 1991: 72–73, 315; this confirms the attribution of the anonymous Year 14 IM 2696 to Taharqa, rather than Shabaka (Jansen-Winkeln 2007–14: III, 29[46.73]).

99   Hourdin 2020.

100 Hourdin 2018: 255–63.

101 Cooney 2000; it appears to have served as the focus for rituals surrounding the king's solar rebirth.

102 Jansen-Winkeln 2007–14: III, 309–13[51.74].

103 Jansen-Winkeln 2007–14: III, 87–92[48.34]; on the phenomenon of the various Osiris chapels of the late Third Intermediate and Saite periods, see Coulon, Hallmann, and Payraudeau 2018.

104 Jansen-Winkeln 2007–14: III, 77[48.19, 20].

105 Jansen-Winkeln 2007–14: III, 77–80[48.21].

106 Fazzini and Bryan 2021: 25–44.

107 Fazzini and Bryan 2021: 45–53, 61–62.

108 Jansen-Winkeln 2007–14: III, 113–15[48.47–49].

109 Jansen-Winkeln 2007–14: III, 115–20[48.50–56].

110 Jansen-Winkeln 2007–14: III, 123–24[48.62–63].

111 Jansen-Winkeln 2007–14: III, 124–25[48.64].

112 Jansen-Winkeln 2007–14: III, 125–26[48.65].

113 Porter and Moss 1952: 149–50; Jansen-Winkeln 2007–14: III, 128[48.70].

114 To judge from some blocks of Taharqa re-used in a Meroitic pyramid there (Jansen-Winkeln 2007–14: III, 128–29[48.71]).

115 Jacquet-Gordon, C. Bonnet, and J. Jacquet 1969.

116 Kawa stela IV (Jansen-Winkeln 2007–14: III, 132–34[48.74], l.9–12).

117 Kawa stelae III [Ny Carlsberg ÆIN 1707] (Jansen-Winkeln 2007–14: III, 129–32[48.73]), VI (Jansen-Winkeln 2007–14: III, 138–41[48.76]), and VII [Ny Carlsberg ÆIN 1713] (Jansen-Winkeln 2007–14: III, 141–42[48.77]).

118 Porter and Moss 1952: 181–84.

119 Porter and Moss 1952: 184–91.

120 Jansen-Winkeln 2007–14: III, 162–79[48.91].

121 Jansen-Winkeln 2007–14: III, 181–82[48.97].

122 Jansen-Winkeln 2007–14: III, 173–80[48.96], 183[48.99].

123 Jansen-Winkeln 2007–14: III, 182–83[48.98].

124 BM EA48116 (Porter and Moss 1952: 396).

125 Babylonian Chronicle 1.iv.16 (Grayson 1975: 84).

126 Somewhere in the northeastern Delta; on Egyptian toponyms used by the Assyrians, see Verreth 1999.

127 Three battles are mentioned in the Babylonian Chronicle (Grayson 1975: 88).

128 Text BM K3082+S2027+K3086 and stela from Zenjirli (Berlin VA2708) (Leichty 2011: 185–86).

129 Cf. Yoyotte 1961.

130 Jansen-Winkeln 2007–14: III, 250[50.6–9].

131 But see Ryholt 2011.

132 Jansen-Winkeln 2007–14: III, 254–55[50.14–16]; the identity of this individual has been much debated; cf. Kahn 2006.

133 Cf. Kitchen 1996: 392 n. 874.

134 Rassam Cylinder (Novotny and Jeffers 2018–23: 233–34 (11.i 110–17).

135 Jansen-Winkeln 2007–14: III, 197–203[48.142].

136 Cf. Depuydt 2006.

137   Louvre IM2640; other stelae from the burial only give the bare year (Porter and Moss 1974–81: 791; Rondot 2022: 202[91]).

138   Louvre IM3733 (Porter and Moss 1974–81: 791–92; Rondot 2022: 203[92]).

139   Rassam Cylinder (Novotny and Jeffers 2018–23: 234[11.i 118–30, ii 5–7]).

140   Nubian Museum stela ex-JE48863 (Jansen-Winkeln 2007–14: III, 236–40 [49.8]); all further quotations in this chapter are from this text, unless otherwise stated.

141   Herodotus II, 52.

142   Versions of the text differ.

143   Location unknown.

144   Three statues of Taharqa found at Nineveh (Vikentiev 1955) were probably among this booty.

145   Rassam Cylnder (Novotny and Jeffers 2018–23: 235–36[11.ii 22–48]).

146   *Strategemata* VII, 3.

147   Jansen-Winkeln 2007–14: III, 229–34 [49.1]; full publication is being prepared by a team led by Essam Nagy.

148   There is no substantive evidence for any kind of coregency between the kings.

149   Blocks Berlin ÄM2096, 2097, and in situ (Jansen-Winkeln 2007–14: III, 245–48[49.22–25]).

150   Cairo JE37888 (Jansen-Winkeln 2007–14: III, 248[49.26]).

151   Cairo CG48603=JE37346 (Jansen-Winkeln 2007–14: III, 248–49[49.27]).

152   Head of a statue of Amun (Ashmolean AM 1922.157 (Jansen-Winkeln 2007–14: III, 240[49.9]).

153   Statues now in Kerma Museum (Jansen-Winkeln 2007–14: III, 235[49.5]).

154   Statues Toledo 49.105 and SNM 1846 (Jansen-Winkeln 2007–14: III, 235–40[49.6–7]).

155   Kendall and Mohamed 2016: 51.

Notes to Chapter 4

1   See Forshaw 2019: 58–62.

2   Cairo JE36327 (Jansen-Winkeln 2007–14: IV, 1619[53.28]). Translation and glosses generally based upon Caminos 1964.

3   For these and other options, see Dodson 2002.

4   Jansen-Winkeln 2007–14: IV, 24[53.35c].

5   See Kahn 2007 for various ideas about the transition from Nubian to Saite rule.

6   For an overview of foreign policy during the early Twenty-sixth Dynasty see Forshaw 2019: 75–92.

7   Jansen-Winkeln 2007–14: IV, 279[54.35].

8   Cf. Leahy 2022.

9   Found at Tanis (Cairo JE67095), Karnak, and Shellal (Jansen-Winkeln 2007–14: IV, 303–304[55.20], 313–14[55.47], 318–19[55.63]).

10   From Tanis.

11   Schmitz 2010.

12   Eide et al. 1994–2000: 286–89[42].

13   Pernigotti 1968.

14   For comparisons, see Gozzoli 1995.

15   Żurawski 2018.

16   Kendall 1991: 308.

17   Valbelle and Bonnet 2019.

18   Porter and Moss 1952: 221.

19   Anderson and Ahmed 2009; cf. Valbelle and Bonnet 2019.

20   For a discussion of the issue see Koch 2014: 400 n. 15.

21   Koch 2014: 402–404; cf. Jansen-Winkeln 2016.

22   Koch 2014: 401–402.

23   Koch 2017.

24   pBerlin P13615 (Erichsen 1942).

25   Jansen-Winkeln 2007–14: III, 82[28].

26   Ryholt 2004.

27   Ryholt 2022.

28   For an overview, see Zibelius-Chen 2006.

29 Cairo JE48866 (Porter and Moss 1952: 217; Grimal 1981: 21–35; Eide et al. 1994–2000: 232–52[37]).
30 For a discussion, see Vrtal 2015.
31 For an overview, see Welsby 1996: 196–205.

Notes to Chapter 5

1 Dunham 1950: 46–47.
2 Porter and Moss 1952: 197; Dunham 1950: 64–66; Lull 2002: 182–83.
3 From the late Twentieth Dynasty, the internal organs had been returned to the body after separate mummifications, meaning that canopic jars were obsolete. However, they had now become such an integral part of the burial outfit that many interments included empty jars, with solid dummies introduced during the Third Intermediate Period.
4 Although partly adopted in Egypt, e.g., the placement of the coffins of Tutankhamun on a bed within his sarcophagus.
5 Dunham 1950: 110–17; Näser and Mazzetti 2020; Doxey 2022.
6 Porter and Moss 1952: 197; Dunham 1950: 67–71; Lull 2002: 183–85.
7 Now Cambridge MA, Peabody Museum, 41-66-50/N3904.0 (Dunham 1950: 118).
8 Porter and Moss 1952: 196; Dunham 1950: 55–59; Lull 2002: 183.
9 For a discussion of this, and other issues concerning the burial of Taharqa, see Kendall 2008.
10 Porter and Moss 1952: 223; Dunham 1955: 7–16; Lull 2002: 185–93. There were once suggestions that Taharqa had possessed a second pyramid (W T 1) at Sedeinga, nearly 350 kilometers away to the north, in which he had actually been buried. However, it has now become clear that the inscribed blocks upon which this attribution was based had been reused: see Leclant 1984; Lull 2002: 193–96.
11 Frankfort 1933.
12 For which see Morfini and Álvarez Sosa 2021; on possible influences on the construction of Taharqa's pyramid, see Traunecker 2022: 236–39.
13 Dodson 1994: 100–101.
14 See Haynes and Leprohon 1987: 23–27.
15 Porter and Moss 1952: 196; Dunham 1950: 60–63; Gasm el Seed 1985; Lull 2002: 196–97.
16 Porter and Moss 1952: 195–97; Dunham 1950: 27–43, 81–90.
17 Dunham 1955: 19–24.
18 Dunham 1955: 25–28.
19 Dunham 1963.
20 Dunham 1963: 366–73.
21 Leahy 1994; 2014.
22 Jansen-Winkeln 2007–14: II, 360[29].
23 Jansen-Winkeln 2007–14: III, 351[10].
24 Jansen-Winkeln 2007–14: III, 352[12].
25 Jansen-Winkeln 2007–14: III, 409–10[136].
26 Leahy 2014: 62–70.
27 Jansen-Winkeln 2007–14: III, 351–52[11].
28 Porter and Moss 1960–64: 772–73; 1972: 476–80; Aston 2009: 263–64.
29 Jansen-Winkeln 2007–14: III, 264–76[48.18].
30 Although such a crypt remained a feature of the chapel of the later Neitiqerti I, it seems not to have been for her burial, as she adopted a stone sarcophagus too large to fit into her crypt. This sarcophagus was placed in a shaft a kilometer to the north, behind Deir el-Medina, as was the case with the sarcophagus of her successor, Ankhnesneferibre (Koch 2017). The crypt under the chapel may have been used as an embalming cache, as had been the case with Amenirdis I's original crypt.
31 Dunham 1955.
32 Dunham 1957: 22–23.
33 Dunham 1957.
34 Dunham 1952.
35 Emery 1938; 1948; Trigger 1969.

Notes to Chapter 6

1   Herodotus II: 137–41, 151.
2   Cf. Aubin 2002: 118–19.
3   See Waddell 1940.
4   Broekman 2015: 20–21.
5   Diodorus I, 65–66.

Notes to Chapter 7

1   Perizonius 1736: 164–96.
2   Perizonius 1736: 188–93.
3   Cf. Hoskins 1835: 360 n. *.
4   Waddington and Hanbury 1822: 170–71.
5   Waddington and Hanbury 1822: 182–83.
6   Wilkinson 1828: 98–99.
7   Wilkinson 1828 and 1830: pl. iii, top left.
8   Wilkinson 1830: 18.
9   Wilkinson 1828 and 1830: pl. iii, top left.
10   Salt 1825: 28–29, pl. iv[24].
11   Felix 1830.
12   Wilkinson 1828: 112.
13   Wilkinson 1835: 515.
14   Wilkinson 1837: 138–40.
15   Sharpe 1876: 141.
16   Lane 2000: 551–52.
17   Rosellini 1833: II, 107–109, 122, 262.
18   Hoskins 1835: 297.
19   Bunsen 1845: 137.
20   Lepsius 1897–1913: V, 256–74.
21   Lepsius 1858: 87–88, pl. xlvii[629, 630].
22   Lepsius 1858: pls. xlvi–xlvii[616–19].
23   Lepsius 1858: pls. lxxi–lxiii[922–87].
24   Berlin ÄM2097 (Jansen-Winkeln 2007–14: III, 246[49.23]).
25   Lepsius 1858: pl. lxviii[768].
26   Lepsius 1858: table 8.
27   Brugsch 1859: 246.
28   Quirke 1995: 17.
29   Waddington and Hanbury 1822; Cailliaud 1826–27.
30   Waddington and Hanbury 1822: 167–69.
31   Waddington and Hanbury 1822: 171–78.
32   Waddington and Hanbury 1822: 176–77.
33   Ruffle 1998.
34   Hoskins 1835.
35   Hoskins 1835: 302–303.
36   Hoskins 1835: 140.
37   Hoskins 1835: 158.
38   Prisse d'Avennes 1847: pls. xxxi–iv.
39   Mariette 1856: 75–77.
40   Ikram and Omar 2021: 25–29.
41   Reisner 1921a: 59–61.
42   Rougé 1863.
43   Mariette 1865.
44   Mariette 1865: 168–69.
45   With an English edition in 1879.
46   Birch 1875: 159–73; Brugsch 1879: 225–73.
47   Birch 1875: 162–63.
48   Hincks 1866: 2–3.
49   Haigh 1868: 81–82.
50   Smith 1868.
51   Haigh 1869.
52   Haigh 1871: 113 n. 1.
53   Brugsch 1879: 268–69.
54   Brugsch 1879: 225–27.
55   For an overview of the development of thinking regarding the origins of the Kushite rulers, see Morkot 2003.
56   Contrasting with earlier views: see Aubin 2002: 235–50.
57   Aubin 2002: 250–65.
58   For which see Aubin 2002: 226–34.
59   Kitchen 1995: 117; for a selection of other examples of gratuitous negativity regarding the Kushites, see Aubin 2002: 227.
60   Cairo JE37488 (Jansen-Winkeln 2007–14: III, 54–55[48.1]).
61   Rougé 1873.
62   Wiedemann 1884–88: II, 590.
63   Wiedemann 1884–88: II, 581–82.
64   Rougé 1873: 12 n. 4.
65   Wiedemann 1884–88: II, 588; this relationship had first been set out in Lieblein 1873: 6–11.

66 And Menkheperre as a King [Remen]y (Maspero 1889: 761–62).

67 Maspero 1889: 751.

68 Turin C.1467.

69 Morkot and Quirke 2001; the Turin museum authorities had already been suspicious of the piece.

70 Maspero 1900: 360–61.

71 Petrie 1905: 296–97.

72 Petrie 1905: 267–68, 278–79, 290–91.

73 Breasted 1905–1906: IV, 481[941].

74 Breasted 1905: 537–61.

75 Erman 1897.

76 https://www.ifao.egnet.net/bases/cachette/.

77 Török 1997a.

78 Griffith 1922.

79 Reisner 1917: 34; on Reisner's work in Nubia, see Manuelian 2022: passim.

80 Owing to the direction of the Nile at Nuri, the conventional equation of north with downstream was reversed at the site. However, Reisner continued to use this convention, but indicated its artificiality by the use of quotation marks.

81 Reisner 1918: 70–72.

82 Reisner 1921b: 21–22.

83 Kendall 1991: 302.

84 Based on the finding of fragments of a vase bearing the prince's name in tomb Nu38 at Nuri (Jansen-Winkeln 2007–14: II, 209[23.9]).

85 Reisner 1921b: 31.

86 Reisner 1919: 43.

87 Reisner 1919: 52.

88 Reisner 1919: 57–58.

89 Reisner 1921b: 33–35.

90 Hall 1925a: 268–69; 1925b: 270–86.

91 Hall 1925a: 269.

92 For a brief history of the excavations see Macadam 1949–55: II, v–vi; for a summary of all the stelae found, see Rondot 2022: 132–37.

93 Listed in Macadam 1949–55: II, xxi.

94 Griffith 1935–38; the paper mistakenly calls the stela "Kawa IX."

95 A collated transcription of which was appended to Griffith's paper (Kuentz 1935–38).

96 Macadam 1949–55: I, 78.

97 Zibelius-Chen 2006: 295–96.

98 Morkot 2000: 145–46, although the likelihood that ⌐Qa⌐tiaa⌐t⌐ should be placed "possibly as early as the Twenty-first Dynasty" had already been raised in Goedicke 1972.

99 Macadam 1949–55: I, 119–31.

100 Dunham and Macadam 1949.

101 For a detailed critique, and wider discussion of Kushite royal succession, see Morkot 1999.

102 Macadam 1949–55: I, 124–25.

103 Macadam 1949–55: I, 120.

104 Robins 1983.

105 Macadam 1949–55: I, 18–20.

106 Kitchen 1996: 165–71.

107 Leclant 1965.

108 Valbelle and Bonnet 2019; Valbelle and Rondot 2022.

109 Jacquet-Gordon, Bonnet, and Jacquet 1969.

110 For an overview of which, see Derricourt 2015: 149–70.

111 Van Sertima 1976: 134.

112 He also writes of "Miamum Nut (who fought with Tafnak's [sic] son, Bocchoris)," following late nineteenth-century thinking.

113 Van Sertima 1976: 135–36.

114 Van Sertima 1976: 139–40 et seqq; for a detailed critique of his Mesoamerican theories, see Haslip-Viera, Ortiz de Montellano, and Barbour 1997.

115 Morkot 2000.

116 Morkot 1999.

117 Morkot 1999: 208.

118 Morkot 1999: 207.

119 Aubin 2002.

120   Bellis 2020.

121   E.g., Murnane 1977: 189–90.

122   E.g., Redford 1999.

123   As argued by Kitchen 2009: 163–64.

124   Aubin 2002: 74–75, 323 n. 87.

125   Cf. Jansen-Winkeln 2006: 258–59, *pace* Kitchen's protestations to the contrary (2009: 163–64).

126   Indeed, although proposed for various pairings of kings in modern histories of ancient Egypt, most alleged cases of coregency turn out to ultimately be means of resolving apparent chronological conundra of the kind presented by the Tang-i Var text, rather than contemporary data left behind by the putative co-rulers (e.g., any double-dating of texts, or representations of the protagonists acting together—rather than simply appearing separately on a wall or other monument).

During the period leading up to Kushite rule, the only known true co-regency (i.e., an anticipatory generational transition, not a case of kings of rival lines ruling in parallel, as was a feature of much of the Third Intermediate Period) is that between Osorkon III and Takelot III. This is attested by an unequivocal father–son double-date (the only such double-date since the Middle Kingdom!). In contextualizing this, one should note that at the time of this unique double-date, Osorkon III was in extreme old age, the coregency having been instituted after Osorkon had held senior positions for some six and a half decades. It was thus probably a "non-standard" arrangement driven by the practical circumstance of the elder king's senility, rather than supporting the idea that coregency was in any way a "normal" matter during this period.

Based on the foregoing, there should be a prima facie assumption *against* assuming the existence of a coregency in the absence of representations of rulers acting together or unequivocal double-dates, no matter how tempting the chronological and other drivers might seem. Given that this alleged coregency of Shabaka and Shabataka was only ever posited to "save" broader chronological assumptions, in the wake of the "Tang-i Var conundrum," it is methodologically unsound to make it the key underpinning of a working hypothesis for the eighth/seventh-century transition. For a detailed discussion of the issues surrounding coregency, see Dodson 2014.

127   Depuydt 1994; Brunet 2005.

128   Broekman 2015: 25; Jurman 2017: 139–45.

129   Bányai 2013.

130   Cf. Broekman 2015: 17.

131   Payraudeau 2014; Bányai 2015; Broekman 2015; 2017a; 2017b; Jurman 2017.

132   Although some skeptics remain (e.g., Morkot 2021: 47).

BIBLIOGRAPHY

Abbreviations for Periodicals

AJA   *American Journal of Archaeology* (Boston)

AncEg   *Ancient Egypt Magazine* (Manchester)

BIFAO   *Bulletin de l'Institut français d'Archéologie orientale du Caire* (Cairo)

BMFA   *Bulletin of the Museum of Fine Arts* (Boston)

BSFE   *Bulletin de la Société française d'Egyptologie* (Paris)

CdE   *Chronique d'Egypte* (Brussels)

CRAIBL   *Comptes rendus des séances de l'Académie des Inscriptions et Belles-Lettres* (Paris)

EgArch   *Egyptian Archaeology: Bulletin of the Egypt Exploration Society* (London)

GM   *Göttinger Miszellen* (Göttingen)

JACF   *Journal of the Ancient Chronology Forum* (Redhill)

JAOS   *Journal of the American Oriental Society* (New Haven, CT)

JARCE   *Journal of the American Research Center in Egypt* (New York/ Washington, DC)

JEA   *Journal of Egyptian Archaeology* (London)

JEH   *Journal of Egyptian History* (Leiden)

JNES   *Journal of Near Eastern Studies* (Chicago)

JSSEA   *Journal of the Society for the Study of Egyptian Antiquities* (Toronto)

LAAA   *Liverpool Annals of Archaeology and Anthropology* (Liverpool)

MDAIK   *Mitteilungen des Deutschen Archäologischen Instituts, Kairo* (Mainz/Berlin)

PSBA   *Proceedings of the Society for Biblical Archaeology* (London)

RdE   *Revue d'Égyptologie* (Louvain)

RevArch   *Revue Archéologique* (Paris)

S&N   *Sudan and Nubia* (London)

SN&R   *Sudan Notes and Records* (Khartoum)

ZÄS   *Zeitschrift für Ägyptische Sprache und Altertumskunde* (Leipzig/Berlin)

Works Cited

Anderson, J.R., and S. eldin M. Ahmed. 2009. "What Are These Doing Here Above the Fifth Cataract?!! Napata Royal Statues at Dangeil." *S&N* 13: 78–86.

Aston, D.A. 2009. *Burial Assemblages of Dynasty 21–25: Chronology—Typology—Developments.* Vienna: Verlag der Österreichischen Akademie der Wissenschaften.

Aubin, H.T. 2002. *The Rescue of Jerusalem: The Alliance between Hebrews and Africans in 701 BC.* New York: Soho.

Bányai, M. 2013. "Ein Vorschlag zur Chronologie der 25. Dynastie in Ägypten." *JEH* 6: 46–129.

———. 2015. "Die Reihenfolge der kuschitischen Könige." *JEH* 8: 115–80.

Bell, B. 1971. "The Dark Ages in Ancient History, I: The First Dark Age in Egypt." *AJA* 75: 1–26.

———. 1975. "Climate and the History of Egypt: The Middle Kingdom." *AJA* 79: 223–69.

Bellis, A.O., ed. 2020. *Jerusalem's Survival, Sennacherib's Departure, and the Kushite Role in 701 BCE: An Examination of Henry Aubin's Rescue of Jerusalem.* Piscataway, NJ: Gorgias Press.

Benson, M., and J. Gourlay. 1899. *The Temple of Mut in Asher.* London: John Murray.

Bierbrier, M.L., ed. 2019. *Who Was Who in Egyptology.* 5th ed. London: Egypt Exploration Society.

Birch, S. 1875. *Egypt from the Earliest Times to B.C. 300.* New York: Scribner, Armstrong and Co.

Bonnet, C. 2000. *Édifices et rites funéraires à Kerma.* Paris: Éditions Errance.

———. 2014. *La ville de Kerma: une capitale nubienne au sud de l'Egypte.* Paris: Favre.

Bonnet, C., and D. Valbelle. 2018. *Les temples égyptiens de Panébès "Le jujubier": à Doukki Gel—Soudan.* Paris: Khéops.

Bonnet, C., D. Valbelle, and S. Marchi. 2020. *Le jujubier: Ville sacrée des pharaons noirs.* Paris: Khéops.

Boraik, M. 2010. "Excavations of the Quays and the Embankment in Front of Karnak Temples: Preliminary Report." *Cahiers de Karnak* 13: 65–78.

———. 2017. "Karnak's Quaysides: The Embankments from the New Kingdom to the Kushito-Saite Period." In *Tombs of the South Asasif Necropolis: New Discoveries and Research 2012–14*, edited by E. Pischikova, 7–21. Cairo: American University in Cairo Press.

Boraik, M., L. Gabolde, and A. Graham. 2017. "Karnak's Quaysides: Evolution of the Embankments from the Eighteenth Dynasty to the Graeco-Roman Period." In *The Nile: Natural and Cultural Landscape in Egypt*, edited by H. Willems and J.-M. Dahms, 97–144. Bielefeld: transcript.

Botta, P.E., and E. Flandin. 1849–50. *Monument de Ninive.* Paris: Imprimerie nationale.

Breasted, J.H. 1905. *A History of Egypt: From the Earliest Times to the Persian Conquest.* New York: Charles Scribner's Sons.

———. 1905–1906. *Ancient Records of Egypt: Historical Documents from the Earliest Times to the Persian Conquest.* 5 vols. Chicago: University of Chicago Press.

Broekman, G.P.F. 2009. "Takeloth III and the End of the 23rd Dynasty." In *The Libyan Period in Egypt: Historical and Cultural Studies into the 21st–24th Dynasties. Proceedings of a Conference at Leiden University, 25–27 October 2007*, edited by G.P.F. Broekman, R.J. Demarée, and O.E. Kaper, 91–101. Leiden: Nederlands Instituut voor het Nabije Oosten; Louvain: Peeters.

———. 2015. "The Order of Succession between Shabaka and Shabataka: A Different View on the Chronology of the Twenty-fifth Dynasty." *GM* 245: 17–31.

———. 2017a. "Genealogical Considerations Regarding the Kings of the Twenty-fifth Dynasty in Egypt." *GM* 251: 13–20.

———. 2017b. "Some Consequences of the Reversion of the Order Shabaka–Shabataka." *GM* 253: 25–32.

Broekman, G.P.F., R.J. Demarée, and O.E. Kaper, eds. 2009. *The Libyan Period in Egypt: Historical and Cultural Studies into the 21st–24th Dynasties. Proceedings of a Conference at Leiden University, 25–27 October 2007.* Leiden: Nederlands Instituut voor het Nabije Oosten; Louvain: Peeters.

Brugsch, H. 1859. *Histoire d'Égypte dès les premiers temps de son existence jusqu'à nos jours.* Leipzig: Hinrichs.

———. 1877. *Geschichte Ägyptens unter den Pharaonen.* Leipzig: Hinrichs.

———. 1879. *A History of Egypt under the Pharaohs, Derived Entirely from the Monuments.* Translated by H.D. Seymour. Edited by P. Smith. London: John Murray.

Brunet, J.F. 2005. "The XXIInd and XXVth Dynasties Apis Bull Conundrum." *JACF* 10: 26–34.

Bunbury, J.M., A. Graham, and M.A. Hunter. 2008. "Stratigraphic Landscape Analysis: Charting the Holocene Movements of the Nile at Karnak through Ancient Egyptian Time." *Geoarchaeology* 23: 351–73.

Bunsen, C.C.J. von. 1845. *Aegyptens Stelle in der Weltgeschichte.* Vol. 3, *Das mittlere und neue Reich.* Hamburg: Friedrich Perthes.

Cailliaud, F. 1826–27. *Voyage à Méroé, au Fleuve Blanc, au-delà de Fâzoql, dans le midi du royaume de Sennâr, à Syouah et dans cinq autres oasis: fait dans les années 1819, 1820, 1821 et 1822.* 4 vols. Paris: Imprimerie Royale.

Caminos, R.A. 1964. "The Nitocris Adoption Stela." *JEA* 50: 71–101.

———. 1998. *Semna–Kumma.* 2 vols. London: Egypt Exploration Society.

Cline, E. 2021. *1177 B.C.: The Year Civilization Collapsed.* Updated ed. Princeton: Princeton University Press.

Cooney, K.M. 2000. "The Edifice of Taharqa by the Sacred Lake: Ritual Function and the Role of the King." *JARCE* 37: 15–47.

Coulon, L. 2022. "Chépénoupet, fille de Piânkhy, Divine Adoratrice d'Amon." In *Pharaon des Deux Terres: l'épopée africaine des rois de Napata*, edited by V. Rondot, 223–25. Paris: Louvre éditions/éditions El Viso.

Coulon, L., A. Hallmann, and F. Payraudeau. 2018. "The Osirian Chapels at Karnak: An Historical and Art Historical Overview Based on Recent Fieldwork and Studies." In *Thebes in the First Millennium BC: Art and Archaeology of the Kushite Period and Beyond*, edited by E. Pischikova, J. Budka, and K. Griffin, 271–93. London: Golden House Publications.

Dallibor, K. 2005. *Taharqo, Pharao aus Kusch: ein Beitrag zur Geschichte und Kultur der 25. Dynastie.* Berlin: Achet.

Darnell, J.C. 2006. *The Inscription of Katimala at Semna: Textual Evidence for the Origins of the Napatan State.* New Haven: Yale Egyptological Seminar.

Davies, W.V. 2001. "Kurgus 2000: The Egyptian Inscriptions." *S&N* 5: 46–58.

———. 2003a. "Kush in Egypt: A New Historical Inscription." *S&N* 7: 52–54.

———. 2003b. "Sobeknakht of Elkab and the Coming of Kush." *EgArch* 23: 3–6.

Depuydt, L. 1994. "Apis Burials in the Twenty-fifth Dynasty." *GM* 138: 23–25.

———. 2001. "Glosses to Jerome's Eusebios as a Source for Pharaonic History." *CdE* 76/152: 30–47.

———. 2006. "Foundations of Day-exact Chronology, 690 BC–332 BC." In *Ancient Egyptian Chronology*, edited by E. Hornung, R. Krauss, and D.A. Warburton, 458–69. Leiden: Brill.

Derricourt, R. 2015. *Antiquity Imagined: The Remarkable Legacy of Egypt and the Ancient Near East.* London: I.B. Tauris.

Dodson, A. 1990. "Crown Prince Djhutmose and the Royal Sons of the Eighteenth Dynasty." *JEA* 76: 87–96.

———. 1994. *The Canopic Equipment of the Kings of Egypt.* London: Kegan Paul International.

———. 1997. "Messuy, Amada and Amenmesse." *JARCE* 34: 41–48.

———. 2002. "The Problem of Amenirdis II and the Heirs to the Office of God's Wife of Amun during the Twenty-sixth Dynasty." *JEA* 88: 179–86.

———. 2009. "On the Alleged 'Amenhotep III/IV Coregency' Graffito at Meidum." *GM* 222: 25–28.

———. 2014. "The Coregency Conundrum." *Kmt* 25/2: 28–35.

———. 2019. *Afterglow of Empire: Egypt from the Fall of the New Kingdom to the Saite Renaissance.* 2nd ed. Cairo: American University in Cairo Press.

———. 2021. *The First Pharaohs: Their Lives and Afterlives.* Cairo: American University in Cairo Press.

Dodson, A., and S. Ikram. 2008. *The Tomb in Ancient Egypt: Royal and Private Sepulchres from the Early Dynastic Period to the Romans.* London: Thames & Hudson.

Doxey, D. 2022. "Les chevaux de Kouch." In *Pharaon des Deux Terres: l'épopée africaine des rois de Napata*, edited by V. Rondot, 376–77. Paris: Musée éditions/El Viso.

Dunham, D. 1950. *The Royal Cemeteries of Kush.* Vol. 1, *El Kurru.* Cambridge, MA: Harvard University Press.

———. 1952. *The Royal Cemeteries of Kush.* Vol. 3, *Decorated Chapels at the Meroitic Pyramids at Meroë and Barkal.* Boston: Museum of Fine Arts.

———. 1955. *The Royal Cemeteries of Kush.* Vol. 2, *Nuri.* Boston: Museum of Fine Arts.

———. 1957. *The Royal Cemeteries of Kush.* Vol. 4, *Royal Tombs at Meroë and Barkal.* Boston: Museum of Fine Arts.

———. 1963. *The Royal Cemeteries of Kush.* Vol. 5, *The West and South Cemeteries at Meroë.* Boston: Museum of Fine Arts.

———. 1970. *The Barkal Temples.* Boston: Museum of Fine Arts.

Dunham, D., and M.F.L. Macadam. 1949. "Names and Relationships of the Royal Family of Napata." *JEA* 35: 139–49.

Eide, T., T. Hägg, R. Holton Pierce, and L. Török, eds. 1994–2000. *Fontes Historiae Nubiorum: Textual Sources for the History of the Middle Nile Region between the Eighth Century BC and the Sixth Century AD.* 4 vols. Bergen: Klassisk institutt, Universitetet i Bergen.

Eigner, D. 1984. *Die monumentalen Grabbauten der Spätzeit in der thebanischen Nekropole.* Vienna: Verlag der Österreichischen Akademie der Wissenschaften.

Einaudi, S. 2014. "Between South and North Asasif: The Tomb of Harwa (TT 37) as a 'Transitional Monument.'" In *Thebes in the First Millennium BC*, edited by E. Pischikova, J. Budka, and K. Griffin, 323–41. Newcastle upon Tyne: Cambridge Scholars Publishing.

Emery, W.B. 1938. *The Royal Tombs of Ballana and Qustul.* 2 vols. Cairo: Government Press.

———. 1948. *Nubian Treasure: An Account of the Discoveries at Ballana and Qustul.* London: Methuen.

Erichsen, W. 1942. "Erwähnung eines Zuges nach Nubien unter Amasis in einem demotischen Text." *Klio: Beiträge zur alten Geschichte* 34: 56–61.

Erman, A. 1897. "Zu den Legrain'schen Inschriften." *ZÄS* 35: 19–29.

Farrulla, S. 2013. "The Enemy Within: Internecine Conflict in the Second Kingdom of Kush." BA Honors thesis, College of William and Mary. https://scholarworks.wm.edu/honorstheses/771/

Fazzini, R.A., and B.M. Bryan. 2021. *The Precinct of Mut at South Karnak: An Archaeological Guide.* Cairo: American University in Cairo Press.

Felix, O. 1830. *Notes on Hieroglyphics*. Cairo: n.p.

Forshaw, R. 2019. *Egypt of the Saite Pharaohs 664–525 bc*. Manchester: Manchester University Press.

Foucart, G. 1924. "Études thébaines: la belle fête de la vallée." *BIFAO* 24: 1–209.

Frame, G. 1999. "The Inscription of Sargon II at Tangi Var." *Orientalia* 68: 31–57.

———. 2021. *The Royal Inscriptions of Sargon II, King of Assyria (721–705 bc)*. Winona Lake, IN: Eisenbrauns.

Frankfort, H. 1933. *The Cenotaph of Seti I at Abydos*. 2 vols. London: Egypt Exploration Society.

Gabolde, L. 2022. "Taharqa, Amon et les merveilles de la cure du Nil en l'an 6 du règne." In *Pharaon des Deux Terres: l'épopée africaine des rois de Napata*, edited by V. Rondot, 246–49. Paris: Louvre éditions/éditions El Viso.

Gasm El Seed, A.A. 1985. "La tombe de Tanoutamon à El Kurru (Ku. 16)." *RdÉ* 36: 67–72.

Gill, D., and M. Vickers. 1996. "Bocchoris the Wise and Absolute Chronology." *Römische Mitteilungen* 103: 1–9.

Goedicke, H. 1962. "Psammetik I. und die Libyer." *MDAIK* 18: 26–49.

———. 1972. Review of Dunham 1970. *AJA* 76: 89.

Gombert-Meurice, F. 2022. "*Chepsesrê* Tefnakht, fondateur de la 26e dynastie." In *Pharaon des Deux Terres: l'épopée africaine des rois de Napata*, edited by V. Rondot, 252–53. Paris: Louvre éditions/éditions El Viso.

Gozzoli, R.B. 1995. "The Nubian War Texts of Psammetichus II: An Essay of Explication." *JSSEA* 25: 46–49.

Grayson, A.K. 1975. *Assyrian and Babylonian Chronicles*. Locust Valley, NY: J.J. Augustin.

Grayson, A.K., and J. Novotny. 2012–14. *The Royal Inscriptions of Sennacherib, King of Assyria (704–681 bc)*. 2 vols. Winona Lake, IN: Eisenbrauns.

Griffith, F.Ll. 1922. "Oxford Excavations in Nubia." *LAAA* 9: 67–124.

———. 1935–38. "A Stela of Tirhaqa from Kawa, Dongola Province, Sudan." *Mélanges Maspero*, 1: *Orient ancien* 2: 423–30. Cairo: Institut français d'archéologie orientale.

Grimal, N.-C. 1981. *Quatre stèles napatéennes au Musée du Caire, JE 48863–48866: textes et indices*. Cairo: Institut français d'archéologie orientale.

Habachi, L. 1959. "The First Two Viceroys of Kush and Their Family." *Kush* 7: 45–62.

Hafsaas, H. 2021. "The C-Group People in Lower Nubia: Cattle Pastoralists on the Frontier between Egypt and Kush." In *The Oxford Handbook of Ancient Nubia*, edited by G. Emberling and B.B. Williams, 157–77. Oxford: Oxford University Press.

Haigh, D.H. 1868. "To the Editor." *ZÄS* 6: 80–83.

———. 1869. "Assyrica." *ZÄS* 7: 3–5.

———. 1871. "Assyrio-Aegyptiaca." *ZÄS* 9: 112–17.

Hakem, A.M.A. 1988. *Meroitic Architecture: A Background of an African Civilisation*. Khartoum: Khartoum University Press.

Hall, H.R. 1925a. "The Eclipse of Egypt." In *The Cambridge Ancient History*, vol. 3: *The Assyrian Empire*, edited by J.B. Bury, S.A. Cook, and F.E. Adcock, 251–69. Cambridge: Cambridge University Press.

———. 1925b. "The Ethiopians and Assyrians in Egypt." In *The Cambridge Ancient History*, vol. 3: *The Assyrian Empire*, edited by J.B. Bury, S.A. Cook, and F.E. Adcock, 270–88. Cambridge: Cambridge University Press.

Haslip-Viera, G., B. Ortiz de Montellano, and W. Barbour. 1997. "Robbing Native American Cultures: Van Sertima's Afrocentricity and the Olmecs." *Current Anthropology* 38: 419–41.

Hassan, F.A. 1997. "Nile Floods and Political Disorder in Early Egypt." In *Third Millennium bc Climate Change and Old World Collapse*, edited by H.N. Dalfes, G. Kukla, and H. Weiss, 1–23. Heidelberg: Springer.

———. 2007. "Droughts, Famine and the Collapse of the Old Kingdom: Re-reading Ipuwer." In *The Archaeology and Art of Ancient Egypt: Essays in Honor of David B. O'Connor*, edited by Z.A. Hawass and J.E. Richards, I, 357–77. Cairo: Conseil Suprême des Antiquités de l'Egypte.

Haynes, J.L., and R.J. Leprohon. 1987. "Napatan Shawabtis in the Royal Ontario Museum." *JSSEA* 17: 18–32.

Hincks, E. 1866. "The Assyrian Sacking of Thebes." *ZÄS* 4: 1–3.

Hölbl, G. 1981. "Die Aegyptiaca des griech-ischen, italienischen und westphönikischen Raumes aus der Zeit des Pharao Bocchoris (718/17–712 v. Chr.)." *Grazer Beiträge* 10: 1–20.

Horton, M. 1991. "Africa in Egypt: New Evidence from Qasr Ibrim." In *Egypt and Africa: Nubia from Prehistory to Islam*, edited by W.V. Davies, 264–77. London: British Museum Press.

Hoskins, G.A. 1835. *Travels in Ethiopia, above the Second Cataract of the Nile: Exhibiting the State of That Country, and Its Various Inhabitants, under the Dominion of Mohammed Ali, and Illustrating the Antiquities, Arts, and History of the Ancient Kingdom of Meroe*. London: Longman, Rees, Orme, Brown, Green & Longman.

Hourdin, J. 2013–15. "Chabataka à Edfou." *Cahiers de Recherches de l'Institut de Papyrologie et d'Égyptologie de Lille* 30: 191–200.

———. 2018. "The Kushite Kiosks of Karnak and Luxor: A Cross-over Study." In *Thebes in the First Millennium* BC: *Art and Archaeology of the Kushite Period and Beyond*, edited by E. Pischikova, J. Budka, and K. Griffin, 255–70. London: Golden House Publications.

———. 2020. "Study of Kushite Architectural Programmes: Taharqa's Columned Porches at Thebes." In *Ancient Egypt 2017: Perspectives of Research*, edited by M.H.T. Lopes, J. Popielska-Grzybowska, J. Iwaszczuk, and R.G. Gurgel Pereira, 77–84. Warsaw: Institute of Mediterranean and Oriental Cultures, Polish Academy of Sciences; Wiesbaden: Harrassowitz.

Howley, K., and P.P. Creasman. 2021. "The Twenty-fifth Dynasty Theban Mortuary Temple of the Vizier Nebneteru, reused by Khonsuirdis and Others." *JEA* 107: 105–14.

Ibrahim Ali, M. 1991. "Les petits souterrains du Sérapéum de Memphis, étude d'archéologie, religion et histoire—Textes inédits." PhD diss., Lyon.

Ibrahim Ali, M., and D. Devauchelle. 2022. "La mort du taureau en l'an 24 de Taharqa: les stèles du Sérapéum de Memphis et la fabri-que de l'Histoire." In *Pharaon des Deux Terres: l'épopée africaine des rois de Napata*, edited by V. Rondot, 188–89. Paris: Louvre éditions/ éditions El Viso.

Ikram, S., and A. Omar. 2021. "Egypt." In *A History of World Egyptology*, edited by A. Bednarski, S. Ikram, and A. Dodson, 25–67. Cambridge: Cambridge University Press.

Jacquet-Gordon, C. Bonnet, and J. Jacquet. 1969. "Pnubs and the Temple of Tabo on Argo Island." *JEA* 55: 103–11.

Jansen-Winkeln, K. 2006. "The Third Intermediate Period: Dyns. 22–24." In *Ancient Egyptian Chronology*, edited by E. Hornung, R. Krauss, and D.A. Warburton, 234–64. Leiden: Brill.

———. 2007–14. *Inschriften der Spätzeit*. 4 vols. Wiesbaden: Harrassowitz.

———. 2016. "Der Nubienfeldzug Psametiks II. und die Stele von Schellal." In *Sapientia Felicitas: Festschrift für Günter Vittmann zum 29. Februar 2016*, edited by S.L. Lippert, M. Schentuleit, and M.A. Stadler, 271–84. Montpellier: Équipe "Égypte Nilotique et Méditerranéenne."

Janssen, J.M.A. 1954. "Over farao Bocchoris." In *Varia historica: aangeboden aan Professor Doctor A.W. Byvanck ter gelegenheid van zijn zeventigste verjaardag*, 17–29. Assen: Van Gorcum.

Jurman, C. 2017. "The Order of the Kushite Kings According to Sources from the Eastern Desert and Thebes. Or: Shabataka Was Here First!" *JEH* 10: 124–51.

Kahn, D. 2001. "The Inscription of Sargon II at Tang-i Var and the Chronology of Dynasty 25." *Orientalia* 70: 1–18.

———. 2006. "A Problem of Pedubasts?" *Antiguo Oriente* 4: 21–40.

———. 2007. "Judean Auxiliaries in Egypt's Wars against Kush." *JAOS* 127: 507–16.

———. 2009. "The Transition from Libyan to Nubian Rule in Egypt: Revisiting the Reign of Tefnakht." In *The Libyan Period in Egypt: Historical and Cultural Studies into the 21st–24th Dynasties. Proceedings of a Conference at Leiden University, 25–27 October 2007*, edited by G.P.F. Broekman, R.J. Demarée, and O.E. Kaper, 139–48. Leiden: Nederlands Instituut voor het Nabije Oosten; Louvain: Peeters.

Kendall, T. 1982. *Kush: Lost Kingdom of the Nile*. Brockton, MA: Brockton Art Museum/Fuller Memorial.

———. 1991. "The Napatan Palace at Gebel Barkal: A First Look at B 1200." In *Egypt and Africa: Nubia from Prehistory to Islam*, edited by W.V. Davies, 302–13. London: British Museum Press.

———. 1999. "The Origin of the Napatan State: El Kurru and the Evidence for the Royal Ancestors." In *Meroitica* 15: *Studien zum antiken Sudan: Akten der 7. Internationalen Tagung für meroitischen Forschungen vom 14. bis. 19 September 1992 in Gosen/bei Berlin*, edited by S. Wenig, 3–117. Wiesbaden: Harrassowitz.

———. 2008. "Why Did Taharqa Build His Tomb at Nuri?" In *Between the Cataracts:* *Proceedings of the 11th Conference for Nubian Studies, Warsaw University, 27 August–2 September 2006*, 1: *Main Papers*, edited by W. Godlewski and A. Łajtr, 117–47. Warsaw: Warsaw University Press.

———. 2009. "Talatat Architecture at Jebel Barkal: Report of the NCAM Mission 2008–2009." *S&N* 13: 2–16.

Kendall, T., and El-H.A. Mohamed. 2016. *A Visitor's Guide to the Jebel Barkal Temples*. Khartoum: Nubian Archaeological Development Organization (Qatar–Sudan). www.jebelbarkal.org/frames/VisGuide.pdf.

Kitchen, K.A. 1995. "Egypt." *Baker Encyclopedia of Bible Places: Towns & Cities; Countries & States; Archaeology & Topography*, edited by J.J. Bimson, 108–21. Grand Rapids, MI: Baker Books.

———. 1996. *The Third Intermediate Period in Egypt (1100–650 B.C.)*. 3rd ed. Warminster: Aris and Phillips.

———. 2009. "The Third Intermediate Period in Egypt: An Overview of Fact and Fiction." In *The Libyan Period in Egypt: Historical and Cultural Studies into the 21st–24th Dynasties. Proceedings of a Conference at Leiden University, 25–27 October 2007*, edited by G.P.F. Broekman, R.J. Demarée, and O.E. Kaper, 161–202. Leiden: Nederlands Instituut voor het Nabije Oosten; Louvain: Peeters.

Koch, C. 2014. "Usurpation and the Erasure of Names during the Twenty-sixth Dynasty." In *Thebes in the First Millennium BC*, edited by E. Pischikova, J. Budka, and K. Griffin, 397–413. Newcastle upon Tyne: Cambridge Scholars Publishing.

———. 2017. "The Sarcophagus of Nitocris (Inv. Cairo TN 6/2/21/1): Further Considerations about the God's Wives' Burial Places." In *Proceedings First Vatican Coffin Conference 19–22 June 2013*, edited by A. Amenta and H. Guichard, I, 231–48. Vatican City: Edizioni Musei Vaticani.

Krauss, R. 1993. "Zur Problematik der Nubienpolitik Kamoses sowie der Hyksosherrschaft in Oberägypten." *Orientalia* 62: 17–29.

Kuentz, C. 1935–38. "Note au précédent article." *Mélanges Maspero*, 1: *Orient ancien* 2: 430–31. Cairo: Institut français d'archéologie orientale.

Lane, E.W. 2000. *Description of Egypt: Notes and Views in Egypt and Nubia, Made during the Years 1825, -26, -27, and -28: Chiefly Consisting of a Series of Descriptions and Delineations of the Monuments, Scenery, &c. of Those Countries; The Views, with Few Exceptions, Made with the Camera-lucida*, edited by J. Thompson. Cairo: American University in Cairo Press.

Leahy, A. 1994. "Kushite Monuments at Abydos." In *The Unbroken Reed: Studies in the Culture and Heritage of Ancient Egypt in Honour of A.F. Shore*, edited by C. Eyre, A. Leahy, and L.M. Leahy, 171–92. London: Egypt Exploration Society.

———. 2014. "Kushites at Abydos: The Royal Family and Beyond." In *Thebes in the First Millennium BC*, edited by E. Pischikova, J. Budka, and K. Griffin, 61–100. Newcastle upon Tyne: Cambridge Scholars Publishing.

———. 2022. "La campagne nubienne de Psammétique II et sa signification historique." In *Pharaon des Deux Terres: l'épopée africaine des rois de Napata*, edited by V. Rondot, 338–41. Paris: Musée éditions/El Viso.

Leclant, J. 1961. *Montouemhat, quatrième prophète d'Amoun, prince de la ville*. Cairo: Institut français d'archéologie orientale.

———. 1963. "Kashta, pharaon, en Egypte." *ZÄS* 90: 74–81.

———. 1965. *Recherches sur les monuments thébains de la XXVe dynastie dite éthiopienne*. Cairo: Institut français d'archéologie orientale.

———. 1984. "Taharqa à Sedeinga." In *Studien zu Sprache und Religion Ägyptens: zu Ehren von Wolfhart Westendorf, überreicht von seinen Freunden und Schülern*, I, 1113–19. Göttingen: F. Junge.

Leichty, E. 2011. *The Royal Inscriptions of Esarhaddon, King of Assyria (680–669 BC)*. Winona Lake, IN: Eisenbrauns.

Lepsius, C.R. 1849–59. *Denkmaeler aus Aegypten und Aethiopien*. 6 vols. Berlin and Leipzig: Nicolaische Buchhandlung.

———. 1858. *Königsbuch der alten Ägypter*. 2 vols. Berlin: Bessersche Buchhandlung.

———. 1897–1913. *Denkmaeler aus Aegypten und Aethiopien, Textband*. 5 vols. Leipzig: J.C. Hinrichs.

Lichtheim, M. 1948. "The High Steward Akhamenru." *JNES* 7: 163–79.

Licitra, N. 2018. "Douze campagnes de fouille au Trésor de Shabaka à Karnak: archéologie d'une institution économique." *BSFE* 199: 38–56.

Licitra, N., C. Thiers, and P. Zignani. 2014. "A Major Development Project of the Northern Area of the Amun-Re Precinct at Karnak during the Reign of Shabaqo." In *Thebes in the First Millennium BC*, edited by E. Pischikova, J. Budka, and K. Griffin, 549–63. Newcastle upon Tyne: Cambridge Scholars Publishing.

Lieblein, J. 1873. *Die aegyptischen Denkmäler in St. Petersburg, Helsingfors, Upsala und Copenhagen*. Christiana: A.W. Brøgger.

Lull, J. 2002. *Las tumbas reales egipcias del Tercer Periodo Intermedio (dinastías XXI–XXV)*. Oxford: Archaeopress.

Macadam, M.F.L. 1949–55. *The Temples of Kawa*. 2 vols. London: Oxford University Press.

Manuelian, P.D. 2022. *Walking among Pharaohs: George Reisner and the Dawn of Modern Egyptology*. New York: Oxford University Press.

Mariette, A. 1856. "Renseignements sur les soixante-quatre Apis trouvés dans les souterrains du Sérapéum: §9. XXVIe Dynastie—cinq Apis." *Bulletin archéologique de l'Athénaeum français* 2: 74–80.

———. 1865. "Quatre pages des archives officielles de l'Éthiopie." *RevArch* NS 12: 161–79.

Maspero, G. 1889. *Les momies royales de Déir el-Bahari*. Paris: Ernest Leroux.

———. 1892. "Notes au jour le jour—IV." *PSBA* 14: 170–204.

———. 1900. *The Passing of the Empires, 850 B.C. to 330 B.C.* London: Society for Promoting Christian Knowledge.

Moret, A. 1903. *De Bocchori rege*. Paris: Ernest Leroux.

Morfini, I., and M. Álvarez Sosa. 2021. "A New 'Osiris Tomb' in Sheikh Abd el-Qur-na—Luxor: From Myth to Architecture." In *Rethinking Osiris: Proceedings of the International Conference, Florence, Italy 26–27 March 2019*, edited by M. Franci, S. Ikram, and I. Morfini, 89–104. Rome: Arbor Sapientiae.

Morkot, R. 1999. "Kingship and Kinship in the Empire of Kush." In *Studien zum antiken Sudan: Akten der 7. Internationalen Tagung für meroitischen Forschungen vom 14. bis. 19. September 1992 in Gosen/bei Berlin*, edited by S. Wenig, 179–229. Wiesbaden: Harrassowitz.

———. 2000. *The Black Pharaohs: Egypt's Nubian Rulers*. London: Rubicon.

———. 2003. "On the Priestly Origin of the Napatan Kings: The Adaptation, Demise and Resurrection of Ideas in Writing Nubian History." In *Ancient Egypt in Africa*, edited by D. O'Connor and A. Reid, 151–68. London: UCL Press.

———. 2007. "Tradition, Innovation, and Researching the Past in Libyan, Kushite, and Saïte Egypt." In *Regime Change in the Ancient Near East and Egypt: From Sargon of Agade to Saddam Hussein*, edited by H. Crawford, 141–64. Oxford: Oxford University Press.

———. 2014. "All in the Detail: Some Further Observations on 'Archaism' and Style in Libyan-Kushite-Saite Egypt." In *Thebes in the First Millennium BC*, edited by E. Pischikova, J. Budka, and K. Griffin, 379–95. Newcastle upon Tyne: Cambridge Scholars Publishing.

———. 2021. "Kings from Kush." *AncEg* 127: 20–27; 128: 42–47.

Morkot, R., and S. Quirke. 2001. "Inventing the 25th Dynasty: Turin Stela 1467 and the Construction of History." In *Begegnungen: Antike Kulturen im Niltal. Festgabe für Erika Endesfelder, Karl-Heinz Priese, Walter Friedrich Reinecke, Steffen Wenig*, edited by C.-B. Arnst, I. Hafemann, and A. Lohwasser, 349–63. Leipzig: Wodtke und Stegbauer.

Müller, M. 2009. "The 'El-Hibeh' Archive: Introduction and Preliminary Information." In *The Libyan Period in Egypt: Historical and Cultural Studies into the 21st–24th Dynasties. Proceedings of a Conference at Leiden University, 25–27 October 2007*, edited by G.P.F. Broekman, R.J. Demarée, and O.E. Kaper, 251–64. Leiden: Nederlands Instituut voor Nabije Oosten.

Murnane, W.J. 1977. *Ancient Egyptian Coregencies*. Chicago: Oriental Institute.

Näser, C., and G. Mazzetti. 2020. "Of Kings and Horses: Two New Horse Skeletons from the Royal Cemetery at el-Kurru, Sudan." *Archaeology International* 23: 122–37. DOI: 10.14324/111.444.ai.2020.10.

Naunton, C. 2014. "Titles of Karakhamun and the Kushite Administration of Thebes." In *Tombs of the South Asasif Necropolis, Thebes: Karakhamun (TT 223) and Karabasken (TT 391) in the Twenty-fifth Dynasty*, edited by E. Pischikova, 103–107. Cairo: American University in Cairo Press.

Novotny, J., and J. Jeffers. 2018–23. *The Royal Inscriptions of Ashurbanipal (668–631 BC), Aššur-etel-ilāni (630–627 BC), and Sîn-šarra-iškun (626–612 BC), Kings of Assyria*. 2 vols. Winona Lake, IN: Eisenbrauns.

O'Connor, D. 1986. "The Locations of Yam and Kush and Their Historical Implications." *JARCE* 23: 27–50.

Parkinson, R. 1999. *Cracking Codes: The Rosetta Stone and Decipherment*. London: British Museum Press.

Payraudeau, F. 2014. "Retour sur la succession Shabako–Shabatako." *NeHeT* 1: 115–27.

Perdu, O. 2002. "De Stéphinatès à Néchao ou les débuts de la XXVIe dynastie." *CRAIBL* 146: 1215–44.

———. 2010. "Le prétendu 'an V' mentionné sur les 'blocs de Piânkhi.'" *RdE* 61: 151–57.

———. 2011. "Les 'blocs de Piânkhi' après un siècle de discussions." In *La XXVIe dynastie, continuités et ruptures: actes du Colloque international organisé les 26 et 27 novembre 2004 à l'Université Charles-de-Gaulle–Lille 3; promenade saïte avec Jean Yoyotte*, edited by D. Devauchelle, 225–40. Paris: Cybele.

———. 2022a. "Étonnants de 'blocs de Piânkhy.'" In *Pharaon des Deux Terres: l'épopée africaine des rois de Napata*, edited by V. Rondot, 226–27. Paris: Louvre éditions/éditions El Viso.

———. 2022b. "Montouemhat, Quatrième prophète d'Amon, Prince de la Ville et Gouverneur de la Haute-Égypte." In *Pharaon des Deux Terres: l'épopée africaine des rois de Napata*, edited by V. Rondot, 228–29. Paris: Louvre éditions/éditions El Viso.

Perizonius, J. 1736. *Ægyptiarum Originum et Temporum Antiquissimorum Investigatio, in qua Marshami Chronologia Funditus Evertitur, Tum Illae Usserii, Cappelli, Pezronii, Aliorumque, Examinantur & Confutantur*, edited by H. van Alphen. Trajecti ad Rhenum: Justum Reers.

Pernigotti, S. 1968. "Il generale Potasimto e la sua famiglia." *Studi Classici e Orientali* 17: 251–64.

Petrie, W.M.F. 1888. *Tanis*. Vol. 2. London: Trübner & Co.

———. 1905. *A History of Egypt from the XIXth to the XXXth Dynasties*. London: Methuen.

Pischikova, E. 2008. "Tomb of Karakhamun (TT 223) in the South Asasif and a 'Lost' Capital." *JARCE* 44: 185–92.

Pischikova, E., ed. 2014. *Tombs of the South Asasif Necropolis, Thebes: Karakhamun (TT 223) and Karabasken (TT 391) in the Twenty-fifth Dynasty*. Cairo: American University in Cairo Press.

———. 2017. *Tombs of the South Asasif Necropolis: New Discoveries and Research 2012–14*. Cairo: American University in Cairo Press.

———. 2021. *Tombs of the South Asasif Necropolis: Art and Archaeology 2015–18*. Cairo: American University in Cairo Press.

Pleyte, W. 1876. "Über zwei Darstellungen des Gottes Horus-Seth." *ZÄS* 14: 49–52.

Pope, J. 2014. *The Double Kingdom under Taharqo: Studies in the History of Kush and Egypt, c. 690–664 BC*. Leiden: Brill.

Porter, B., and R.B. Moss. 1952. *Topographical Bibliography of Ancient Egyptian Hieroglyphic Texts, Reliefs and Paintings*. Vol. 7, *Nubia, Deserts, and Outside Egypt*. Oxford: Clarendon Press.

———. 1960–64. *Topographical Bibliography of Ancient Egyptian Hieroglyphic Texts, Reliefs and Paintings*. Vol. 1, *The Theban Necropolis*. 2nd ed. Oxford: Clarendon Press.

———. 1972. *Topographical Bibliography of Ancient Egyptian Hieroglyphic Texts, Reliefs and Paintings*. Vol. 2, *Theban Temples*. 2nd ed. Oxford: Clarendon Press.

———. 1974–81. *Topographical Bibliography of Ancient Egyptian Hieroglyphic Texts, Reliefs and Paintings*. Vol. 3, *Memphis*. 2nd ed. by J. Málek. Oxford: Clarendon Press/Griffith Institute.

Priese, K.-H. 1970. "Der Beginn der Kuschitischen Herrschaft." *ZÄS* 98/1: 16–32.

———. 1977. "Eine verschollene Bauinscrift des frühmerotischen Königs Aktisanes vom Gebel Barkal." In *Ägypten und Kusch*, edited by E. Endesfelder, K.-H. Priese, W.-F. Reineke, and S. Wenig, 343–67. Berlin: Akademie-Verlag.

Prisse d'Avennes, E. 1847. *Monuments égyptiens: bas-reliefs, peintures, inscriptions, etc., d'après les dessins exécutés sur les lieux*. Paris: Firmin Didot Frères.

Quirke, S. 1995. "The Quartzite Lintels of Senusret III, King of Egypt." *British Museum Magazine* 23: 16–17.

Redford, D.B. 1999. "A Note on the Chronology of Dynasty 25 and the Inscription of Sargon II at Tang-i Var." *Orientalia* 68: 58–60.

Reisner, G.A. 1917. "Excavations at Napata, the Capital of Ethiopia." *BMFA* 15: 25–34.

———. 1918. "Known and Unknown Kings of Ethiopia." *BMFA* 16: 67–82.

———. 1919. "Outline of the Ancient History of the Sudan, Part IV: The First Kingdom of Ethiopia, Its Conquest of Egypt, and Its Development into a Kingdom of the Sudan (1100–250 BC)." *SN&R* 2: 35–67.

———. 1921a. "Historical Inscriptions from Gebel Barkal." *SN&R* 4: 59–75.

———. 1921b. "The Royal Family of Ethiopia." *BMFA* 19: 21–38.

———. 1931. "Inscribed Monuments from Gebel Barkal." *ZÄS* 66: 76–100.

Ridgway, D. 1999. "The Rehabilitation of Bocchoris: Notes and Queries from Italy." *JEA* 85: 143–52.

Ritner, R.K. 2009. *The Libyan Anarchy: Inscriptions from Egypt's Third Intermediate Period*. Atlanta: Society of Biblical Literature.

Robins, G. 1983. "A Critical Examination of the Theory that the Right to the Throne of Ancient Egypt Passed through the Female Line in the 18th Dynasty." *GM* 62: 67–77.

Rondot, V., ed. 2022. *Pharaon des Deux Terres: l'épopée africaine des rois de Napata*. Paris: Louvre éditions/éditions El Viso.

Rosellini, I. 1833. *I monumenti dell'Egitto e della Nubia: disegnati dalla Spedizione Scientifico-Letteraria Toscana in Egitto*. Vol. 1, *Monumenti Storici*. Pisa: Nicoló Capurro.

Rougé, E. de. 1863. "Inscription historique du roi Pianchi-Mériamoun." *RevArch* NS 8: 94–127.

———. 1873. "Étude sur quelques monuments du règne de Tahraka." *Mélanges d'archéologie égyptienne et assyrienne* 1: 11–23, 85–91.

Ruffle, J. 1998. "Lord Prudhoe and His Lions." *S&N* 2: 82–87.

Russman, E.R. 1974. *The Representation of the King in the XXVth Dynasty*. Brussels: Fondation Égyptologique Reine Élisabeth; Brooklyn: The Brooklyn Museum.

———. 1997. "Mentuemhat's Kushite Wife (Further Remarks on the Decoration of the Tomb of Mentuemhat, 2)." *JARCE* 34: 21–39.

Ryholt, K.S.B. 1997. *The Political Situation in Egypt during the Second Intermediate Period c. 1800–1550 BC*. Copenhagen: Museum Tusculanum Press.

———. 2004. "The Assyrian Invasion of Egypt in Egyptian Literary Tradition: A Survey of the Narrative Source Material." In *Assyria and Beyond: Studies Presented to Mogens Trolle Larsen*, edited by J.G. Dercksen, 483–510. Leiden: Nederlands Instituut voor het Nabije Oosten.

———. 2011. "New Light on the Legendary King Nechepsos of Egypt." *JEA* 97: 61–72.

———. 2022. "Taharqa contre le griffon." In *Pharaon des Deux Terres: l'épopée africaine des rois de Napata*, edited by V. Rondot, 406–407. Paris: Louvre éditions/éditions El Viso.

Salt, H. 1825. *Essay on Dr. Young's and M. Champollion's Phonetic System of Hieroglyphics: With Some Additional Discoveries, by Which It May Be Applied to Decipher the Names of the Ancient Kings of Egypt and Ethiopia*. London: Valpy.

Sauneron, S., and J. Yoyotte. 1952. "La campagne nubienne de Psammétique II et sa signification historique." *BIFAO* 50: 157–207.

Schmitz, P.C. 2010. "The Phoenician Contingent in the Campaign of Psammetichus II against Kush." *JEH* 3: 321–37.

Schweinfurth, G. 1886. *Alte Baureste und hieroglyphische Inschriften im Uadi Gasus*. Berlin: Königlich-Preussische Akademie der Wissenschaften.

Sharpe, S. 1876. *The History of Egypt, from the Earliest Times till the Conquest by the Arabs A.D. 640.* 6th ed. London: George Bell.

Simpson, W.K. 1962. "Nubia: 1962 Excavations at Toshka and Arminna." *Expedition* 4/4: 36–46.

———. 1963. *Heka-Nefer and the Dynastic Material from Toshka and Arminna.* New Haven: Peabody Museum of Natural History of Yale University; Philadelphia: University of Pennsylvania Museum of Archaeology and Anthropology.

Smith, G. 1868. "Egyptian Campaigns of Esarhaddon and Assur-bani-pal." *ZÄS* 6: 93–99.

Spencer, A.J. 1989. *Excavations at El-Ashmunein.* Vol. 2, *The Temple Area.* London: British Museum Publications.

Thijs, A. 2015. "From the Lunar Eclipse of Takeloth II back to Shoshenq I and Shishak." In *Solomon and Shishak: Current Perspectives from Archaeology, Epigraphy, History and Chronology. Proceedings of the Third BICANE Colloquium held at Sidney Sussex College, Cambridge 26–27 March, 2011*, edited by P. James and P.G. van der Veen, 42–60. Oxford: Archaeopress.

Török, L. 1995. "The Emergence of the Kingdom of Kush and Her Myth of the State in the First Millennium BC." In *Actes de la VIIIe conférence internationale des études nubiennes*, vol. 1: *Communications principales*: 203–28.

———. 1997a. *Meroe City, an Ancient African Capital: John Garstang's Excavations in the Sudan.* London: Egypt Exploration Society.

———. 1997b. *The Kingdom of Kush: Handbook of the Napatan–Meroitic Civilization.* Leiden: Brill.

———. 2009. *Between Two Worlds: The Frontier Region between Ancient Nubia and Egypt, 3700 BC–500 AD.* Leiden: Brill.

Traunecker, C. 2022. "Tombeaux de l'élite et tombeaux de rois: de la montagne thébaine à la quatrième cataracte, une brève histoire des palais funéraires de Thèbes et de Napata." In *Pharaon des Deux Terres: l'épopée africaine des rois de Napata*, edited by V. Rondot, 232–39. Paris: Louvre éditions/éditions El Viso.

Trigger, B.G. 1969. "The Royal Tombs at Qustul and Ballâna and Their Meroïtic Antecedents." *JEA* 55: 117–28.

Valbelle, D., and C. Bonnet. 2019. "The Cache of Dukki Gel (Pa-nebes)." In *Handbook of Ancient Nubia*, edited by D. Raue, II, 667–74. Berlin and Boston: De Gruyter.

———. 2022. "Doukki Gel. La ville d'Amon du Jujubier et les statues des rois de Napata." In *Pharaon des Deux Terres: l'épopée africaine des rois de Napata*, edited by V. Rondot, 332–35. Paris: Louvre éditions/éditions El Viso.

Valbelle, D., and V. Rondot. 2022. "Doukki Gel et ses statues." In *Pharaon des Deux Terres: l'épopée africaine des rois de Napata*, edited by V. Rondot, 358–67. Paris: Louvre éditions/éditions El Viso.

Van Sertima, I. 1976. *They Came before Columbus: The African Presence in Ancient America.* New York: Random House.

Vercoutter, J. 1960. "The Napatan Kings and Apis Worship (Serapeum Burials of the Napatan Period)." *Kush* 8: 62–76.

Verreth, H. 1999. "The Eastern Egyptian Border Region in Assyrian Sources." *JAOS* 119: 234–47.

Vikentiev, V. 1955. "Quelques considérations à propos des statues de Taharqa trouvées dans les ruines du palais d'Esarhaddon." *Sumer* 11: 111–16.

Vittmann, G. 1974. "Zur Lesung des Königsnamen ⸢𓏏⸣." *Orientalia* 43: 12–16.

von Beckerath, J. 1997. *Chronologie des pharaonischen Ägypten: die Zeitbestimmung der ägyptischen Geschichte von der Vorzeit bis 332 v. Chr.* Mainz: Philipp von Zabern.

Vrtal, V. 2015. "Egyptian Inscriptions of Natakamani and Amanitore." In *There and Back Again—the Crossroads II: Proceedings of an International Conference Held in Prague, September 15–18, 2014*, edited by J. Mynářová, P. Onderka, and Peter Pavúk, 465–92. Prague: Charles University Faculty of Arts.

Waddell, W.G., trans. 1940. *Manetho*. Cambridge, MA: Harvard University Press; London: William Heinemann.

Waddington, G., and B. Hanbury. 1822. *Journal of a Visit to Some Parts of Ethiopia*. London: Murray.

Weigall, A.E.P. 1907. *A Report on the Antiquities of Lower Nubia (the First Cataract to the Sudan Frontier) and Their Condition in 1906–7*. Oxford: Oxford University Press.

Welsby, D.A. 1996. *The Kingdom of Kush: The Napatan and Meroitic Empires*. London: British Museum Press.

Wiedemann, A. 1884–88. *Ägyptische Geschichte*. 3 vols. Gotha: Perthes.

Wilkinson, J.G. 1828. *Materia hieroglyphica: Containing the Egyptian Pantheon, and the Succession of the Pharaohs, from the Earliest Times to the Conquest by Alexander, and Other Hieroglyphical Subjects; with Plates, and Notes Explanatory of the Same*. Malta: Government Press.

———. 1830. *Extracts from Several Hieroglyphical Subjects, Found at Thebes and Other Parts of Egypt, with Remarks on the Same*. Malta: Government Press.

———. 1835. *Topography of Thebes and General View of Egypt: Being a Short Account of the Principal Objects Worthy of Notice in the Valley of the Nile, to the Second Cataract and Wadee Samneh, with the Fyoom, Oases, and Eastern Desert, from Sooez to Berenice; with Remarks on the Manners and Customs of the Ancient Egyptians and the Productions of the Country, &c, &c*. London: John Murray.

———. 1837. *The Manners and Customs of the Ancient Egyptians: Including Their Private Life, Government, Laws, Arts, Manufactures, Religion, Agriculture, and Early History; Derived from a Comparison of the Paintings, Sculptures, and Monuments Still Existing, with the Accounts of Ancient Authors*. Vol. 1. London: John Murray.

Yoyotte, J. 1961. "Les principautés du Delta au temps de l'anarchie libyenne." In *Mélanges Maspero* 1/4: 121–81. Cairo: Institut français d'archéologie orientale.

Zibelius-Chen, Z. 2006. "The Chronology of Nubian Kingdoms from Dyn. 25 to the End of the Kingdom of Meroe." In *Ancient Egyptian Chronology*, edited by E. Hornung, R. Krauss, and D.A. Warburton, 284–303. Leiden: Brill.

Żurawski, B. 2018. "Where Was the 'Land of Shas'? Some Comments on Psamtik II's Expedition to the South Caused by the Recent Archaeological Discoveries in the Southern Dongola Reach." In *Across the Mediterranean—Along the Nile: Studies in Egyptology, Nubiology and Late Antiquity Dedicated to László Török on the Occasion of His 75th Birthday*, edited by T.A. Bács, A. Bollók, and T. Vida, I, 455–75. Budapest: Hungarian Academy of Sciences.

SOURCES OF IMAGES

All images by author unless otherwise stated.

1.   Martin Davies.
4.   Bottom: adapted from Lepsius 1849–59: I, pl. 125.
8b.   Macadam 1949–55: II, pl. vi.
8c.   Macadam 1949–55: II, pl. vii.
8d.   Reisner 1931: 83[62].
9a.   Martin Davies.
9b.   Caminos 1998: pls. 15–20.
10.   Main image: Martin Davies.
11.   Dyan Hilton.
13.   Inset: Leclant 1963: fig. 1.
14.   Adapted from Theban Mapping Project.
16.   Photo: Benson and Gourlay 1899: pls. xx[1], xxii[5]. Drawing: Foucart 1924: pl. ix[B].
17.   Bottom: Reisner 1931: pl. v.
20.   Museum of Fine Arts, Boston.
22.   Mission française de fouilles de Tanis/Christelle Desbordes.
23.   Top: Dyan Hilton.
24.   Inset: Kendall and Mohamed 2016: 54, fig. 2.
25.   Trustees of the British Museum.
30.   Lepsius 1849–59: V, pl. 4.
34.   Left: Metropolitan Museum of Art. Right: Dyan Hilton.
35.   Salima Ikram.
38.   Hesamdroodgar, via Wikipedia Commons.
40.   Metropolitan Museum of Art.

41.	Trustees of the British Museum.
43.	Top: Dyan Hilton.
50.	Trustees of the British Museum.
51.	Trustees of the British Museum.
53.	Top: Lepsius 1849–59: V, pl. 15.
55.	Close-up: Dyan Hilton.
61.	Top: Stephen P. Harvey.
71.	Left: Richard Mortel via Wikipedia Commons. Right: Trustees of the British Museum.
76.	© Osiris Ptah Nebankh Research Project.
78.	Adapted from Schweinfurth 1886: pl ii.
79.	Left: Sauneron and Yoyotte 1952: pl. iv.
81.	Dyan Hilton.
82.	Right: Dyan Hilton.
87.	Center right: Dyan Hilton.
88.	Left: Trustees of the British Museum.
96.	Museum of Fine Arts, Boston.
97.	Museum of Fine Arts, Boston.
99b–d.	Museum of Fine Arts, Boston.
101.	Top: Dyan Hilton. Bottom: Dunham 1955: pl. iiiB.
102.	Bottom: Museum of Fine Arts, Boston.
103.	Trustees of the British Museum.
107.	Museum of Fine Arts, Boston.
108.	Top: Dyan Hilton.
112.	Bottom right: Metropolitan Museum of Art.
114.	Top: Dyan Hilton.
115.	Bottom: Museum of Fine Arts, Boston.
116.	Top: John Hodgins.
117.	Dyan Hilton.
118.	Dyan Hilton.
119.	Emery 1948: pl. 9.
122.	Waddington and Hanbury 1822: pl. opp. pp. 158, 159, 167.
123.	Waddington and Hanbury 1822: pl. opp. p. 176.
124.	Dyan Hilton.
125.	Left: Egypt Exploration Society. Right: Petrie 1888: pl. ix.
126.	L. Frank Baum, courtesy †David Moyer.
128.	Map and stelae after Macadam 1949–55: II, pls. 4–12; 1:pls. 6, 8, 10, 12, 14.
130.	Campbell Price.

INDEX

KING OF EGYPT/EGYPT-KUSH
KING OF KUSH
RULING QUEEN OF KUSH
Alphanumerics following names represent tomb numbers